We hold these truths to be self-evident: that all men and women are created equal; that they are endowed by their Creator with certain inalienable rights; that among these are life, liberty, and the pursuit of happiness; that to secure these rights governments are instituted, deriving their just powers from the consent of the governed. Whenever any form of Government becomes destructive of these ends, it is the right of those who suffer from it to refuse allegiance to it, and to insist upon the institution of a new government. . . . But when a long train of abuses and usurpations, pursuing invariably the same object, evinces a design to reduce them under absolute despotism, it is their duty to throw off such government, and to provide new guards for their future security. Such has been the patient sufferance of the women under this government, and such is now the necessity which constrains them to demand the equal station to which they are entitled. . . .

DECLARATION OF SENTIMENTS, JULY 1848

ALSO BY GEOFFREY C. WARD

Treasures of the World: The Maharajahs

Before the Trumpet: Young Franklin Roosevelt, 1882–1905

A First-Class Temperament: The Emergence of Franklin Roosevelt

The Civil War: An Illustrated History
(with Ken Burns and Ric Burns)

American Originals: The Private Worlds of Some Singular Men and Women

Tiger-Wallahs: Encounters with the Men Who Tried to Save the Greatest of the Cats
(with Diane Raines Ward)

Baseball: An Illustrated History
(with Ken Burns)

Constant Companion: The Unknown Story of the Intimate
Friendship Between Franklin Roosevelt and Margaret Suckley

The West: An Illustrated History

The Year of the Tiger

ALSO BY KEN BURNS

The Civil War: An Illustrated History
(with Geoffrey C. Ward and Ric Burns)

Baseball: An Illustrated History
(with Geoffrey C. Ward)

The Shakers: Hands to Work, Hearts to God
(with Amy S. Burns)

Lewis & Clark
(with Dayton Duncan)

NOT FOR OURSELVES ALONE

THE STORY OF ELIZABETH CADY STANTON AND SUSAN B. ANTHONY

NOT FOR OURSELVES ALONE

The Story of Elizabeth Cady Stanton and Susan B. Anthony

AN ILLUSTRATED HISTORY

by
GEOFFREY C. WARD

based on a documentary film by
KEN BURNS *and* PAUL BARNES
written by
GEOFFREY C. WARD

with a preface by
KEN BURNS

introduction by
PAUL BARNES

and contributions by
MARTHA SAXTON
ANN D. GORDON
ELLEN CAROL DUBOIS

ALFRED A. KNOPF   NEW YORK   1999

This Is a Borzoi Book
Published by Alfred A. Knopf

Copyright © 1999 by
The American Lives Film Project, Inc.

www.randomhouse.com

Knopf, Borzoi Books, and the colophon are registered trade-
marks of Random House, Inc.

Library of Congress Cataloging-in-Publication Data
Ward, Geoffrey C.
    Not for ourselves alone : the story of Elizabeth Cady
Stanton and Susan B. Anthony : an illustrated history /
by Geoffrey C. Ward ; based on a documentary film by
Ken Burns and Paul Barnes, written by Geoffrey C. Ward ;
with a preface by Ken Burns ; introduction by Paul Barnes ;
and contributions by Martha Saxton, Ann D. Gordon,
Ellen Carol DuBois.
        p.   cm.
    Includes bibliographical references and index.
    ISBN 0-375-40560-7 (alk. paper)
    1. Stanton, Elizabeth Cady, 1815–1902.   2. Anthony,
Susan B. (Susan Brownell), 1820–1906.   3. Feminists—
United States Biography.   4. Suffragists—United States
Biography.   5. Women's rights—United States—His-
tory—19th century.   6. Women—Suffrage—United
States—History—19th century.   I. Saxton, Martha.
II. Gordon, Ann D. (Ann Dexter)   III. DuBois, Ellen
Carol   IV. Title.
HQ1412.W36   1999
305.42'092'273—dc21   99-31056
                                                CIP

Manufactured in the United States of America

First Edition

Endpapers: Suffrage parade in New York, 1915

Frontispiece: Susan B. Anthony and Elizabeth Cady Stanton on the porch of Anthony's Rochester home, c. 1895

Contents

Our Big Time

On November 2, 1920, for the first time in history, more than eight million American women went to the polls and exercised their newly won right to vote in precincts all over the country: a caravan of automobiles shuttled seventy residents of a home for elderly women to the polls on the Upper West Side of Manhattan. In Rhode Island, a woman candidate for state office could not contain her joy: "Now we know what a political earthquake is," she said. In Philadelphia, large numbers of women voters turned out—despite a new city ordinance meant to discourage them by insisting that women confess their age to the registrars. In Atlanta, seventy-five black women went to the polls only to have their ballots nullified by technicalities by nightfall. In Baltimore, an elderly judge who had overseen elections in one precinct for twenty years found himself with little to do; according to the *Baltimore Sun*, "the women had taken almost everything out of his hands." "I'm going to let them carry the ballot box downtown," the judge said. Of the twenty nuns at St. Catherine's Normal Institute in the same city, ten went to the polls. "I only wish I had an airship," said a nun who had been prevented from voting because she was from out of town, "so I could go home to Texas and participate."

Across the country—from the mountains of Utah, Wyoming, Colorado, and Idaho, where women had voted for years—to the farm communities of the Midwest and the small towns of New England and the

Suffragists marching to finish the great work begun by Elizabeth Cady Stanton and Susan B. Anthony, New York City, May 12, 1912

Deep South, it was the same: an energy, a deep, abiding, democratic energy was being released, and in many ways the American Revolution was coming to fruition. Thomas Jefferson had proclaimed in 1776 that equality would be the bedrock of a new American government. But it took another 144 years for women finally to achieve full citizenship in the United States, and the two women who had fought longest and hardest for women's rights, Elizabeth Cady Stanton and Susan B. Anthony, had not lived long enough to cast a ballot themselves.

For most of the life of this Republic, we have formally told our history from the top down. This is essentially the history of the State, focusing on generals and presidents, on the story of Great Men, constructed on the erroneous assumption that this myopic view of our past eventually engages everyone in the American narrative and touches experiences common to us all. It does not. It does exhibit, or has exhibited, an understandable arrogance, and we, as a people, have often been forced to rely on family memory and community recollection to make political history somehow meaningful.

In recent years, though, we have begun to see our past from a variety of new perspectives, finding in the million heroic acts of ordinary citizens—history from the bottom up this time—a new and sustaining vision of the ongoing pageant of human events in America. As we explore these new historical approaches, we are confronted daily with an increasingly vivid sense of their central importance to the whole of American studies. Yet often our wonder and excitement at these new areas of discovery is tempered by an almost inexpressible outrage that these heretofore "hidden histories" have been so long kept from public view, smothered by the drumbeat of the old, decidedly sentimental version of events. Nowhere is this outrage more pronounced than in the remarkable, complicated, and inspiring story of the struggle for women's rights.

In the summer of 1988, during the production of a documentary film series on the history of the Civil War—a series that struggled in every one of its episodes to show the war from a variety of personal as well as objective viewpoints—my editor Paul Barnes regaled our small staff each day at lunch with his infectious enthusiasm for Elisabeth Griffith's biography of Elizabeth Cady Stanton, a name I only vaguely recognized. As retold around the table by Paul, Stanton's story came alive for all of us, and I decided that summer to add her name to a list of film portraits we were planning to produce in the years to come, films on Thomas Jefferson, Lewis and Clark, Mark Twain, and Frank Lloyd Wright.

It took us more years than we expected, but eventually Paul (who was persuaded to leave his editing machine to produce the film with me) and I started work on what has proven to be one of the most satisfying experiences of our professional lives. Eventually we decided to enlarge our scope by transforming the two-part miniseries we envisioned into a dual biography, pairing Stanton with her longtime friend and protégé, the more well known (perhaps "less obscure" is the better and more honest phrase) Susan B. Anthony. The completed three-hour film, upon which this volume is based, details not only the dramatic and sometimes poignant fifty-year relationship between these two remarkable women, but is in effect the story of women's rights in the nineteenth century. The documentary became, as well, an anatomy of a nascent political movement, filled as all great

movements are with success and retreat, compromise and conviction, individual heroism and transcendent rhetoric. In the end, the story of these two women touched themes that speak to the deepest and most profound parts of all of our personal, indeed spiritual and psychological, lives.

These two women are most responsible for the largest social transformation in American history, a transformation that—unlike Jefferson's Declaration of Independence, which proclaimed the equality only of white males—affected a majority of American citizens and has provided the model for a host of other twentieth-century agitations.

When these two wonderfully different and equally brilliant women, Elizabeth Cady Stanton and Susan B. Anthony, were born in the first fifth of the nineteenth century, women in America had fewer rights than a male inmate of an insane asylum. Women were prevented from attending college, and barred from the pulpit and all professions. Those who dared speak in public in this democracy were thought indecent. No women could serve on a jury and most were considered "incompetent" to testify in court. They could not sign contracts, keep or invest earnings, own or inherit property; they had no rights in divorce, including the custody of the children they bore. In fact, women were the property of their husbands, who were entitled—by law—to their wives' wages and bodies. And the ballot by which women might have voted to improve their status was denied to them by law. Nowhere in America—nowhere in the world—did women have the right to vote.

When Stanton and Anthony passed from the scene in the opening days of the twentieth century, most of the aforementioned (to us self-evident) rights had been achieved for women in America—and these two remarkable women could rightfully take credit for much of that progress: "They are women's history of the nineteenth century," the biographer Kathleen Barry proudly insists. And when the vote for women finally came, the Nineteenth Amendment to the United States Constitution that gave them that right was word for word what Stanton and Anthony had been submitting and resubmitting to Congress for decades.

Looking back over the complicated expanse of the twentieth century, ninety-eight-year-old Ruth Dyk, speaking in an interview for our film, remembered the feverish excitement of the push for the vote when she was just a girl—her mother was quite active in the movement. "This was our big time," she said of the suffragist marches that paraded up and down Beacon Hill in Boston, and when the vote was won, Ruth was overjoyed: "We had worked so long, we had worked so hard. We never thought it would happen. . . . If you had worked for years to do it, if you believed in it, if you thought great things were going to come out of it—great in terms of the position of women in our culture, position of women in their jobs, position of women everywhere, and this was going to improve that . . . I mean lives would be changed."

"Remember, in those days, women were in the kitchen. Men did the voting. And they let them do the voting. They weren't interested," says Ethel Hall, of Long Island, now 100 years old. She, too, vividly recalled for us the excitement for the new movement: "a woman in Cold Spring Harbor . . . rode a white horse all the way to Albany trying to educate people along the way on why women should have the vote." But Ethel also remembered the worries and doubts she and many others had, the undertow of all the hubbub for rights: "I remember the women suffragettes. They seemed rather bold and unladylike to venture out in the world . . . they were a little bit unladylike, but when we got the vote, we were thankful to them. We had to wake up, too."

On November 2, 1920, Ethel voted for the first time in Rockville Centre, New York. She had turned twenty-one the previous April and was just starting her career, teaching English and math to eighth-graders. With an impish shrug, she admits on camera that she followed her father's advice and voted Republican—"for Warren G. Harding of Teapot Dome!" But then Ethel Hall, born in the waning moments of the nineteenth century, alive and well at the dawn of the twenty-first, smiled an even deeper smile and told us of the great pride she felt that day and still feels, a pride that speaks not only to her own personal transformation, but to the two great women who had made that development possible. In the last moments of the interview she gave, Ethel paused and in a strong clear voice said, "I had just been graduated from college, and up there we were taught the slogan, 'Not for ourselves alone, but that we must teach others.' I felt [voting] was something I could do for my country. And I was very happy about it."

Not for ourselves alone.

Ken Burns
Walpole, New Hampshire

Introduction

Elizabeth Cady Who?

This book and the film project that inspired it had their genesis in the work of the biographer Elisabeth Griffith. Back in 1984, when Ken Burns and I were working on *The Statue of Liberty*, I happened to read in the *New York Times Book Review* a review of *In Her Own Right*, Griffith's life of Elizabeth Cady Stanton. I had never heard of Stanton, and I had always been a history buff. It was one of my favorite subjects in high school and college. As I read the review, I was amazed at all that this woman had done back in the nineteenth century.

I mentioned it to my friend Geoff Ward, the historian and screenwriter, who happened to have a copy of Griffith's book in his library. He gave it to me, and as I read it, my admiration for Stanton grew—along with my astonishment that this great American woman had never been mentioned in any of my history courses. I was not alone in my ignorance: none of my college-educated friends, female or male, knew anything at all about Stanton; nor did they know anything about her friend and partner, Susan B. Anthony, other than that she appeared on a rarely seen silver dollar.

I suggested to Ken that we select Stanton as one of the subjects for our *American Lives* series for public television, and when I had outlined her story, he immediately agreed. (Later, we decided to enlarge the film's scope to include Anthony, as well.) My interest in this project is also personal. I grew up in the fifties and sixties surrounded by women—my mother and three sisters. My father worked second shift, three to eleven, and I hardly ever saw him. My older brother was fourteen years older than I and almost always out of the house when I was growing up. So from a very young age I was acutely aware of the pressures my mother and sisters were under to conform to the "role" women were supposed to assume and maintain.

My mother was a difficult, troubled individual, and I think much of her dissatisfaction with her life stemmed from the fact that she never really felt comfortable with the role of wife and mother that she had felt she had no choice but to assume. Her own mother had refused to let her go to high school because boys also attended, and so my mother's education ended at grade school. She married at eighteen, eager to leave her mother's supervision, and quickly had two children. Three more followed at regular seven-year intervals, and from family stories I surmise they came whenever there were major rumbles of discontent in my parents' marriage.

The happiest I ever remember my mother being was when I was about five and she, assuming I was her last child, took a part-time job as a saleswoman at a local candy store. My oldest sister, Carole, was old enough to take care of me so that my mother could go to work. Suddenly she had a life of her own outside the home. For the first time, she had her own money and was able to buy herself clothes, things for our home, and extras for us kids. She had a set of new friends apart from the family, too, and was developing a new social life. She seemed like a different woman, and her happiness spread throughout our family.

Then, when I was seven, my mother and father sat me down and told me that I was going to have a new brother or sister. Even at that age I could tell that my mother was not happy at the prospect. But this was 1957, and my mother had been raised a Catholic—though she was no longer a practicing one. There was no possible alternative to having the child. My father made her give up her job as well, and all the new friendships she had made while working quickly fell away.

Perhaps because she was forty years old, it was a difficult pregnancy. My mother was ill for months after my sister was born and had to undergo a hysterectomy. The baby suffered from colic. By then my oldest sister was married, and the bulk of the child care fell to my mother. She changed dramatically after that. Her mothering now seemed to be performed by rote—something she had to do, not something she wanted to do. She was often angry and withdrawn and fell into silences for days at a time, sitting in front of the television set night after night until it was time for bed.

One would think that with all of her own disappointments she might have encouraged her daughters to pursue a different life. Instead, she ruled them with an iron hand, always pushing them into behaviors that were socially acceptable for women. My brother and I had unlimited freedom, but my sisters were always under strict curfews and denied permission to do many things. When my middle sister expressed an interest in pursuing a career in business, my mother discouraged her. When my oldest sister became pregnant three months before her planned Catholic wedding, my mother made her cancel all the elaborate preparations and marry immediately, with only close family attending. She would not allow her daughter to wear white. Through it all, I could not fathom why a woman so unhappy in her own limited choices would wish so fiercely to see her daughters limit theirs.

Watching the growth of the women's movement in the seventies, I was immediately sympathetic. It seemed at the time to be entirely new, born out of all the questioning of authority and traditions that went on in the sixties. I had no idea then that the women's movement had a history, that many of the issues it raised had their roots in the nineteenth century, in the work of Stanton and Anthony and all the other courageous and freethinking women with whom they worked.

When I discovered all this through Elisabeth Griffith's biography of Stanton—and the works of Kathleen Barry, Ellen Carol DuBois, Ann D. Gordon and all the other historians and biographers I have read since—I grew more and more convinced that had this history been well known, had every eighth-grade textbook had a chapter on the 1848 Seneca Falls Women's Rights Convention and another on Stanton and Anthony's work for woman suffrage (as it was termed in their day), my mother and my sisters might have been aware that other women had been asking for more choices in their lives, for more equality with men, for a change in the restrictive social rules by which they lived, might have recognized some kindred spirits and taken on Stanton and Anthony as their role models, their heroines.

It is my hope that our film and this book will help at least a little to end the long silence surrounding these extraordinary women and their contribution to the ongoing evolution of our American democracy. Then, with the next generation of American women—and men—I won't have to say the name Susan B. Anthony and find it recognized only in relation to a coin, or say the name Elizabeth Cady Stanton and receive the response "Elizabeth Cady *who?*"

Paul Barnes
Walpole, New Hampshire

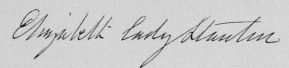

NOT FOR OURSELVES ALONE

THE STORY OF ELIZABETH CADY STANTON AND SUSAN B. ANTHONY

Mormon family in Salt Lake City, c. 1855

SO ENTIRELY ONE ARE WE

1

On the evening of November 12, 1895, passersby on Thirty-ninth Street on Manhattan's West Side noticed something still thought unusual even in New York: large groups of well-dressed women hurrying along the street, unaccompanied by men. They were converging on the big yellow-brick Metropolitan Opera House at the corner of Broadway. "Parties of women . . . without escorts, women unaccustomed to being out that way," a reporter for the *New York Times* noted, found safety in numbers: "One woman said as she entered the Opera House with her party, 'I feel just as though I belonged to a shoal of fishes.'"

The women who crowded the sidewalk, pushed their way into the lobby, and began to move toward their seats in the lofty, glittering interior—more than three thousand of them, along with only a handful of men—had not turned out merely to hear music. They had come to attend a historic event, a great "Reunion of Pioneers and Friends of Woman's Progress," and the boxes that framed the stage in front of them were festooned with flowers and banners belonging to women's organizations: the Woman's Christian Temperance Union, in white with gold letters; the Professional Woman's League, all in gold; the Woman's Press Club, in violet, yellow, and white; the Republican Woman's Club, in patriotic red, white, and blue. At center stage stood three ornately carved chairs, the back and arms of each wound with red roses. Behind the chair in the center was a vast oval of white chrysanthemums with the name STANTON picked out in crimson immortelles.

It was the eightieth birthday of Elizabeth Cady Stanton, the woman who had launched the women's-rights movement in 1848 and had helped lead it ever since. Its celebration was to be the central theme of the evening, and when four sisters named Parke began playing a cornet fanfare and the guest of honor started to make her stately way onstage, a diminutive but corpulent figure in black, leaning on a cane with one hand and clinging with the other to the arm of her son Theodore, the entire audience rose to flutter handkerchiefs in tribute. Stanton was nearly blind now and very frail, but as she carefully took her seat and composed herself amid the flowers, one woman in the crowd thought she looked, "with her majestic face crowned with its beautiful white hair, like a queen upon her throne."

The official hostess for the evening sat at Stanton's left: Mrs. Mary Lowe Dickinson was president of the Woman's National Council of the United States, which claimed 700,000 members all across the country. But sitting at Stanton's right hand, as she had sat for better than forty years, was her close friend and strongest ally, Susan B. Anthony. She was herself seventy-five years old that fall but still routinely working harder than women half her age. In the first seven months of the year alone she had traveled to thirteen states to speak. Then, while addressing a crowd at Lakeside, Ohio, in late July, she had collapsed onstage with what may have been a small stroke—"the whole of me coming to a sudden standstill," she remembered, "like a clap of thunder under a clear sky." She was the best-known woman in America, and as she recuperated, reporters from all over the country kept a death watch outside the house; one Chicago paper telegraphed its man on the scene: "50,000 words if still living, no limit if dead." Anthony had chafed under the enforced rest—"do-nothingness," she called it—and it had taken her nearly three months to get back on her feet. But onstage at the Metropolitan Opera House, she now seemed to one reporter "as erect and alert as ever" as, one by one, younger women, many of whom she had helped train for leadership, rose to recount the progress that women had made in the fields of religion, education, and philanthropy since she and Stanton had begun their work.

The birthday celebration for her old friend had been Anthony's brainchild, but she had been careful to remain behind the scenes until now—not wanting

Suffrage pioneers and their admirers gather for Elizabeth Cady Stanton's eightieth birthday in New York City, November 12, 1895: In this group portrait, made on the stage of the Metropolitan Opera House, the guest of honor is seated at the center, with Susan B. Anthony directly to her right. The bearded man behind them is John Hutchinson, the last of the Hutchinson Family Singers, an old ally who had toured the country signing temperance and abolition anthems long before the Civil War.

*Reassuring news from a newspaper clipping in one of Susan B.
Anthony's scrapbooks*

the evening to seem merely "a mutual admiration
affair," she said—and the National American Woman
Suffrage Association, of which she was president, was
just one of several sponsors. But the symbolism of
seeing the two trailblazers sitting side by side was not
lost on the audience. "Together they have trodden
the flinty stones," said a message from Clara Barton;
"together they opened the way for all womanhood
through all time."

The two women could not have been more different. Stanton had been born to wealth and comfort, and was for many years the housebound mother
of seven. She was witty and hospitable, fond of good
food and fine clothes, an enthusiastic devotee of after-

noon naps. But she was also an uncompromising revolutionary—a "many idead woman," her daughter Harriot Stanton Blatch proudly called her—for whom winning the vote was always just one item on a comprehensive agenda aimed at improving the status of all women in every area of life.

Anthony was a Quaker farmer's daughter who had chosen early not to marry; alone among the earliest advocates of woman suffrage, she had remained self-supporting all her life. She was plainspoken, disciplined, single-minded, but she had learned to be a canny tactician as well, willing to tack to the left or to the right if by so doing she could steer the woman-suffrage movement closer to its goal. Though she never held public office and would not live to cast a legal vote, she had already become the nation's first great woman politician, "Aunt Susan" to a whole generation of young women.

Stanton herself had once tried to explain the nature of their partnership. "I am the better writer," she said, "[and] she the better critic. She supplied the facts and statistics, I the philosophy and rhetoric, and together we have made arguments that have stood unshaken by the storms of . . . long years; arguments that no man has answered. Our speeches may be considered the united product of our two brains. So entirely one are we that . . . not one feeling of envy or jealousy has ever shadowed our lives."

Their arguments had indeed proved unassailable, and they had determined early on that they should always stand together: "To the world we always seem to agree and uniformly reflect each other," Stanton wrote. "Like husband and wife, each has the feeling that we must have no differences in public." But behind the scenes, the real story was more complicated—and more interesting—filled with instances of love and loyalty, envy and betrayal; raising larger questions of principle and compromise, means and ends, and the meaning of independence itself.

Finally, it was time to hear from the guest of honor. Mrs. Dickinson introduced her as "the Mother of the heart-life stirring in us all." The crowd rose once again, a sea of waving handkerchiefs. Only Stanton's obvious frailty returned them to their seats; no one wanted to force her to stand too long.

Women in the front rows saw that there were tears in her eyes. "I thank you all very much for the tributes of love, respect, and gratitude," she said, her rich voice penetrating to the farthest balcony. "I am well aware that these demon-

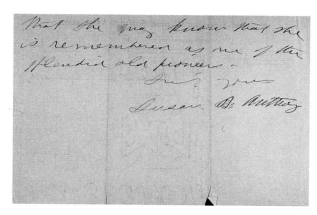

A letter from Anthony that accompanied an invitation to Stanton's 1895 celebration, intended for the mother of Edwin Marsh, one of the Rochester election inspectors who had been jailed twenty-three years earlier for permitting Anthony to cast her vote

Stanton in 1895. "I have been affected to tears more than once during these days of triumph," she wrote in her diary the day after her eightieth birthday celebration. "Knowing myself, conscious of all my shortcomings, remembering how I have left undone so many things I should have done, I often feel myself unworthy of these generous praises, the out-pouring of so much love and friendship from so many unexpected sources."

strations are not so much tributes to me as an individual as to the great idea that I represent—the enfranchisement of women."

She was too weak to remain on her feet, she said. A younger colleague would read her remarks for her. She started for her chair, then turned to the audience again, a smile playing across her lips: "Before I sit down I want to say one word to the men who are present. I fear you think the 'new woman' is going to wipe you off the planet, but be not afraid. All who have mothers, sisters, wives or sweethearts will be very well looked after."

The old idea that man was made for himself, and woman for him, that he is the oak, she the vine, he the head, she the heart, he the great conservator of wisdom, . . . she of love,—will be reverently laid aside with other long since exploded philosophies of the ignorant past.

Susan B. Anthony

Philadelphia family, c. 1846

Then she sat and listened along with the audience as her words were read aloud. While she was never one to discourage praise and had heard precious little of it in recent years, she was too impatient to bask in it for long. Nor did she want to waste valuable time saying predictable things about votes for women, the cause with which she'd been most clearly identified since 1848: the vote was coming, she was sure, though she would not live to see it. "I cannot work in the same old ruts any longer," she'd recently told a friend. "I have said all I have to say on the subject of suffrage." And she saw little point in further belaboring the discredited notion that women must confine themselves to "woman's sphere"—being daughters and wives and mothers and nothing else. "That ground," she wrote, "has been traveled over so often there is not a single tree nor flower nor blade of grass to be found anywhere."

For Elizabeth Cady Stanton there was always more interesting, more important work to do, and even on this self-consciously sentimental occasion, meant to bring women of many opinions together, she could not resist challenging her listeners. If women were to continue on the path of progress, she said, Christianity itself needed to be reformed:

> Nothing that has ever emanated from the brain of man is too sacred to be revised and corrected. Our National Constitution has been amended fifteen times, our English system of jurisprudence has been essentially modified in the interest of woman to keep pace with advancing civilization. And now the time has come to amend and modify the canon laws, prayer-books, liturgies and Bibles. . . . Woman's imperative duty at this hour is to demand a thorough revision of creeds and codes, Scriptures and constitutions.

Anthony sat quietly as Stanton's words were read out to the increasingly restive audience. She was privately disappointed that Stanton had not rested her case "after describing the wonderful advances made in state, church, society and home, instead of going on to single out the church and declare it to be especially slow in accepting the doctrine of equality of women." Criticism of the churches would unnecessarily alienate many of the women present, she thought, and would provide still another distraction from her lifelong effort to win the vote, which she believed would arm all women everywhere with the weapon they needed to transform the country and the world.

But Anthony was accustomed to such embarrassments—Stanton could never be kept for long from expressing what she believed to be essential truths about woman's condition, no matter whom they might offend. The next day Anthony journeyed uptown to Stanton's West Side apartment, where an artist was waiting to make a plaster cast of her hand linked with that of her great friend. Cast in bronze, it was meant to be still another symbol of one of the most fateful friendships in American history.

I WISH YOU WERE A BOY!

Three years later, at the age of eighty-two, Elizabeth Cady Stanton published her autobiography, *Eighty Years and More*. It was intended, she wrote, simply to "amuse and benefit the reader." It was also clearly meant to win converts to her cause. It is a selective chronicle—important historical events are overlooked; Stanton's long and complicated marriage is only lightly touched upon; and the facts of her girlhood are artfully arranged to provide the reader with an understanding of the world from which she came and the personal impact upon her of the orthodox patriarchal society against which she led her lifelong rebellion, and against which she wanted her mostly female readers to rebel as well.

"Our parents were as kind, indulgent and considerate as the Puritan ideas of those days permitted," she said of her earliest years, "but fear rather than love, of God and parents alike, predominated. Add to this our timidity in our intercourse with servants and teachers, and our dread of the ever-present devil, and the reader will see that under such conditions, nothing but strong self-will and a good share of hope and mirthfulness could have saved an ordinary child from becoming a nullity."

There was never anything ordinary about the little girl who was born in the finest house in Johnstown, New York, on November 12, 1815. Nor was there ever any danger that she would become a "nullity" or fail for a moment during her long life to demonstrate less than her full measure of self-will or hope or mirthfulness.

She was the eighth child born to Judge Daniel Cady and his wife, Margaret Livingston. Her mother was tall and stately, the daughter of an officer in the Rev-

Judge Daniel and Margaret Livingston Cady, the parents of Elizabeth Cady Stanton; and their home in Johnstown, New York (in the foreground of the photograph opposite). In her reminiscences, Stanton portrayed both her parents and her hometown as grim, stifling to a lively little girl determined to question everything.

olution, a member of one of New York state's oldest and most aristocratic clans. The Livingstons had once ruled a large part of the Hudson Valley like feudal lords and had never entirely abandoned the notion that they were somehow set apart from—and a little above—their fellow citizens. In some respects, Elizabeth ran true to that form: she would proudly call herself a "Daughter of the Revolution" to the end of her life and often conveyed the sense that her views should prevail simply because she held them. But her mother nonetheless remains a minor character in her autobiography, little more than a "queenly" disciplinarian determined to spoil her daughter's fun. In her mother's eyes, Stanton wrote, "everything I liked and enjoyed was messy or injurious . . . and everything I disliked was just the thing."

It was Elizabeth's father who mattered most to her; it was for his approval that she yearned, against his patriarchal strictures that she would fight all her life. He was short, canny, and conservative, a former shoemaker's apprentice whose advantageous marriage had helped make him a prosperous man—under the property law that then prevailed, his bride's entire inheritance had become his own at the moment the two exchanged vows. He had gone on to make himself rich in real estate while pursuing a distinguished career in law and politics: circuit court judge, state legislator, Whig congressman, eventually associate justice of the New York Supreme Court. In everything he did, his daughter wrote, he was "a conservative's conservative."

Elizabeth remembered her girlhood as an unbroken string of revolts—against the "petty tyranny" of the Scots nurses her mother hired to care for her and her sisters; against the matching red dresses that her mother insisted be worn by all the girls; against the dour, unforgiving Calvinism of her family's Presbyterian faith. "[E]verything we like to do is a sin," she remembered telling one of her nurses, "and . . . everything we dislike is commanded by God or someone on earth. I am so tired of that everlasting no! no! no! At school, at home, everywhere it is *no!*" She was often punished by her mother for what were called "tantrums," she recalled, but she was sure her protests had in fact been "justifiable acts of rebellion against the tyranny of those in authority."

From the first, she remembered being angered by the injustices to women she saw everywhere around her. Her earliest memory, she claimed, was the disappointing response of family friends to the birth of her younger sister Catherine, when she herself was only four. Visitor after visitor, she recalled, said, "What a pity it is she's a girl!" Her father's law students teased her about her perpetual indignation. When she showed them a new necklace, one explained that "if in due time you should be my wife, those ornaments would be mine; I could take them and lock them up, and you could never wear them except with my permission. I could even exchange them for a box of cigars, and you could watch them evaporate in smoke."

Stanton revisited her childhood many times in lectures and articles, altering or omitting details as she went, but there were two incidents she rarely failed to include. The first took place when she was a small girl, she said, and had been present in her father's office when a tearful woman named Flora Campbell came to plead for help. Without consulting her, Campbell explained, her husband had mortgaged the farm that had been her inheritance from her father; now his creditors were taking it over. What should she do? Where could she and her children go? Judge Cady was sympathetic but largely helpless. Campbell had no legal recourse, he said; under current law her inheritance was her husband's to do with as he saw fit. Cady could provide her with a place to live on one of his many properties, but otherwise there was nothing he could do. Elizabeth—to whom the judge had seemed all-powerful until that moment—told Flora Campbell not to worry; she promised to go through her father's law books with a pair of scissors, snipping out every statute that was unfair to women. Her father gently took her aside and explained that the law was the law. "When you are grown up, and able to prepare a speech," she remembered his telling her, "you must go down to Albany and talk to the legislators; tell them all you have seen in this office—the sufferings of the [women], robbed of their inheritance . . . and if you can persuade them

There would be more sense in insisting on man's limitations because he cannot be a mother, than on a woman's because she can be. Surely maternity is an added power and de-

California family, mid-1850s

velopment of some of the most tender sentiments of the human heart and not a "limitation" . . .

"But it unfits her for much of the world's work."

Yes, and it fits her for much of [it]; a large share of human legislation would be better done by her because of this deep experience. . . . If one-half the effort had been expended to exalt the feminine element that has been made to degrade it, we should have reached the natural equilib-rium long ago. Either sex, in isolation, is robbed of one-half its power for the accomplishment of any given work.

ELIZABETH CADY STANTON

to pass new laws, the old ones will be a dead letter." "Thus," Stanton wrote, "the future object of my life was foreshadowed and my duty plainly outlined by him who was opposed to my public career when, in due time, I entered upon it."

The second incident to which she repeatedly returned in her writings occurred in 1826, when she was eleven. Elizabeth and her sisters were a source of pleasure and pride to Judge Cady, but his hopes for his family's future always lay with his sons. Three boys had died in infancy. The fourth, Eleazar, was twenty that summer and just home from completing his studies at Union College. "We all . . . felt," Elizabeth remembered, "that this son filled a larger place in our father's affection . . . than his five daughters together."

But Eleazar, too, fell ill and died. Daniel Cady was shattered, Elizabeth remembered:

> I still recall . . . going into the large, darkened parlor to see my brother and finding the casket, mirrors and pictures all draped in white, and my father seated by his side, pale and immovable. As he took no notice of me, after standing a long while, I climbed upon his knee, when he mechanically put his arm about me and with my head resting against his beating heart we both sat in silence, he thinking of the wreck of all his hopes in the loss of a dear son, and I wondering what could be said or done to fill the void in his breast. At length, he heaved a deep sigh and said: "Oh, my daughter, I wish you were a boy!" Throwing my arms about his neck, I replied: "I will try to be all my brother was."

She resolved to be "manly" from then on, she recalled, by which she said she meant "learned and courageous," and she hurled herself into activities then thought exclusively male. She learned to jump ditches and four-foot fences on horseback, challenged male students to debate, and, alone among the girls at Johnstown Academy, studied Greek with the boys, doing so well that she took home the second prize in the annual competition. Her goal in all of this, she remembered, was to hear her father say, "Well, a girl is as good as a boy, after all." But he never did. Instead, shown proof after proof of her ability, he would sigh that he still wished she were a boy, "and I," Stanton wrote, "not knowing why he felt thus, would hide my tears of vexation."

Both these stories—calculated to spark empathy and anger in female readers with their own experiences of patronization by men—seem too good literally to have been true in every detail. It is hard to imagine that Judge Cady, who appears to have opposed his daughter's every attempt to build an independent life for herself outside the home, could ever actually have urged her to make speeches in public. And in some earlier accounts of her girlhood Stanton herself wrote that she had resolved to take on the Johnstown boys in Greek well before the death of her brother. But literal truth mattered less to her than the lessons to be drawn from experiences with which she hoped all women could identify.

Stanton's schoolmistress Emma Willard and her Troy Female Seminary, the first endowed institution for the education of girls in America. "She was a splendid-looking woman," Stanton recalled, "then in her prime, and fully realized my idea of a queen."

TROY FEMALE SEMINARY.

This Institution offers the accumulated advantages of nearly fifty years of successful operation. Every facility is provided for a thorough course of useful and ornamental education, under the direction of a corps of more than twenty professors and teachers. The members of the Institution have the benefit of Lectures of the highest order, on

SCIENCE, HISTORY, LITERATURE, ART, &C. &C.,

And the use of a valuable Library, an extensive Philosophical Apparatus, a well selected Cabinet of Minerals, and Shells, Maps, Charts, and Models.

Superior Music Teachers are constantly employed in the Seminary. Great Attention is given to the French Language.

The teachers reside in the family, and adapt their instructions to its use in conversation.

THE CLASSES IN DRAWING AND PAINTING, IN OIL AND WATER COLORS,

Are under the direction of instructors of long experience and tried ability. A large and choice collection of Pictures is constantly before them for study and for patterns.

The pupils are received into the family of the principals, in which every arrangement is made for their physical education and the improvement of their manners and morals. They occupy private rooms, two in each, the rooms of the female teachers and that of an experienced nurse being among those of the young ladies.

Circulars containing more particular information may be obtained by application to the principals, Mr. or Mrs. JOHN H. WILLARD, Troy, N. Y.

In 1830, Elizabeth was fifteen and eager to continue her education. She wanted to attend Union College, the institution her late brother had attended, the school to which some of her male classmates from Johnstown Academy were going. But neither Union nor any other college in America would then admit a female student. "My vexation and mortification knew no bounds," she remembered. Nor did Judge Cady think much of the revolutionary idea of secondary education for young women. It would be better, she remembered his saying, if she contented herself with attending the circuit courts with him from time to time, enjoyed "balls and dinners," and learned "how to keep house and make puddings."

Three years earlier, Margaret Cady had borne her husband still another son. When he, too, died in infancy, she suffered a nervous breakdown, and Elizabeth's older sister Tryphena took over the running of the household for a time. Tryphena's husband, Edward Bayard, now came to Elizabeth's rescue; he persuaded her father that three years at the Troy Female Seminary, run by Emma Willard, would do the girl no harm.

Willard was a pioneer in women's education who argued that young women would be better wives and mothers if they studied algebra and history and music. Elizabeth admired her headmistress and enjoyed the company of the other girls, but she found childish the great fuss her fellow students made about boys. "My own experience," she wrote later, "proves to me that it is a grave mistake to send boys and girls to separate institutions. . . . The stimulus of sex promotes a healthy condition of the intellectual and moral faculties, and gives to both a development they never can acquire alone." All her life she would champion the cause of coeducation.

And it was while attending Willard's school that she underwent an ordeal that affected her own emotional equilibrium for a time—and encouraged the lifelong religious skepticism that would one day lead her to mount an assault on Christian scripture itself. In 1831 she attended a six-week revival conducted by the greatest American evangelist of the nineteenth century, Charles Grandison Finney. He was tall and grave, a former lawyer with a huge voice who believed that every man and woman had personally to be confronted by the choice between salvation and damnation. Stanton never forgot him or forgave his impact upon her. He was a "terrifier of human souls," she said:

The evangelist Charles Grandison Finney and his second wife, Elizabeth Ford Atkinson, in 1850. Stanton never abandoned her conviction that Finney's fire-and-brimstone sermons did more harm than good, but she was delighted when, after she had helped to launch the women's movement, Mrs. Finney took her aside to confide that "you have the sympathy of a large proportion of the educated women with you," even if "these women dare not speak out their sympathy."

> I can see him now, his great eyes rolling around the congregation and his arms flying about in the air like those of a windmill. . . . [H]e described hell and the devil and the long procession of sinners being swept down by rapids, about to make the awful plunge into the burning depths of liquid fire below. . . . He suddenly halted and, pointing his index finger at the supposed procession, he exclaimed: "There, do you not see them!"
>
> I was wrought up to such a pitch that I actually jumped up and gazed in the direction to which he pointed while the picture glowed before my eyes and remained with me for months afterward.

Highly strung, brought up to believe literally in "the ever-present devil," Stanton was deeply shaken. "Fear of the Judgment seized my soul," she remembered. "Visions of the Lost haunted my dreams. Mental anguish prostrated my health." She fell ill and left school for a time, but even at home she found herself so frightened that she felt compelled to wake her father night after night "to pray for me lest I should be cast into the bottomless pit before morning." It took weeks for her to get over her terror, and the experience left her convinced that it was criminal to "shadow the minds of the young with . . . gloomy superstitions, . . . with fears of the unknown and the unknowable to poison all their joy in life."

Once again, her brother-in-law Edward Bayard proved her salvation. He encouraged her to read widely, to interest herself in the latest findings of what then passed for science—phrenology, homeopathy, animal magnetism. Eventually, she wrote, and with Bayard's help, "religious superstition gave place to rational ideas based on scientific facts and . . . as I looked at everything from a new standpoint, I grew more and more happy." She would one day get to know Charles Finney, whose antislavery sentiments and belief in the responsibility of each individual for his or her own fate she shared, but she remained convinced that the fear his kind of evangelism encouraged did "incalculable harm to the very souls he sought to save."

The seven carefree years that followed her graduation from school in 1833, she remembered, were the most pleasant of her girlhood. She was small, attractive, and vivacious and delighted in singing, dancing, flirting—and beating at chess the law students who gathered in the family parlor in the evenings. There was one awkwardness. Edward Bayard, ten years her senior, had been her friend and confidant within the family. Now, according to a story told by her daughter Harriot Stanton Blatch long after her mother's death, he became something more: they fell in love, and he proposed that he leave his wife and run away with Elizabeth. Unwilling to wound her sister, she turned him down, and he vowed never to be alone with her again.

She spent several weeks each summer in Peterboro, New York, the home of her mother's cousin Gerrit Smith. He was one of the richest men in America, heir to a vast fortune and more than a million acres of land in three states. He was also one of the most generous, an enthusiastic backer of every kind of reform—vegetarianism, temperance, abolitionism. His palatial house was a stopping place for advocates of all sorts of views, as one frequent guest remembered:

There you might meet a dozen wealthy and refined visitors from the metropolitan cities; a sprinkling of negroes from the sunny South on their way to Canada; a crazy Millerite or two, who, disgusted with the world, thought it destined to be burned up at an early day; an adventurer who wanted Mr. Smith to invest largely in some utterly impracticable patent right, while the throng would be checkered with three or four Indians of the neighborhood, the remnants of the once powerful Oneidas, who remembered [Smith's wealthy] father, and felt pretty sure that they could get something out of his munificent son. The high-born guests had come to enjoy themselves during the summer solstice at this fine rural retreat, and they always had a good time. As to the rest, they were never sent empty away, especially the negroes and the Indians, the former accepting cash in hand and good advice about the best route to Canada, while the latter departed in good time with shoulders stooping under burdens of flour, beef, and other edibles. But Mr. Smith never was known

to invest in any of the patent rights, and he took not a single share of stock in the scheme for burning up the world.

Elizabeth loved it all. Her own home was quiet, constrained, and conservative. "To go anywhere else after a visit" to her cousins, she once said, was "like coming down from the divine heights into the valley of humiliation." "Every member of their household is an abolitionist," she marveled, "even to the coachman." In the Smiths' parlor she listened to ceaseless talk of politics and radical reform and found listeners willing to consider her own burgeoning opinions as well. "I had become interested in the anti-slavery and temperance questions . . . ," she recalled. "I felt a new inspiration in life and was enthused with new ideas of individual rights and the basic principles of government."

And there, in October of 1839, she met a man who must have seemed the living embodiment of those new ideas. Henry Brewster Stanton was ten years older than she, tall, handsome, unattached, and, she remembered, "then considered the most eloquent and impassioned orator on the anti-slavery platform." Born in Connecticut into a family with as impeccable a Revolutionary pedigree as her

The Gerrit Smith house at Peterboro, New York, the village that Smith's fur-trading father, Peter Smith, had founded and then named for himself

Elizabeth Cady about the time she met her future husband, Henry Stanton

own, he had begun life as a journalist, then been so inspired by the same Charles Finney who had terrified Elizabeth that he abandoned law and journalism and enrolled at Lane Seminary in Ohio, intending to become a clergyman. But when he and several fellow students began to agitate against slavery and were ordered to stop doing so by the trustees, they withdrew from the school in what came to be called the Lane Rebellion. Stanton then became one of seventy full-time agents for the American Anti-Slavery Society, celebrated for his ability to make his listeners both laugh and cry and for the courage with which he faced down angry mobs. (Later in life he was proud to say that he'd survived a total of two hundred of them—had in fact been attacked in every northern state from Indiana to Maine except Vermont, which alone "abstained from that fascinating recreation.")

Just before meeting Elizabeth, he had helped foster still another revolt within the ranks of abolitionism itself, urging his fellow members of the American Anti-Slavery Society to form a new Liberty party, pledged to the overthrow of slavery through political means. To the first generation of abolitionists like William Lloyd Garrison and Wendell Phillips, slavery remained an evil that could be expunged only by "moral suasion"; for them to take part in electoral politics under a Constitution that sanctioned slavery was to compromise with wickedness.

To Stanton, Gerrit Smith and the other founders of what would soon become the Liberty Party, however, it was simple realism, and Elizabeth would come to agree. She had nothing but admiration for Garrison's high-minded stand and uncompromising rhetoric, she wrote a friend, but "so long as we are governed by human laws, I should be unwilling to have the making & administering of those laws left entirely to the selfish & unprincipled part of the community, which would be the case should all our honest men refuse to mingle in political affairs."

One glorious October morning, Stanton took Elizabeth on a long ride through the woods. "As we were returning home," she recalled, "we stopped often to admire the scenery and, perchance, each other. When walking slowly through a beautiful grove, he laid his hand on the horn of the saddle and, to my surprise, made one of those charming revelations of human feeling which brave knights have always found eloquent words to utter, and to which fair ladies have always listened with mingled emotions of pleasure and astonishment."

Elizabeth accepted Henry Stanton's proposal—and quickly found herself once again the center of controversy within the family. Gerrit Smith warned that her father would never agree to the marriage, and Judge Cady bore out the grim prediction. "I understand [Stanton] has no trade or profession," he told Smith. "Mr. Stanton's present business cannot be regarded as a business for life. If the object of the Abolitionists be soon accomplished he must be thrown out of business—

and if success does not crown their efforts—the rank and file will not much longer consent to pay salaries."

Edward Bayard was against the marriage, too, and in the face of strenuous objections from the two men whose good opinion she had always prized above all others, Elizabeth wavered and, finally, dutifully, broke off the engagement: "Hitherto, my apprehensions had all been of death and eternity," she wrote; "now life itself was filled with fears."

But Henry Stanton was a persistent suitor, flooding her with letters begging her to reconsider. Elizabeth had come to love him—and already loved his cause. When he told her in the winter of 1840 that he was about to sail for London as a delegate to the first World Anti-Slavery Convention in London and planned to remain abroad for eight long months, she reversed herself.

They were married in Johnstown on May 1, 1840. No one knows how Judge Cady was reconciled to the wedding; possibly, in exchange for his grudging acquiescence, he elicited a promise that when the newlyweds returned from England, his son-in-law would agree to come and study law with him so that he could support his daughter in the manner to which she was accustomed. In any case, the bride insisted on two changes in the ceremony. She and Henry agreed to strike the word "obey"—theirs was meant to be a marriage between equals—and she kept her own name. Henceforth, she would be known, not as "Mrs. Henry Stanton," as custom dictated, but as "Elizabeth Cady Stanton."

Ten days later, the newlyweds boarded the *Montreal* at New York for England. Marriage had done nothing to dampen Elizabeth's high spirits. Even before the ship left the dock she startled the other passengers by playing tag on deck with her sister Margaret's husband, who had come to see her off. Once at sea, she accepted a dare from the captain to be hauled in a chair up to the top of the mast so that she could enjoy the view only male passengers were customarily given the opportunity to see. She also took obvious pleasure in trouncing at chess the most celebrated man aboard, her husband's close ally and the presidential candidate of the brand-new Liberty Party, James G. Birney.

Birney's radicalism did not extend to his personal life; in every other realm save his opposition to slavery, he was a conservative Alabamian who, Elizabeth recalled, "soon perceived that I needed toning down before reaching England." "You went to the masthead in a chair," he chided her, "which I think very unladylike. [And] I heard you call your husband 'Henry' in the presence of strangers, which is not permissible in polite society. You should always say, 'Mr. Stanton.' "

Elizabeth Cady Stanton laughed off the criticism. Armed by her own girlhood with what she herself remembered as "a good degree of self-esteem," she had already decided that the rules that governed the behavior of other women would not apply to her.

THE WORST GIRL OF ALL BEING

Susan B. Anthony did not share her great friend's literary gifts. "Whenever I take my pen in hand," she confessed to her first biographer, "I always seem to be mounted on stilts." Nor did she share Stanton's fondness for drawing universal lessons from arranging and rearranging the events of her own girlhood. As an adult, she was a whirlwind, so relentlessly active that she left little time for the sort of self-examination that might have helped explain precisely how a shy, self-conscious young woman seemingly consumed with self-doubt managed within a very few years to transform herself into an utterly self-reliant political leader whose boldness matched that of any other woman of her time.

Some part of the answer—but only part—clearly lay within the home in which she spent her first eighteen years. Elizabeth Cady Stanton's rebelliousness represented a deliberate breaking-away from a determinedly traditional household. Anthony's rebellion was no less intense, her independent spirit and willingness to go it alone in some ways still more remarkable, but both were at least in part in keeping with the traditions preached and practiced by her family. Her parents believed it was the first duty of every human being to do what he or she could to be useful to the world, a conviction they somehow managed to convey to all six of their children who survived into adulthood. Both their sons would play active roles in the Kansas struggle against slavery; both of Susan's married sisters sup-

Daniel and Lucy Read Anthony, the parents of Susan B. Anthony, supported their daughter's early drive for autonomy.

ported her work for suffrage, while her unmarried youngest sister, Mary, would fight for it openly, often at her side.

The elder Anthonys identified early with each of the two causes to which Susan would first devote herself—temperance and abolitionism—and were entirely sympathetic when she finally fixed upon women's rights as her life's work. Although she became America's most celebrated proponent of a woman's right to remain single and completely independent, she was devoted to her family and would draw all her life on the support and encouragement of every member of it.

Susan Brownell Anthony was born near Adams, Massachusetts, on February 15, 1820. Her father, Daniel, was a Quaker farmer so devout that toys, games, and music were all barred from his house for fear they might distract the children from what was called the Inner Light—the God who lived within every soul—and so committed to pacifism that he refused to vote or pay taxes to a government willing to wage war. When the tax collector came to call, he placed his purse on the table and said, "I shall not voluntarily pay these taxes; If thee wants to rifle my pocketbook, thee may do so." And he shared fully in the Quaker belief that men and women were equal before God; his own sister was a Quaker elder and respected preacher.

But Daniel Anthony's relationship with the Friends was never simple. He was made to apologize to the Meeting for his "misconduct" in marrying Susan's mother, Lucy Read, a Baptist; was brought before the congregation again to explain why he had dared go "out of plainness" by wearing a handsome cape purchased in

The birthplace and early home of Susan B. Anthony, built by her father at the base of Mount Greylock, near Adams, Massachusetts

The Friends' Meeting House at Adams, where Anthony often heard her father's sister preach

New York, and was finally read out of Meeting altogether because—in order to provide local young people a place in which to learn to dance other than in taverns, where alcohol was served—he had opened up his attic as a dancing school. (The fact that he had been careful to keep his own children from taking part in the dancing did not sway the elders.) Susan inherited from her father a host of Quaker qualities—humility, austerity, egalitarianism—along with a deep distrust of orthodoxy.

Her mother was a shy, reticent woman, so modest she is said never to have so much as mentioned any of her pregnancies—Susan was the second of eight children—to a living soul other than her husband and her mother. She had given up the simplest pleasures to marry her Quaker husband—singing, dancing, brightly colored clothing—and accepted with good grace even the criticism of her husband's Quaker neighbors who overheard her humming lullabies to her babies. And when the time came, she agreed that her children should all become members of the Friends' Meeting. She herself, though, never became a Quaker, claiming always that she was "not good enough."

Not long after Susan was born, her father harnessed the stream that twisted through his farm to power a small cotton mill and staffed it with young women from the surrounding hills; unlike Elizabeth Cady Stanton, who would have to develop her empathy for working-class women secondhand, Susan B. Anthony was surrounded from earliest childhood by women who earned their own livelihoods. As many as eleven mill girls sometimes boarded in the Anthony home. Lucy Read Anthony had to not only care for her own children but look after these boarders as well. She did so without complaint, but her daughters were all expected to help, and from early girlhood Susan was accustomed to an almost ceaseless round of work—sewing, cleaning, hauling water, preparing three meals a day for as many as sixteen people, and washing up again once they had finished eating. When her enemies in later years charged that because she had never married she couldn't possibly understand the supposed advantages of remaining within "woman's sphere," the memory of her mother's sacrifices and her own sometimes arduous girlhood must have made her smile.

Susan was precocious enough to have learned to read before the age of four, but she is said to have strained her eyes so badly that they crossed. The left one eventually straightened itself, but the right would remain out of alignment all her life, a source of sufficient self-consciousness that in later years she would rarely allow that side of her face to be photographed. She seems to have been unusually conscientious, too. When, at the age of eleven, she earned three dollars substituting at one of her father's looms for two weeks, she used every penny of it to buy three blue teacups for her overworked mother, and when the male foreman left and she suggested that one of the women be appointed to replace him, she was disappointed when her father said that putting a woman in charge would never do.

In 1826, Daniel Anthony moved his family to nearby Battenville, built himself a handsome fifteen-room house, and began running several mills for a local businessman. By 1835 he had become one of the most important men in the community.

Susan attended the district school until the male teacher reached long division and refused to teach it to her, either because he did not believe girls needed such lofty knowledge or because he secretly hadn't mastered it himself. In any case, her father pulled her out of the classroom and started a home school for his children and the women who worked in his mills. Daniel Anthony taught classes himself at first, then hired a series of teachers, including Mary Perkins, trained by the educational pioneer Mary Lyon. Susan was accustomed to the young women who worked in her father's mills, but Mary Perkins was different—an independent, unmarried woman who had been "fashionably educated."

Beginning in the summer of Susan's fifteenth year, Daniel Anthony saw to it that she and her older sister, Guelma, took teaching jobs themselves, first acting as governesses in the homes of family friends, then taking over classrooms in the district school at one dollar and fifty cents a week—roughly one quarter of the salary that had been paid to the men they replaced. Inequities in pay between men and women were abstractions to Elizabeth Cady Stanton; they would remain vivid memories to Susan B. Anthony.

Man's intellectual superiority cannot be a question until woman has had a fair trial. When we shall have freedom to find our own sphere, when we shall have had our colleges, our professions, our trades, for a century, a comparison then may be justly instituted.   Elizabeth Cady Stanton

California seamstress, c. 1880

When neighbors criticized Daniel Anthony for allowing his daughters to earn their own wages, he was unperturbed: "I am fully of the belief that shouldst thou never teach school a single day afterwards," he assured Guelma, "thou wouldst ever feel to justify thy course . . . Thou wouldst seem to me to be laying the foundation for thy far greater usefulness."

Anthony believed his daughters' usefulness—and their sense of self-reliance—would be enhanced by further education as well, and in the autumn of 1837, he escorted seventeen-year-old Susan to the same Quaker boarding school near Philadelphia at which Guelma had already spent a year.

Deborah Moulson's Female Seminary offered a remarkably substantive curriculum for a girl's school of that time: "Arithmetic, Algebra, Literature, Chemistry, Philosophy, Physiology and Bookkeeping." Susan enjoyed her studies, although what she called the "nonconformance" of her eyes sometimes embarrassed her when she tried to read aloud in class. But not even the presence of her older sister could allay her fervent longing for her large and loving family: "Oft times when in the act of committing lessons," she wrote in her journal, "will the enduring allurements of home rush upon my mind, and surely it requires all the fortitude that I can command to overcome such feelings."

Those feelings were only intensified by the school's founder and headmistress, Deborah Moulson, whose primary purpose was the "inculcation of the principles of Humility, Morality and love of Virtue"—principles she sought to inculcate in Susan B. Anthony with a relentlessness that even in an age of severity and repression seems to have bordered on the psychotic.

The pages of Susan's diary are filled with examples of her teacher's grim zeal. A single instance of "levity and mirthfulness" was enough for Moulson to compare Susan and seven other girls to Judas Iscariot. When Susan and some of her friends failed to remember minute details of one Sunday's sermon, they were warned that God would strike them dead if they did not pay better heed.

The headmistress was hard on all her girls, but she seems to have singled out Susan for special severity. And Susan, already self-conscious and almost obsessively self-critical, seems to have been especially vulnerable to her assaults. Moulson used even her own frail health—she was in fact slowly dying of tuberculosis—to undercut her pupils. When Susan failed to dot an *i* in one of her exercises, the headmistress declared that all "the distress she had [herself] undergone in mind and body" was entirely due to her students' shortcomings. "This was like an Electrical shock to me," Anthony confided to her diary. "I rushed upstairs to my room where, without restraint I could give vent to my tears. . . . Indeed I do consider myself such a bad creature that I can not see any who seems worse."

Nothing the overly conscientious, desperately homesick girl could think to do met with her teacher's approval. When she tried to sweep the cobwebs from the classroom ceiling and accidentally damaged the lock and hinges of her teacher's desk, she confessed what she had done the moment Moulson entered the room. In front of the whole class, the headmistress icily refused to acknowledge Susan's apology, preferring instead that she contemplate her wickedness in silence and thereby learn still more humility. Sixty years later, Anthony told her biographer, the memory of that humiliation still made her "turn cold and sick at heart."

Susan's time at Miss Moulson's seminary served to reinforce her sense of her own unworthiness, her frustration at being unable ever to meet the moral standards she set for herself. "Sometimes," she told a friend, "I feel as if I were the worst girl of all being."

Her ordeal did not last long. At the end of her first term, her father came to take her and Guelma home: he could no longer pay their tuition. The country was in the grip of a depression, and Daniel Anthony himself was faced with bankruptcy. That summer, his handsome home, his store and factory and household goods—including even the "underclothes of wife and daughters" and "Mr. and Mrs. Anthony's spectacles"—were put up for public auction, and he was eventually forced to move his family to a crossroads settlement called Hardscrabble and start over.

Her father's failure would alter Susan's life forever. She had originally taught school in the summertime merely because he believed it would strengthen her character and encourage her sense of self-sufficiency. Now she had no choice: to help keep the family afloat, Susan would have to leave home and seek full-time teaching jobs wherever she could find them. It was to be her "sad lot," she wrote that year, "to mingle with strangers." This was more than adolescent melodrama; for her to be forced to make her way alone among people who did not all employ Quaker speech or follow Quaker ways was a break with everything she had known.

In the spring of 1839, Susan took up her duties as the assistant teacher at Eunice Kenyon's boarding school in New Rochelle, New York. She was anxious and fearful at first, and still more so when Kenyon went home on leave and the nineteen-year-old found herself in charge: the responsibility was great, she wrote, and the work "very trying." She insisted on strict discipline in the classroom, and when she sent one student to bed without supper, the girl's mother and grandmother stormed into the school, demanding to speak to the head teacher. Susan defiantly urged them to do so, then collapsed in tears: "I hope [Eunice] will not be such a fool as I was to cry but hold to her rights," she wrote, "and I know she will as she possesses and feels more independence than I fear I ever shall."

Anthony was always hardest on herself, but she was hard on others as well. Even the austere Presbyterianism against which Elizabeth Cady Stanton had revolted struck her as dangerously frivolous: "The dress of the communicants bespeaks nothing but vanity of heart," she wrote after visiting a Presbyterian service one Sunday; "curls, bows and artificials displayed in profusion . . . surely if their hearts were not vain and worldly, their dress would not be."

She stayed at home when the rest of the town turned out to see President Martin van Buren pass through, in part because he was said to enjoy "all-debasing Wine." Her devotion to temperance drove her to write her own good-natured uncle a hastily scrawled letter chastising him for having dared to drink ale on special occasions. "[I]t is a great thing to say what one will not do before having any experience," he answered. "Thy aunt Ann Eliza says to tell thee we are temperate drinkers. We should think from the shape of thy letter that thou thyself hadst had a good horn from the contents of the cider barrel, a part being written one side up and a part the other way, and it would need someone in nearly the same predicament to keep track of it. We hope thy cranium will get straightened when the answer to this is written."

Anthony was not amused. Nor was she pleased when she learned in the summer of 1839 that Guelma planned to marry a mutual childhood friend. Her older sister was her closest confidante and had been her chief source of solace during her year of boarding school. Now she felt abandoned, just as she would throughout her life when unmarried women who were especially close to her chose to marry. "I have no dear sister to whom I can freely open my heart and in whom I can confide my little griefs . . . ," she noted in her diary. "My feelings are inexpressible, therefore I will not try to say any more in reference to them."

Susan attended her sister's wedding in September of 1839, just a few weeks before Henry Stanton began his courtship of Elizabeth Cady. By the time the Stantons were married the following spring, Anthony was back at work, teaching this time at a district school in Center Falls. She was still lonely, still unhappy at being away from home, but there were also signs that her self-confidence and assertiveness were beginning to grow: Just a few months earlier, the angry complaints of the mother of one of her pupils had reduced her to tears. Now, she told her first biographer, when a loutish older boy repeatedly defied her, she "proceeded to use the rod. He fought viciously but she finally flogged him into complete submission."

A NEW BORN SENSE OF DIGNITY AND FREEDOM

The international Anti-Slavery Convention in London for which the newlywed Stantons had eagerly set sail just ten days after their wedding in the spring of 1840 had been hailed by Henry Stanton's friend John Greenleaf Whittier as "the world's convention," a convocation of "the pledged philanthropy of the earth." But it did not live up to its billing: Of the 500 delegates listed in its official proceedings, 425 were British, 69 were American, 5 were French, and 1 was a Spaniard. And every single one of them was male.

In recent years, American women had won for themselves the right to play an active role in antislavery agitation, and seven of their number had come to London expecting to be full-fledged delegates. But in Britain such a thing was still

In Benjamin Robert Haydon's rendering of the international Anti-Slavery Convention held in London in 1840, women are shown carefully segregated from

the male delegates on the convention floor. Henry Stanton is the man with sideburns seated second from the right in the front row.

unthinkable, and the British & Foreign Anti-Slavery Society, which sponsored the event, was determined that no woman be seated on the convention floor: if the ladies wished to hear the gentlemen debate, they were told, they would have to sit in a separate, roped-off chamber just off the floor of Freemasons Hall. When some of the American delegates—including Wendell Phillips and Henry Stanton—objected to "disfranchising one half of creation," they were overwhelmingly outvoted. William Lloyd Garrison, arriving late, refused to take his seat in protest. "I can take no part in a convention that strikes down the most sacred rights of all women," he said.

Elizabeth Cady Stanton was not a delegate—she had come to London only as her husband's spouse—but she shared fully in the female delegates' "humiliation and chagrin." "It struck me as very remarkable," she recalled, "that abolitionists, who felt so keenly the wrongs of the slave, should be so oblivious to the equal wrongs of their own mothers, wives, and sisters. . . . To me there was no question so important as the emancipation of women from the dogmas of the past."

Between sessions, Stanton remembered, back at the boardinghouse where many of the Americans stayed, the women "kept up a brisk fire morning, noon, and night . . . on the unfortunate gentlemen." In those dinner-table debates, Stanton took particular note of the way Lucretia Mott, a Quaker woman delegate from Philadelphia, dealt with the opposition: "Calmly and skillfully Mrs. Mott parried all their attacks, now by her quiet humor turning the laugh on them, and then by her earnestness and dignity silencing their ridicule and sneers." Stanton would adopt those techniques as her own: many years later, Susan B. Anthony would still be marveling at Stanton's ability to give her audiences "the rankest radical sentiments, but all so cushioned they didn't hurt."

But there was more to Stanton's admiration for Mott than tactics. "Mrs. Mott was to me an entire new revelation of womanhood," Stanton remembered. "I sought every opportunity to be at her side, and continually plied her with questions. I had never heard a woman talk what, as a Scotch Presbyterian, I had scarcely dared to think. . . . When I first heard from her lips that I had the same right to think for myself that Luther, Calvin and John Knox had, and the same right to be guided by my own convictions, I felt at once a new born sense of dignity and freedom."

The feeling was mutual. Mott wrote that she found Stanton "bright, open, lovely . . . I love her now as one belonging to us," and she urged her younger admirer to ground herself in the women's-rights writings of Mary Wollstonecraft, Frances Wright, and the Grimké sisters.

"As the convention adjourned, the remark was heard on all sides," Stanton continued, " 'It is about time some demand was made for new liberties for women.' As Mrs. Mott and I walked home, arm in arm . . . we resolved to hold a convention as soon as we returned home to America, and form a society to advocate the rights of women."

It would take eight years for Elizabeth Cady Stanton and Lucretia Mott to make good on that pledge, eight years during which Stanton showed every outward sign of becoming a conventional young matron.

Sarah (left) and Angelina Grimké

At a time when women were expected to remain silent outside their homes, Angelina and Sarah Grimké spoke up, and in so doing helped pave the way for Stanton, Anthony, and all the other advocates of women's rights who came after them. Daughters of a prominent slave-holding family from Charleston, they left their home and abandoned their Episcopal faith rather than sanction slavery, moved north to Philadelphia, and joined the Society of Friends.

In 1836, Angelina wrote *An Appeal to the Christian Women of the South*, thought so inflammatory that some Southern postmasters destroyed any copies that fell into their hands. In it she not only called slavery a sin, but declared blacks and whites equal—a minority view even among abolitionists. "Female slaves," Angelina Grimké wrote, "are our countrywomen; they are our sisters."

The Grimkés soon began to speak as well as write, appearing before small groups of women at first in friendly parlors, but eventually in front of large mixed audiences in churches and lecture halls all over New England, to the fury of conservative clergymen. Angelina Grimké was especially powerful on the platform; the abolitionist orator Wendell Phillips remembered, "She swept the chords of the human heart with a power . . . such as had never been heard from a woman."

But when the Grimkés began to blend into their anti-slavery rhetoric calls for women's rights, even some of their antislavery allies began to criticize them. John Greenleaf Whittier accused the sisters of forgetting "the great and dreadful wrongs of the slave in a selfish crusade against some paltry grievance . . . some trifling oppression, political or social, of their own."

"If we surrender the right to *speak* in public this year," replied Angelina, "we must surrender the right to petition next year, and the right to *write* the year after, and so on. What *then* can *woman* do for the slave, when she herself is under the feet of man and shamed into *silence?*"

"I ask no favors for my sex," Sarah wrote in her *Letters on the Equality of Sexes and the Condition of Women* (1838). "All I ask of our brethren is that they will take their feet from off our necks and permit us to stand upright on the ground which God has deigned us to occupy."

In 1838, at the urging of Henry Stanton and others, Angelina Grimké became the first woman ever to speak to a legislative body, testifying on behalf of the right to petition government about slavery before a committee of the Massachusetts State Legislature. "I was so near fainting," she remembered, "that my heart almost died within me . . . but our Lord and Master gave me his arm to lean on and in great weakness, my limbs trembling under me, I stood up and spoke for nearly two hours."

Shortly after that their public careers came to an end. Angelina married fellow abolitionist Theodore Weld. Sarah moved in with them, and all three turned their attention to raising Angelina's three children and running a boarding school to make ends meet (two of Stanton's sons were among their pupils). But the Grimké sisters never retreated from their belief in equality. When they discovered in 1868 that two mulatto youths named Archibald and Francis Grimké were the illegitimate sons of their own brother and a slave, they immediately acknowledged them as their nephews, welcomed them into the Weld home, and encouraged them to complete their studies at Harvard Law School and Princeton Theological Seminary. One of them, Archibald Grimké, would become a prominent member of the National Association for the Advancement of Colored People.

After returning to the United States, the Stantons lived for nearly four years with the Cadys while Henry learned the law from Elizabeth's father and then struggled to establish his own practice. In 1845, they moved to Boston, where Henry opened a practice and began pursuing a career in antislavery politics. Elizabeth gave birth to three boys—Daniel, Henry, and Gerrit—during these early years of her marriage and reveled in running her own household:

> When first installed as mistress over an establishment, one has the same feeling that a young minister must have in taking over a congregation. It is a proud moment in a woman's life to reign supreme within four walls, to be the one to whom all questions of domestic pleasure and economy are referred, and to hold in her hand that little family book in which the daily expenses . . . are duly registered. I studied up everything pertaining to housekeeping, and enjoyed it all. . . . My love of order and cleanliness was carried throughout from parlor to kitchen, from the front door to the back. . . . I put my soul into everything and hence enjoyed it.

But even then she was restless, eager to absorb everything around her. "I am enjoying myself more than I ever did in any city," Stanton wrote a friend. "I attend all sorts & sizes of meetings & lectures. I consider myself in a kind of a moral museum." She got to know the region's most eminent writers and reformers—Whittier, Bronson Alcott, Nathaniel Hawthorne, Ralph Waldo Emerson, and the liberal minister Theodore Parker—and Elizabeth never missed an antislavery convention, delighting both in "the fiery eloquence of the abolitionists and the amusing episodes that occurred when some crank was suppressed and borne out on the shoulders of his brethren." She walked four miles to church and back in order to hear Parker invoke an androgynous "Mother and Father of us all," and she marveled at the thunderous oratory of the ex-slave Frederick Douglass, who reminded her of an African prince as "around him sat the great antislavery orators of the day, earnestly watching the effect of his eloquence on [an] immense audience that laughed and wept by turns, completely carried away by the wondrous gifts of his pathos and humor."

"All sorts of new ideas are seething . . . ," she wrote her mother, "but I haven't either time or place to enumerate them and if I did you and my good father would probably balk at most of them."

Elizabeth Cady Stanton flourished in Boston; Henry Stanton did not. His first law partnership broke up when he refused on principle to represent a liquor dealer in court; the Liberty Party, to which he devoted much of his time, never built a

Lucretia Coffin Mott was a Quaker minister, an agent for the Underground Railroad, a founder of the first Female Anti-Slavery Society, and a forceful speaker, but her greatest contribution to American reform may have been her role as mentor to Elizabeth Cady Stanton. She was a "broad, liberal thinker," Stanton remembered, and "opened to me a new world of thought."

A rare abolitionist button from the 1850s features a miniature daguerreotype of black and white hands joined in amity.

Frederick Douglass presented this 1848 daguerreotype of himself to Susan B. Anthony. "The cause of the slave," he would later write, "has been peculiarly woman's cause."

strong base; and he began to attribute the headaches and catarrh that continually plagued him to the damp, cold winds off the Atlantic.

In 1847, the Stantons moved to the little mill town of Seneca Falls in central New York and started over. Judge Cady, who owned considerable acreage in the area, gave them a house at 32 Washington Street. It would officially be their home for sixteen years—Elizabeth would give birth to two more boys and two girls within its walls—but Henry Stanton was only rarely there. He devoted most of his time to his law clients and to pursuing a largely unsuccessful career in antislavery politics in Albany and New York, moving over the years from the Liberty Party to the Free-Soil Party to the antislavery wing of the Democrats and, eventually, to the Republicans.

Meanwhile, Elizabeth was left alone to care for the household. She came to hate small-town life—the muddy roads, the domestic drudgery, the ill-trained help, the overly conventional townspeople whom she shocked by raising a flag to denote the birth of each new baby in an age when childbirth was not to be mentioned in polite company. She also found herself enmeshed in the troubled domestic lives of some of the Irish immigrant families that lived nearby. "If a drunken husband was pounding his wife, the children would run for me," she recalled, and she was sometimes called upon to help deliver babies as well: "[W]ho can measure the mountains of sorrow and suffering endured in unwelcome motherhood in the abodes of ignorance, poverty, and vice, where terror-stricken women and children are the victims of strong men frenzied with passion and intoxicating drink?"

Above all, she suffered, she remembered, "from mental hunger" in Seneca Falls, could find nothing that would "bring into play my higher faculties." And, from the first, she saw in the lives of other women echoes of her own dissatisfaction.

The general discontent I felt with woman's portion as wife, mother, housekeeper, physician, and spiritual guide, the chaotic conditions into which everything fell without her constant supervision, and the wearied, anxious look of the majority of women impressed me with a strong feeling that some active measures should be taken to remedy the wrongs of society in general, and of women in particular. . . . It seemed as if all the elements had conspired to impel me to some onward step. I could not see what to do or where to begin.

If God has assigned a sphere to man and one to woman, we claim the right ourselves to judge His design in reference to us. . . . We think that a man has quite enough to do to find out his own individual calling, without being taxed to find out also where every woman belongs.

Elizabeth Cady Stanton

Family group, c. 1845

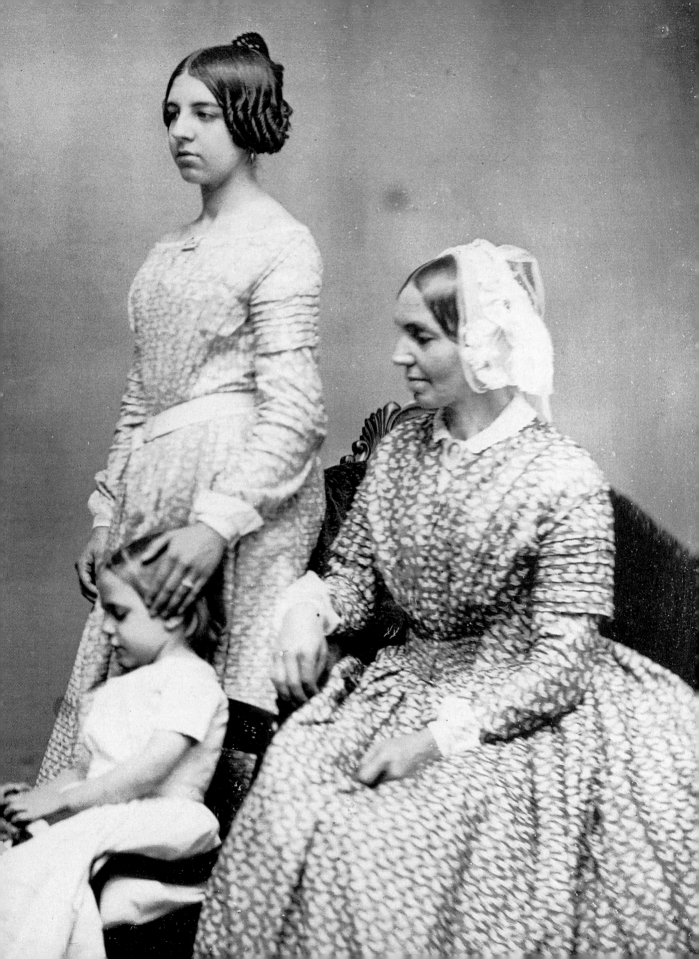

ALL SAY THE SCHOOL MARM LOOKS BEAUTIFUL

By 1845, the fortunes of the Anthony family had begun to improve. An inheritance from Susan's maternal grandfather permitted Daniel Anthony to purchase a farm just outside Rochester.

Susan helped with the move, but she did not stay at home for long. Independence evidently now appealed to her, and the following spring she accepted appointment as headmistress of the female department of the Canajoharie Academy. She would be responsible for twenty to twenty-five girls and be paid roughly one hundred dollars a year, all of which was now hers to spend as she liked.

At Canajoharie, she quietly abandoned the "plain language" she had always spoken at home, and—now that her father was back on his feet—she could afford to abandon the plain style of dress as well. "I've got my wardrobe pretty well replaced. No, *placed* for the first time," she told her mother. "I have a new pearl straw gypsy hat trimmed in white ribbon with fringe on one edge and a pink satin stripe on the other, with a few white roses and green leaves for inside trimming."

And when, dressed in her new finery, she presided over the first quarterly examination at her school, she took pleasure in reporting home not only that every-

The Canajoharie Academy, on the left, and the teachers' living quarters next door— Anthony's world from 1846 to 1849

Liberated from Quaker plainness, the twenty-eight-year-old Anthony had her daguerreotype portrait made at Canajoharie in 1848, proudly wearing a new dress she described in a letter to her mother—"plaid, white, blue, purple, and brown, has two puffs around the skirt, cups to the sleeves, with puffs & buttons where they end and puff at the rist . . . & a new colaret about my neck."

thing had gone well, but that "all say the school marm looks beautiful and I heard some of the scholars expressing fear that *some one* should be smitten and they thus deprived of a teacher."

Several men evidently were smitten: two widowers with children proposed marriage; a younger man took Anthony on carriage rides through the countryside; another, whom she privately called "very handsome, sleek as a ribbon," often called at the school just to see her. She even agreed to attend a dance, something no Quaker was permitted to do, only to have her escort make the grievous error of taking a drink: "I, next time I consent to go," she wrote as soon she got home, "must have a total abstinence man to accompany me. I cannot think of going to a dance with one whose highest delight is to make a fool of himself."

She had had "plenty" of beaux as a young woman, Anthony assured her first biographer, and she was pursued by occasional suitors well into middle age, but she turned them all away. She would be pilloried for that decision all her life, but there is no evidence that she ever regretted it: "I'm sure no man could have made me happier than I am," she said toward the end of her long life, and she offered a female interviewer her own official rationale: "I never felt I could give up my life of freedom to become a man's housekeeper. When I was young if a girl married poor she became a housekeeper and a drudge. If she married wealthy, she became a pet and a doll. Just think, had I married at twenty, I would have been a drudge or a doll for 55 years. Think of it!"

In any case, the obvious pleasure Susan felt in her growing independence continued to be alloyed with dutiful guilt. "I really believe Mother would feel bad if she knew how happily my time is passed," she confessed to one of her sisters, "how seldom I cried to see her." But she stayed away from home for two years nonetheless, and by 1848 even her new life was beginning to bore her. Running her half of the Canajoharie school had once seemed a terrifying prospect. Now it seemed too easy, demanded too little of her ferocious energy. "A weariness has come over me that the short spring vacation did not in the least dispel," she told her parents. "I have a pleasant school of 20 scholars, but I have had to manufacture the interest duty compels me to exhibit. I am anxious they should learn, but feel almost to shrink from the task, energy & something to stimulate is wanting."

Like Elizabeth Cady Stanton at Seneca Falls, Susan B. Anthony was increasingly dissatisfied. She was tired of "theory," she told her mother, and looking for a way to take practical action toward "a happier and more glorious world."

SENECA FALLS, NEW YORK, JULY 19–20, 1848

Stanton, too, was searching for a way to "remedy the wrongs of society and of woman in particular." She would find it on a warm July day in 1848, when she received an invitation to tea from Jane and Richard Hunt, Quaker friends who lived in neighboring Waterloo; Lucretia Mott and her husband would also be there.

Stanton eagerly accepted, and there, she recalled—sitting at the Hunts' tea table with the woman she admired most, alongside two other women with Quaker backgrounds, Mary Ann McClintock and Lucretia Mott's younger sister, Martha Coffin Wright, "I poured out . . . the torrent of my long-accumulating discontent, with such vehemence and indignation that I stirred myself as well as the rest of the party to do and dare anything." Stanton's vehemence—and the responsive chord her discontents struck in her listeners—inspired them to hold a "public meeting for protest and discussion."

Nothing like it had ever been attempted anywhere before. Eighteen-forty-eight was a year of revolution. Paris mobs toppled the King of France. Rome declared

Revolutionaries: (clockwise from top left) Jane Hunt, Mary Ann McClintock, and Martha Coffin Wright

The New York Tribune headlines just some of the revolutions underway around the world at the time of the Seneca Falls Convention.

NEW-YORK TRIBUNE.
THREE DAYS
LATER FROM EUROPE.
ARRIVAL OF THE EUROPA.
DISCOVERY OF ANOTHER PLOT IN PARIS.
PLAN OF THE INSURGENTS
MEASURES OF THE GOVERNMENT.
CANNON PLANTED IN THE STREETS OF PARIS.
RUMORS AND ALARMS.
PROGRESS OF INSURRECTION IN SPAIN.
DEATH TO THE CARLIST CHIEFS.
SPREAD OF THE CHOLERA IN RUSSIA.
RESIGNATION OF THE PIEDMONTESE MINISTRY.
A REPUBLIC IN MOLDAVIA.
Germany Still Troubled.
IRELAND ON THE POINT OF INSURRECTION
MEAGHER ARRESTED AND IN JAIL!
Bloodless Collision between the Troops & People.
Both Sides Arming for the Struggle.
BRITISH CHARTISTS ARMING.
MONEY MARKET FIRM.
State of the Corn and Provision Market
LITTLE CHANGE IN COTTON.
The Cunard steamer *Europa*, Captain LOTT, which sailed from Liverpool at ? M on the 15th, reached Halifax at 5 P

itself a republic and drove the pope from the Vatican. There were uprisings in Prague, Berlin, Vienna, Venice, Milan, Naples, Warsaw. But the brief, unsigned notice that Stanton and her friends placed in the *Seneca County Courier* on July 11 of that year signaled the start of a revolution that would have more lasting consequences than any of the others.

WOMAN'S RIGHTS CONVENTION.
A convention to discuss the social, civil and religious condition and rights of Woman will be held in the Wesleyan Chapel, at Seneca Falls, N.Y., on Wednesday and Thursday, the 19th and 20th of July current, commencing at 10 o'clock a.m.

Having declared their intention to hold a convention, Stanton recalled, the women weren't really sure what to do next. Meeting around a circular mahogany table in Mary Ann McClintock's parlor in Waterloo, they were at first "as helpless and hopeless as if [we] had been suddenly asked to construct a steam engine." Finally, they decided to draft a statement for the convention to consider—a Declaration of Sentiments, they called it—that would enumerate the rights of women just as Thomas Jefferson's Declaration had enumerated those of men. All five women contributed their thoughts, but it was Stanton's decision to model the statement after the document whose message of equality and natural rights was familiar to every American, and it is Stanton's voice that rings most clearly from its pages.

The first women's-rights convention in history got off to a late start: the key to the chapel could not be found at first, and Stanton had to send a young nephew in through an open window to unlock the doors. That day only women were allowed to attend, but on the next day, July 20, the convention was open to all, and more than three hundred women and men filed into the chapel, local people mostly, many of them Quakers and Congregationalists, some supporters of the new Free-Soil Party for which Henry Stanton was now actively campaigning. They would all be asked to vote the Declaration of Sentiments up or down.

When none of the women who had organized the convention felt qualified to act as chair, Lucretia Mott's husband, James, agreed to preside. But it fell to Elizabeth Cady Stanton to present the document. She had never before addressed a public meeting, let alone one attended by a crowd that was what was then called "promiscuous"— made up of men as well as women. Still, she managed to get through the Declaration, and that afternoon sixty-eight women fixed their signatures to it and thirty-two men were recorded as "present in favor of the movement."

Stanton next offered eleven additional resolutions for the convention to ratify. Ten would pass without dissent, but number nine declared it "the duty of the women of this country to secure to themselves their sacred right to the elective franchise."

Nowhere on earth did women have the right to vote. Henry Stanton had favored the Declaration, but thought asking for suffrage would make the whole proceeding "a farce" and—according to one of his children—had left town rather than be embarrassed by it. Even Lucretia Mott was concerned. "Lizzie," she told Stanton, "Thou wilt make the convention ridiculous."

Stanton with her sons Henry Jr., left, and Neil, about 1848. "It appears that my machinery is capable of running a long time," she would tell a friend a few years later. "Of course I may burst my boiler screaming to boys to come out of the cherry trees and to stop throwing stones, or explode from accumulated steam of a moral kind that I dare not let off, or be hung for breaking the pate of some stupid Hibernian for burning my meat or pudding on some company occasion. My babies, the boys and these Irish girls, as well as the generally unsettled condition of the moral, religious and political world, are enough to fret to pieces the best constructed machinery. Some days I feel a general giving way, but I find that a new sun brings me fresh courage and vigor."

Stanton held firm, telling her listeners:

Strange as it may seem to many, we now demand our right to vote according to the declaration of the government under which we live. We should not feel so sorely grieved if no man who had not attained the full stature of a Webster, Clay, Van Buren or Gerrit Smith could claim the right of elective franchise. But to have drunkards, idiots, horseracing rum-selling rowdies, ignorant foreigners, and silly boys fully recognized, while we ourselves are thrust out from all the rights that belong to citizens, is too grossly insulting to . . . be longer quietly submitted to. The right is ours. Have it we must. Use it we will. The pens, the tongues, the fortunes, the indomitable wills of many women are already pledged to secure this right.

Despite her brave words, there were in fact only a handful of women yet pledged to secure the right to vote, and privately she feared that she would be unable to persuade her listeners. Her friend Frederick Douglass was in the audience and asked for permission to speak. Without the vote, he told his listeners, women would be unable to change the laws that treated them unfairly. His exact words that day are lost, but a few days later he made an argument that must have been very similar in his own newspaper, the *North Star*:

All that distinguishes man as an intelligent and accountable being is equally true of woman; and if that government only is just which governs by the free consent of the governed, there can be no reason in the world for denying to woman the exercise of the elective franchise, or a hand in making and administering the laws of the land. Our doctrine is that "right is of no sex."

Douglass's eloquence helped carry the day. The resolution passed, and the convention adjourned.

News of it traveled fast. William Lloyd Garrison applauded the "Woman's Revolution" in his *Liberator*. Horace Greeley was cautiously sympathetic in his *New York Tribune*. "It is easy to be smart, to be droll, to be facetious in opposition to the demands of these Female Reformers," he wrote, "and in decrying assumptions so novel and opposed to established habits and usages, a little wit will go a great way. . . . However unwise and mistaken the demand, it is but the assertion of a natural right and as such must be conceded."

But most editorial writers ridiculed the whole idea of women acting on their own. "The women folks have just held a convention up in New York, and passed a sort of 'Bill of Rights,' " said the *Lowell* (Massachusetts) *Courier*, "affirming it their right to vote, to become teachers, legislators, lawyers, divines, and do all and [sundry] the 'lords' . . . now do. They should have resolved at the same time that it was obligatory [for] the 'lords' aforesaid to wash dishes, . . . handle the broom, darn stockings, . . . wear trinkets, look beautiful, and be as fascinating as those blessed morsels of humanity whom God gave to preserve that rough animal man, in something like reasonable civilization."

"A woman is nobody. A wife is everything," echoed the *Philadelphia Public Ledger and Daily Transcript*. "A pretty girl is equal to ten thousand men, and a mother is, next to God, all powerful. . . . The ladies of Philadelphia, therefore, under the influence of the most serious, sober second thoughts, are resolved to maintain their rights as Wives, Belles, Virgins and Mothers, and not as Women."

Under this kind of ridicule, some of the signers of the Declaration of Sentiments asked that their names be withdrawn, Elizabeth Cady Stanton recalled, but she did not retreat an inch. She saw even bad publicity as useful to her cause. "It will start women thinking, and men, too," she assured Lucretia Mott, "and when men and women think about a new question, the first step is taken. The great fault of mankind is that it will not think."

Making people think would be Stanton's life's work, and she did not shrink from a fight if needed. When Seneca Falls clergymen joined in the critical chorus, charging that Scripture precluded a public role for women, she hit back hard in the local paper. The Bible, she wrote, should be the "great Charter of Human Rights." Instead, it was "too often perverted by narrow, bigoted, sectarian teachers as to favor all kinds of oppression, and to degrade and crush humanity itself. No reform has ever been started but the Bible, falsely interpreted, has opposed it. Wine drinking was proved to be right by the Bible. Slavery was proposed as an institution of the Bible. War, with its long train of calamities and abominations is proved to be right by the Bible. . . . Let the people no longer trust to their blind guides, but read and reason for themselves." Such views did not endear her to her more pious neighbors; one remembered that she made it a point never to be seen with a woman who held such opinions.

But soon, small groups of women and a scattering of sympathetic men began to meet in other New York towns, and in Ohio, Pennsylvania, and Massachusetts, all galvanized by Stanton's Declaration.

It had been seventy-two years since the Declaration of Independence. It would be seventy-two more before women attained the full citizenship that Elizabeth Cady Stanton and her friends had now declared to be their birthright. But the struggle for women's rights had begun, and Stanton was already sure that it would soon be "*the* issue of the day. All other reforms, however important they may be, cannot so deeply affect the interests of humanity."

Stanton herself was becoming a celebrity. The demands of running her household kept her close to home, but she was determined to make her presence felt anyway. She began contributing articles to a temperance monthly, *The Lily*. At first she coyly signed them "Sunflower," then she boldly affixed her initials —"E.C.S." She wrote about temperance and suffrage, but she also took on other

The Stanton home at Seneca Falls

topics occupying the minds of middle-class women: schools, housekeeping, child care.

She was particularly exercised by sewing:

As an amusement it is contemptible; as an educator of head or heart, worthless; as a developer of muscle, of no avail; as a support, the most miserable of trades. It is a continued drain on sight and strength, on health and life, and it should be the study of every woman to do as little of it as possible. . . . What use is all the flummering, puffing, and mysterious folding we see in ladies' dresses? What use in ruffles on round pillow cases, night caps, and children's clothes? What use in making shirts for our lords in the wonderful manner we now do, with all those tiny plaits, and rows of stitching down before, and round the collars and wrist bands? Why, all these things are done, to make the men, children, women, chairs, sofas, and tables look pretty. . . . If the women for the last fifty years had spent all the time they have wasted in furbelowing their rags, in riding, walking, or playing on the lawn with their children, the whole race would look ten times as well as they do now.

There was no reason, she added, why boys shouldn't learn to sew.

Seriously, I see no reason why boys should be left to roam the streets, day and night, wholly unemployed, a nuisance to everybody, and a curse to themselves,

Sisters, c. 1850

It is our duty to assert and reassert this right [to vote], to agitate, discuss and petition, until our political equality be fully recognized. Depend upon it, this is the point to attack, the stronghold of the fortress—the one woman will find it most difficult to take—the one man will most reluctantly give up; therefore, let us encamp right under its shadow—there spend all our time, strength and moral ammunition, year after year, with perseverance, courage and decision.

ELIZABETH CADY STANTON

whilst their sisters are over-taxed at home to make and mend their clothes. It will be a glorious day for the emancipation of those of our sex who have long been slaves to the needle, when men and boys make their own clothes, and women make theirs in the plainest possible manner.

Eventually, Horace Greeley offered Stanton a far wider audience in the pages of his *Tribune*. From the first, she proved a masterful polemicist. In a time when political rhetoric was often self-consciously overwritten, her best writings were crisp, clear, and to the point. Asked to send some remarks to a women's-rights convention being held in Ohio in the spring of 1850, she laid out the case against the men who ruled her world with the wit and gusto that would characterize her prose throughout her life.

They tax our property to build Colleges, then pass a special law prohibiting any woman to enter there. A married woman has no legal existence; she has no more absolute rights than a slave on a Southern plantation. She takes the name of her master, holds nothing, owns nothing, can bring no action in her own name; and the principle on which she and the slave is educated is the same. The slave is taught what is considered best for him to know—which is nothing; the woman is taught what is best for her to know—which is little more than nothing; man being the umpire in both cases. A woman cannot follow out the impulses of her own immortal mind in her sphere, any further than the slave can in his sphere. Civilly, socially, and religiously, she is what man chooses her to be—nothing more or less—and such is the slave. It is impossible for us to convince man that we think and feel exactly as he does, that we have the same sense of right and justice, the same love of freedom and independence. Some men regard us as devils, and some as angels; hence one class would shut us up in a certain sphere for fear of the evil we might do, and the other for fear of the evil that might be done to us; thus, except for the sentiment of the thing, for all the good it does us, we might as well be thought the one as the other. But we ourselves have to do with what we are and what we shall be.

A REFORMER

Two weeks after the gathering at Seneca Falls, a second women's-rights convention, which Elizabeth Cady Stanton helped organize, was held in the Unitarian Church in Rochester. The Declaration of Sentiments was again adopted. So were new resolutions, including one that called for equality of all women "of whatever complexion."

Among those who attended—and signed the Declaration—were Mr. and Mrs. Daniel Anthony of Rochester and their youngest daughter, Mary. Already committed to both temperance and abolition, they found women's rights a congenial cause as well. Susan was not there. Still teaching school at Canajoharie, she had in any case then been "rather inclined to deride [the convention's] principles," she told a friend many years later. "Politics seemed a great deal farther away than paradise and the most radical reformer had not the prophetic eye which could discern the woman politician." She did not then think the vote very important, either; her own father never voted, after all. (Daniel Anthony would not do so until 1860, when, finally convinced that slavery could be ended only by force of arms, he cast his first ballot, for Abraham Lincoln.)

Besides, she now had a cause of her own. Sometime in 1848 she had helped form a local chapter of the Daughters of Temperance. She delivered her first public address as its "Presiding Sister" on March 2, 1849. It was an appeal to the ladies of the town to enlist in "our great cause, the cause of Virtue, Love and Temperance," and clearly a great event in her life: "I was escorted into the hall by the Committee where were assembled about 200 people," she proudly told her mother. "The room was beautifully festooned with cedar and red flannel. On the south side was printed in large capitals of evergreen the name of 'Susan B. Anthony.' I hardly knew how to conduct myself amidst so much kindly regard."

Intemperance, she told her listeners that day, was "the blighting mildew of all our social connexions," and women—as "the sex that fashions the Social and Moral State of Society"—had an inescapable duty to help bring about its eradication. It was time, she said, for "all our young ladies [to] come forth and boldly declare themselves on the side of reform. . . ."

> Then arises the question how are we to accomplish the end desired. I answer, not by centering all our benevolent feelings upon our own home circle . . . not by caring naught for the culture of no minds, save those of our own darlings. No, No, the gratification of the selfish impulses alone can never produce a desirable change in the moral aspect of society. . . . If we say we love the cause and then sit down at our ease, surely do our actions speak the lie.

She would deliver that same message with undiminished fervor for the rest of her life. As a girl, she had been dutifully determined to overcome every one of her own weaknesses, and she would never abandon her drive to set the right sort of example for her family and small circle of female friends. "Daniel," she wrote to her brother that same year, "let us strive to have right on our side come what will, & then we shall have one comfort which the guilty know not, & that is a conscience void of offence, an inward joy which none but the doers of good can know. That I may not be permitted to deviate from the path of my duty is my daily & hourly prayer to God."

But that narrow path had steadily broadened. For more than ten years she had poured all of her zeal into improving the characters of the children entrusted to her care. Now, at twenty-nine, she was beginning to see that there might be a way to play a part in transforming the larger world—and in the coming years it would sometimes seem that the world itself was too small to contain all her energy and zeal. "In ancient Greece she would have been a stoic," Stanton once wrote of Anthony; "in the era of the Reformation, a Calvinist; in King Charles's time, a Puritan; but in the Nineteenth Century, by the very law of her being, she is a reformer."

Her growing resolve to find something more to do with her life received the most vivid possible reinforcement just a few days after her successful speech, when the cousin with whom she had been boarding gave birth to a little girl and then developed what turned out to be a fatal illness. Anthony nursed her day and night for months, cooking and cleaning and washing for the whole household as well—labors for which the woman's remarkably benighted husband seemed to think she deserved not a word of thanks. In his mind, such work was simply the duty of an unmarried woman, an "old maid."

Anthony loved her cousin and was saddened by her death. But she also resented being taken for granted. "It seems to me that no one feels that it is any thing out of the common course of things for me to sacrifice my every feeling, almost every principle," she complained to her brother Daniel, "to gratify those with whom I mingle." "I often feel that I have not a disinterested friend," she told one of her sisters, "not one who loves me for my very self, but many who endure my presence because they may derive some service from me." Over the years, Anthony would often rush to the side of family members when they were seriously ill, but she was also determined never again to allow herself to be exploited, "the drudge and burdenbearer of the family."

That autumn, Susan B. Anthony resigned her teaching position at the school —where, she reported, guests at a farewell dinner hailed her as "the smartest woman that was now or ever in Canajoharie"—and went home to Rochester. Her parents, realizing how tired she was of teaching, had offered to let her run the family farm while she decided what she might do next; her father was now selling insurance to supplement the family's income and needed the help in any case.

She threw herself into farm work, but as soon as she could she also began edging steadily into the outside world. She joined the local Daughters of Temperance soon after moving to Rochester and before long was organizing suppers and fairs, then traveling to neighboring towns to show other women how to do the same. From the first, she exhibited organizational skills and a willingness to work that soon earned her the nickname "Napoleon."

But in 1850, the national debate over slavery began to overshadow even temperance in Anthony's mind. Her father had long since separated from those ortho-

dox Quakers who did not see it as part of their religious duty to combat slavery, and when Congress passed the Fugitive Slave Act that year, placing federal power behind the slave-catchers, it seemed only to confirm for father and daughter alike the inherent wickedness of a government that countenanced slavery. The Anthonys did all they could to help runaways make their way north to Canada on the Underground Railroad, and their farm became a Sunday-afternoon meeting place for like-minded Quakers, often joined by antislavery activists from all over the northeast. Frederick Douglass, Wendell Phillips, John Brown, and William Lloyd Garrison all dined at the family table. Susan "always superintended these Sunday dinners," she told her earliest biographer, "and was divided between her anxiety to sustain her reputation as a superior cook and her desire not to miss a word of the conversation in the parlor."

She evidently missed very few words. Temperance and abolition began to merge in her mind: when she spoke at a Rochester "Temperance Festival" in February

The Anthony farmhouse outside Rochester. In the years before the Civil War it was a weekly rendezvous for Garrisonian abolitionists pledged to "immediate and unconditional emancipation." "Anti-slavery has made me richer and braver in spirit," Anthony wrote in 1855. "It is the school of schools for the full and true development of the nobler elements of life."

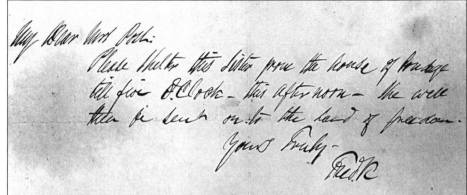

A note from Frederick Douglass asks the Anthonys' Rochester friend Amy Post to hide a runaway slave until another agent can carry her on to the next station on the Underground Railroad.

Abigail Kelley Foster

of 1851, she exhorted the women in her audience to develop as much sympathy for slave women in the South as they had for the battered wives of drunkards.

Abigail Kelley Foster visited the Anthony farm with her husband, Stephen, that same winter. She was herself a former schoolteacher and had defied convention—and the hostility of mobs that hated both her antislavery message and the fact that a woman dared deliver it—to become a fearless antislavery speaker. Foster saw Susan's eagerness to become more involved in the abolitionist struggle, invited her to come along with her on a week-long speaking tour, and then offered to help her get started as an abolitionist agent on her own.

Anthony demurred, though Foster's example stayed with her. Despite the extraordinary energy and capacity for getting things done she had already begun to display, despite her desire to make a broader impact on the world, she remained unsure of her ability to communicate to others the importance of the causes that now consumed her.

At Seneca Falls that same winter, Elizabeth Cady Stanton bore a fourth son, Theodore Weld Stanton. "He bounded on the stage of life, with great ease comparatively!!" she reported to her cousin and closest friend, Elizabeth Smith Miller. "I was sick but a few hours, did not lie down half an hour before he was born but worked round as hard as I could all night to do up the last things I had to do," and she was up again the morning after the birth, writing letters.

Stanton always prided herself on the relative effortlessness with which she brought children into the world in an era when pregnancy was considered an illness from which mothers needed weeks to recover, but there were now four boys to look after. Stanton was a loving parent who believed that her children should be given all the freedom she felt she had been denied as a girl. She rarely spanked them, did not require them to attend any church, refused even to wake them in the morning in the hope they would learn to discipline themselves. Her offspring—

Abolition provided the founders of the women's movement with their first taste of equality. In this rare daguerreotype made at an anti–Fugitive Slave Act convention at Cazenovia, New York, on August 22, 1850, Frederick Douglass sits at the table at left surrounded by fellow members of the American Anti-Slavery Society, male and female, black and white. The man standing behind Douglass is thought to be Gerrit Smith. The bonneted woman in the center may be Abigail Kelley Foster, who first urged Anthony to become an abolitionist speaker.

And Ain't I a Woman?

In the spring of 1851, women in an Akron, Ohio, church tried to hold a women's rights convention, only to be drowned out by a raucous band of jeering clergymen. Then, Sojourner Truth asked to be allowed to speak. She was a former slave and itinerant Methodist preacher from upstate New York—her real name was Isabella; she had taken a new name, she said, at the urging of God himself.

The clergymen jeered at her, too, until she pointed a long bony finger at them, and began to speak, ridiculing those who had dared claim that women were too delicate to survive in the larger world beyond the home:

Sojourner Truth peddled cartes de visite *of herself like this one to finance her speaking. "I sell the shadow," she said, "to support the substance."*

The man over there says women need to be helped into carriages and lifted over ditches, and to have the best place everywhere. Nobody ever helps me into carriages or over puddles, or gives me the best place—and ain't I a woman? . . . Look at my arm! I have ploughed and planted and gathered into barns, and no man could head me—and ain't I a woman? I could work as much and eat as much as a man—when I could get it—and bear the lash as well! And ain't I a woman? I have borne thirteen children, and seen most of 'em sold into slavery, and when I cried out with my mother's grief, none but Jesus heard me—and ain't I a woman?

Before she finished, even some of the clergymen had begun to applaud. She would soon become a legend in suffrage as well as antislavery circles.

Anthony wrote that she "combined in herself as an individual the two most hated elements of humanity. She was black, and she was a woman, and all the insults that could be cast upon color and sex were together hurled at her, but there she stood, calm and dignified, a grand wise woman who could neither read nor write, and yet with deep insight could penetrate the very soul of the universe about her."

After the Civil War the suffrage movement split in two. Most former abolitionists believed black men should receive the ballot before women got the vote. Truth sided with those, like Stanton and Anthony, who argued the two must go through together. "There is a great stir about colored men getting their rights," she said, "but not a word about the colored women; and if colored men get their rights, and not colored women theirs, . . . the colored men will be masters over the women, and it will be just as bad as it was before."

there would eventually be seven of them—were lively, fractious, irrepressible. The older boys delighted in cursing, sometimes hauled the younger ones up onto the roof, organized stone-throwing expeditions against their Irish neighbors. Stanton herself once privately admitted that her boys were "miserable little underdeveloped vandals." She would reluctantly send the two eldest boys, Daniel and Neil, off to boarding school later in the year, and further eased her domestic burdens by hiring an able housekeeper named Amelia Willard, who stayed with her for decades. But she remained largely confined to her home and village, still firing off salvos on women's rights but unable to take the field herself.

Martha Saxton

Women Without Rights

In 1920, when women acquired suffrage at last, many—probably most—Americans of both sexes still believed that differences between men and women equipped them for different life paths and responsibilities. Although many favored giving the vote to women, many were ambivalent at best. A century earlier, almost all Americans believed God had ordained different duties for the sexes, and the idea of women voting was laughable.

During the philosophical upheaval that accompanied the Revolution, a handful of men and women speculated about an enlarged role for women in public. Abigail Adams, alive to the fervor for self-determination all around her, urged her husband, John, in 1776, to restrain husbands from too much power over their wives: "Remember, all men would be tyrants if they could." John, more cranky perhaps than sympathetic about this call for independence from a new quarter, replied that he was already seeing in too many places the unwelcome signs of self-assertion. Bolder than Mrs. Adams, Mary Wollstonecraft, an English witness to the French Revolution, suggested in *A Vindication of the Rights of Woman* (1792) that society might benefit from enfranchising women and no longer regarding them as simply sexual and domestic creatures. Her ideas, however, were discredited after her death with the revelation that she had given birth to a baby out of wedlock. As one disapproving writer of moral volumes for girls wrote, "The female Quixote broke her lance vindicating the 'Rights of Woman,' and no one sympathized in her defeat."

That the details of Wollstonecraft's personal life scandalized Americans and for more than a hundred years utterly eclipsed her ideas underscores the point that most Americans agreed that women's important contributions were to be made at home and that chastity was a far more significant achievement than political thought. Everything women managed to do beyond the home would be considered secondary to and contingent on their virtuous domestic behavior.

While Americans of the revolutionary generation gave no thought to suffrage for women, many did think about the issue Abigail Adams raised with John: women, and married women in particular, had few legal protections. Women went from being daughters—dependent on their fathers—to wives and the marital status of femes coverts, meaning without a

In 1776, Abigail Adams vainly urged her husband, John, to see to it that the Declaration of Independence apply to women as well as men. "If particular care and attention is not paid to the Ladies," she warned, "we are determined to foment a Rebellion."

legal identity separate from their husbands. Married women could not own property in their own names, and if they earned money, it did not legally belong to them. Their husbands also had claim to their labor, disposition over their children in everyday life, and automatic custody in the event of separation or divorce. Legally speaking, a woman came into her own as a widow; but many women, in an age of frequent and dangerous childbirth and medical care that was more likely to harm than to help, never became widows and lived lives whose conditions depended almost wholly upon the temperaments and wishes of their husbands. The Revolution resolved those questions temporarily by confirming that women's obligations to their husbands substituted for obligations that, as citizens, they would have to the state. Legal thinkers defended coverture, the device through which women lost their civil identity and rights, as women's protection from taxes, jury duty, and the draft.

The Revolution seemed to settle questions about the legal status of women in traditional, patriarchal ways (although, later in the century, feminists would succeed in rectifying some of these inequities more quickly than they would in procuring the vote), but it left open the precise definition of their role in the new republic. Americans, never doubting that housekeeping and family should be women's foremost concerns, saw in this work new significance in the wake of our severing ties with the old world. Moral writers increasingly described the raising of virtuous citizens by women as absolutely vital to the new nation's ability to stay free from the corruptions of Europe. Lydia Maria Child dedicated her influential book on child rearing to American women "on whose intelligence and discretion the safety and prosperity of our republic so much depend." In a country with no clear hierarchy, few formal institutions, and a rapidly expanding market economy, nurturing virtue in each citizen became a task of anxious concern. Tempta-tion to greed, envy of the rich, and materialism were everywhere. Similarly, social mobility and the consequent proximity of respectable people to the "rude and the vicious"—Mrs. Child's terms for most servants—were said to place innocent girls in danger of sexual corruption. Mothers were to shield their children from the infinite varieties of vice and provide them with exacting consciences that would ensure hard work and self-discipline.

Mrs. Child directed her advice to white women of what would become the middle class. Their husbands were increasingly absent from the home on business, giving mothers' responsibilities a new urgency. Child, who was also an abolitionist, knew that such advice was of little use to slave mothers, of whom there were some half a million in 1820, and who had few opportunities to protect their children from mistreatment or sale. Most put in long days in the field and left their children in the care of older slave women or other children. When slave mothers on Landon Carter's plantation fought to have more time to nurse their infants, Carter had them whipped and reduced their breaks to three half-hour intervals a day. Poor white mothers were also often unable to stay home with their children, and for the urban poor, in any case, home might be little more than a shared attic or a shed. These women had to pick up whatever work—usually laundering and cooking—they could, and neighbors often played as large a part in raising urban children as mothers did.

For all women, however they experienced it, motherhood was, with its risks and responsibilities, a far more defining part of their lives than it is now. In 1810, women on average bore eight children and could expect to spend six years pregnant and eight years nursing. Except for the invention of forceps, techniques for helping mothers deliver babies had not changed much for centuries (and the enthusiastic use of that new tool caused new problems even as it alleviated old ones). Although numbers are extremely unreliable, it appears that about 20 percent of adult women's deaths were from childbirth in the late colonial and early national period. The most common aftereffects of childbirth were lifelong weakness and illness.

More devastating even than the risks of childbirth was the 50 percent mortality rate of children under the age of ten. Not surprisingly, the death of children preoccupied American women. Their letters and diaries are full of mourning. Benjamin Franklin's sister wrote her brother after the death of her daughter that "she was Every thing to me. Sorrows roll over me like waves of the sea. I am hardly allowed time to fetch my breath. . . . I have now, in the first flow of my grief, been almost ready to say, 'What have I more?' " Death sometimes took all a mother's children. Women were the front-line mourners, with responsibility for preparing the corpses and leading and containing the family grief. Advice to grieving mothers was plentiful and usually emphasized the glories of the world to come. Lydia Child wrote, "Tell him the brother, or sister, or parent he loved is gone to God; and that the good are far happier with the holy angels, than they could have been on earth; and that if we are good, we shall in a little while go to them in heaven."

Only housekeeping rivaled motherhood, in its endlessly duplicating responsibilities, for the preeminent position in women's lives. All mothers, wealthy, poor or slave, urban or rural, were expected to manage their homes. Wealthy women had servants or slaves to help them, but even they had to supervise a wide variety of chores in households that still produced many of their own necessities—soap, candles, fabrics, clothing, bed linens, preserved foods—in addition to the regular work, such as laundry and cooking, which were performed without running water or any source of heat but fire. For poorer women the challenge was making do with little while feeling the sting of the increasing wealth of the emerging middle class.

The reward for shouldering without complaint the onerous tasks of home and family life was high praise for the "feminine" excellences of obedience to male authority, a submissive demeanor, unwavering attention to the family, and a well-developed capacity for self-sacrifice. Reverence for these qualities characterized the flowering of middle-class culture.

The nineteenth century saw domestic life grow steadily more complex and elaborate. There were more and more objects to enjoy, but more to take care of as well; better cooking utensils and foods, but higher expectations for variety and taste in meals; more cleaning devices but higher standards for a clean home. Some devices like the icebox—a tin-lined wooden box, sitting on a block of ice cut from a winter lake and stored in an icehouse that helped keep perishable food during the summer—were clearly conveniences. But the impact of the sewing machine, introduced toward the end of the antebellum period, was more complicated: one woman wrote that she had been told it would leave her with nothing to do; instead, "it monopolizes our time."

By far, the worst domestic chore was laundry, the only one that Catharine Beecher, author of the widely read *A Treatise on Domestic Economy for the Use of Young Ladies at Home and at School* (1841), recommended farming out if possible. Indeed, it was the first chore that women with any discretionary money at all paid other women—always poor and usually black or Irish—to do. For one wash, one boiling, and one rinse, someone had to fetch fifty gallons (about four hundred pounds) of water from the well or stream. The laundress had to sort the clothes by color and material, soak them overnight, then drain off the excess water and pour hot suds (probably from soap she made herself, a lengthy process that involved tending a vat of boiling animal fat, ashes, and lye) onto the clothes. She then had to scrub and wring out the clothes, cover them with water again, and boil them on the stove, moving the concoction around with a wash stick. Then she rubbed the dirty spots with soap once more and rinsed them—the whites first in plain water and then again in bluing. If she were using river water from the Mississippi, for example, she had to know the secret of clearing mud from water as well. Wash day was usually followed by a day devoted to ironing, which required the laundress to heat on the stove (and keep hot) a number of irons of various dimensions to handle the range of problems posed by flat fabrics, skirts, sleeves, and ruffles. Ironing may have been a little more welcome on a cold winter's day but was uniquely unpleasant in the heat of the summer.

When women were not attending to their children or performing domestic tasks, two major social movements engaged their imaginations and aspirations: religious awakenings and the spread of education for women. These movements touched so many because they helped provide hope and meaning to the isolated and difficult lives most women lived. The two forces would ultimately change the conditions under which most women lived their lives, although they would not necessarily point all women directly toward suffrage. Women as well as a growing number of men wished to improve the education available to girls, picking up a theme reformers had discussed since before the Revolution. Benjamin Rush, doctor, scientist, and active member of the Revolutionary generation, argued in 1787 that women needed to be educated in order to fulfill the most important duty of their lives: making the men they married and mothered virtuous. He had high hopes for the transformation women's education would cause: "It would require a lively imagination to describe, or even to comprehend, the happiness of a country where knowledge and virtue were generally diffused among the female sex."

Molding entertaining wives had long been a motive for educating wealthy girls. The daughters of merchants and planters received an education in reading, writing, French and possibly Italian (classics were reserved to boys), some history and moral philosophy, along with piano or guitar and an assortment of exotic skills like drawing on velvet, grotto-making (arranging oyster shells to resemble miniature caves), and painting fans to protect the face when sitting near a fire.

After the Revolution public schools and Sunday schools began to compete with private academies for female students. The underlying motives were a mixture of religious, moral, and civil, reflecting the dominant place of Christianity in the project of educating "republican mothers." In rural areas where public schools were few or nonexistent (there were none in the South until after the Civil War), Sunday schools were the only source of education for many. Girls routinely outnumbered boys in Sunday schools.

Emma Willard's "Plan for Improving Female Education," which she presented to the legislature of New York State in 1819, laid out a description and justification of rigorous education for women, which differed little from that offered by Dartmouth, Amherst, or Brown, but positioned it safely inside the sacred circle of domestic duties. To contemporary readers it seems paradoxically both liberating and restricting, but in its day its revolutionary aspects were the most clearly visible. Some perceptive con-

Mary Wollstonecraft's turbulent private life undercut the impact of her early feminist writings, but when Stanton and Anthony published the first volume of their History of Woman Suffrage *in 1881, they listed her first among the nineteen women "Whose Earnest Lives and Fearless Words" had been their "constant Inspiration."*

temporaries found it too radical in justifying education that might lead women out of intellectual dependence upon their husbands. As early as the 1820s, Willard's Troy Female Seminary graduates were going west and south to teach in newly established towns in places like Ohio, Indiana, Illinois, Missouri, and Alabama. Teaching became the first "respectable" profession for women who did not wish to marry right away. With the growing number of academies for women, more and more women went as far as California and Oregon to teach. Most stayed, married, and raised families, becoming important and respected members of their new communities.

Increasing literacy among women also provided the basis for a fast-growing women's literary culture. By the time of the Civil War many of the most popular American novelists were women, including Harriet Beecher Stowe, Susanna Rowson, and Catharine Maria Sedgwick.

The movement to improve women's education coincided and overlapped with the other great movement of the early nineteenth century: a series of religious revivals beginning in Cane Ridge, Kentucky, in 1801, continuing and echoing all over the country and known as the Second Great Awakening. The centerpiece of these revivals was the conversion of a frightened sinner to a redeemed life, forgiven by Christ. Converts, who first had to confront their utter helplessness and dependence upon Jesus Christ, found themselves immeasurably strengthened by the absolution of their sins, by the help of the Lord in fighting new temptations, and, perhaps most of all, by the tremendous spiritual and social power of the community of converts into which they had stepped.

The infusion of power triggered by an evangelical conversion was especially heady for the weakest elements of society: most women, African-Americans, and Native Americans. Women were the most numerous converts in the Second Great Awakening, the most numerous members of early evangelical churches, and the most zealous participants in revivals. While the revivals were as intensely patriarchal as the family life they reinforced, women were equal at the communion table (where they outnumbered men two to one) and in God's eyes. They were also more given to trances and various other kinds of ecstatic behavior, and were much more likely to bring other members of their families to church membership. In the fluid environment of camp meetings, women felt free to explore a full range of spiritual and mystical leanings and to define an individual spiritual style. Many men stood in awe of their greater expressivity and were willing to be influenced by it.

Most reform movements of the nineteenth century were powered by men and women who had been converted in an evangelical revival and had found there the piety and spiritual conviction to attack social evils, such as drunkenness, Sabbath breaking, men's sexual impurity, prostitution, slavery, and even the subordination of women, although at first that cause had little of the popularity of antislavery or temperance. Evangelical men and women breathed urgency into a wide variety of activities, including child rearing and maintaining family relations, with the ferocity of their commitment to perfect Christian life.

Frances Wright, Scottish-born utopian socialist and freethinker, believed that American women would assume "their places as thinking beings" long before their European sisters did. She paved the way for Stanton, Anthony, and their contemporaries by daring to advocate women's rights on lecture platforms in Eastern and Midwestern cities during the late 1820s and 1830s.

The evangelical zeal of white middle-class women nullified time-honored distinctions between the private activities in which they engaged and the public activities that had been reserved to men. By participating in reform movements, women redefined where they could go and what they could do. Under the Christian aegis, female soldiers in the wars against sin were able to help remodel institutions like prisons, hospitals, and insane asylums, adding their ideas to the developing institutional life of the young republic.

Some women wished to reform the church itself. White women tended, however, to be unwilling to break free of all the rules. Harriet Livermore, the "Pilgrim Stranger," became an itinerant preacher, even preaching to Congress, but she never challenged biblical ideas of female inferiority. Mary Sibley, an evangelical Presbyterian from St. Louis, contented herself with teaching Sunday school, exhorting congregations, distributing Bibles, and leading private spiritual sessions with her students and family—everything but preaching in a church, because St. Paul had said, "Let your women keep silence in the churches . . . if they will learn anything, let them ask their husbands at home" (Corinthians 14:34 and 35), verses that had kept most American women silent in church since the arrival of the Pilgrims.

A few African-American women committed to a more radical egalitarianism took their ministries farther. An illiterate woman known simply as Old Elizabeth became an itinerant Methodist preacher in Maryland and Virginia before the Civil War. The best-known black woman preacher was Sojourner Truth, who was also that rare creature, a worker for woman suffrage. But most women of the early nineteenth century did not have her experience or vision. They led lives that were by our standards circumscribed: they believed that both their duties and their rewards lay at home. Their access to public questions lay largely along religious paths. Spirituality was more likely to claim their attention and lift their spirits than politics. Reading and writing were precious skills that helped them through their arduous days. Only the accumulated weight of countless small personal changes occurring over many decades brought a substantial number of women to question, tentatively at first, the divine origin of the prohibition keeping them from taking their convictions to the polls.

Declaration of Sentiments

The precise authorship of the document that launched the women's movement in 1848 is unclear—five women are thought to have had a hand in its composition—but Elizabeth Cady Stanton's indignation at women's plight and her remarkable rhetorical power are evident in every paragraph.

When, in the course of human events, it becomes necessary for one portion of the family of man to assume among the people of the earth a position different from that which they have hitherto occupied, but one to which the laws of nature and of nature's God entitle them, a decent respect to the opinions of mankind requires that they should declare the causes that impel them to such a course.

We hold these truths to be self-evident: that all men and women are created equal; that they are endowed by their Creator with certain inalienable rights; that among these are life, liberty, and the pursuit of happiness; that to secure these rights governments are instituted, deriving their just powers from the consent of the governed. Whenever any form of Government becomes destructive of these ends, it is the right of those who suffer from it to refuse allegiance to it, and to insist upon the institution of a new government, laying its foundation on such principles, and organizing its powers in such form, as to them shall seem most likely to effect their safety and happiness. Prudence, indeed, will dictate that governments long established should not be changed for light and transient causes; and accordingly all experience hath shown that mankind are more disposed to suffer, while evils are sufferable, than to right themselves by abolishing the forms to which they were accustomed. But when a long train of abuses and usurpations, pursuing invariably the same object, evinces a design to reduce them under absolute despotism, it is their duty to throw off such government, and to provide new guards for their future security. Such has been the patient sufferance of the women under this government, and such is now the necessity which constrains them to demand the equal station to which they are entitled.

The history of mankind is a history of repeated injuries and usurpations on the part of man toward woman, having in direct object the establishment of an absolute tyranny over her. To prove this, let facts be submitted to a candid world.

He has never permitted her to exercise her inalienable right to the elective franchise.

He has compelled her to submit to laws, in the formation of which she had no voice.

He has withheld from her rights which are given to the most ignorant and degraded men—both natives and foreigners.

Having deprived her of this first right of a citizen, the elective franchise, thereby leaving her without representation in the halls of legislation, he has oppressed her on all sides.

He has made her, if married, in the eye of the law, civilly dead.

He has taken from her all right in property, even to the wages she earns.

He has made her, morally, an irresponsible being, as she can commit many crimes with impunity, provided they be done in the presence of her husband. In the covenant of marriage, she is compelled to promise obedience to her husband, he becoming to all intents and purposes, her master—the law giving him power to deprive her of her liberty, and to administer chastisement.

He has so framed the laws of divorce, as to what shall be the proper causes, and in case of separation, to whom the guardianship of the children shall be given, as to be wholly regardless of the happiness of women—the law, in all cases, going upon a false supposition of the supremacy of man, and giving all power into his hands.

After depriving her of all rights as a married woman, if single, and the owner of property, he has taxed her to support a government which recognizes her only when her property can be made profitable to it.

He has monopolized nearly all the profitable employments, and from those she is permitted to follow, she receives but a scanty remuneration. He closes against her all the avenues to wealth and distinction which he considers most honorable to himself. As a teacher of theology, medicine, or law, she is not known.

He has denied her the facilities for obtaining a thorough education, all colleges being closed against her.

He allows her in Church as well as State, but a subordinate position, claiming Apostolic authority for her exclusion from the ministry, and, with some exceptions, from any public participation in the affairs of the Church.

He has created a false public sentiment, by giving to the world a different code of morals for men and women, by which moral delinquencies which exclude women from society, are not only tolerated, but deemed of little account in man.

He has usurped the prerogative of Jehovah himself, claiming it as his right to assign for her a sphere of action, when that belongs to her conscience and to her God.

He has endeavored, in every way that he could, to destroy her confidence in her own powers, to lessen her self-respect, and to make her willing to lead a dependent and abject life.

Now, in view of this entire disfranchisement of one-half the people of this country, their social and religious degradation—in view of the unjust laws above mentioned, and because women do feel themselves aggrieved, oppressed, and fraudulently deprived of their most sacred rights, we insist that they have immediate admission to all the rights and privileges which belong to them as citizens of the United States.

In entering upon the great work before us, we anticipate no small amount of misconception, misrepresentation, and ridicule; but we shall use every instrumentality within our power to effect our object. We shall employ agents, circulate tracts, petition the State and National legislatures, and endeavor to enlist the pulpit and the press in our behalf. We hope this Convention will be followed by a series of Conventions embracing every part of the country.

Firmly relying upon the final triumph of the Right and the True, we do this day affix our signatures to this declaration.

Lucretia Mott, Harriet Cady Eaton, Margaret Pryor, Elizabeth Cady Stanton, Eunice Newton Foote, Mary Ann McClintock, Margaret Schooley, Martha C. Wright, Jane C. Hunt, Amy Post, Catharine F. Stebbins, Mary Ann Frink, Lydia Mount, Delia Mathews, Catharine C. Paine, Elizabeth W. McClintock, Malvina Seymour, Phebe Mosher, Catharine Shaw, Deborah Scott, Sarah Hallowell, Mary McClintock, Mary Gilbert, Sophrone Taylor, Cynthia Davis, Mary Martin, P. A. Culvert,

Susan R. Doty, Rebecca Race, Sarah A. Mosher, Mary E. Vail, Lucy Spalding, Lavinia Latham, Sarah Smith, Hannah Plant, Lucy Jones, Sarah Whitney, Mary H. Hallowell, Elizabeth Conklin, Sally Pitcher, Mary Conklin, Susan Quinn, Mary S. Mirror, Phebe King, Julia Ann Drake, Charlotte Woodard, Martha Underhill, Dorothy Matthews, Eunice Barker, Sarah R. Woods, Lydia Gild, Sarah Hoffman, Elizabeth Leslie, Martha Ridley, Rachel D. Bonnel, Betsey Tewksbury, Rhoda Palmer, Margaret Jenkins, Cynthia Fuller, Eliza Martin, Maria E. Wilbur, Elizabeth D. Smith, Caroline Barker, Ann Porter, Experience Gibbs, Antoinette E. Segur, Hannah J. Latham, Sarah Sisson

The following are the names of the gentlemen present in favor of the movement:

Richard P. Hunt, Samuel D. Tillman, Justin Williams, Elisha Foote, Frederick Douglass, Henry W. Seymour, Henry Seymour, David Spalding, William G. Barker, Elias J. Doty, John Jones, William S. Dell, James Mott, William Burroughs, Robert Smalldridge, Jacob Matthews, Charles L. Hoskins, Thomas McClintock, Saron Phillips, Jacob Chamberlain, Jonathan Metcalf, Nathan J. Milliken, S. E. Woodworth, Edward F. Underhill, George W. Pryor, Joel Bunker, Isaac Van Tassel, Thomas Dell, E. W. Capron, Stephen Shear, Henry Hatley, Azallah Schooley

The following resolutions were discussed by Lucretia Mott, Thomas and Mary Ann McClintock, Amy Post, Catharine A. F. Stebbins, and others, and were adopted:

WHEREAS, The great precept of nature is conceded to be, that "man shall pursue his own true and substantial happiness." Blackstone in his Commentaries remarks, that this law of Nature being coeval with mankind, and dictated by God himself, is of course superior in obligation to any other. It is binding over all the globe, in all countries and at all times; no human laws are of any validity if contrary to this, and such of them as are valid, derive all their force, and all their validity, and all their authority, mediately and immediately, from this original; therefore,

RESOLVED, That such laws as conflict, in any way, with the true and substantial happiness of woman, are contrary to the great precept of nature and of no validity, for this is "superior in obligation to any other."

RESOLVED, That all laws which prevent woman from occupying such a station in society as her conscience shall dictate, or which place her in a position inferior to that of man, are contrary to the great precept of nature, and therefore of no force or authority.

RESOLVED, That woman is man's equal—was intended to be so by the Creator, and the highest good of the race demands that she should be recognized as such.

RESOLVED, That the women of this country ought to be enlightened in regard to the laws under which they live, that they may no longer publish their degradation by declaring themselves satisfied with their present position, nor their ignorance, by asserting that they have all the rights they want.

RESOLVED, That inasmuch as man, while claiming for himself intellectual superiority, does accord to woman moral superiority, it is pre-eminently his duty to encourage her to speak and teach, as she has an opportunity, in all religious assemblies.

RESOLVED, That the same amount of virtue, delicacy, and refinement of behavior that is required of woman in the social state, should also be required of man, and the same transgressions should be visited with equal severity on both man and woman.

RESOLVED, That the objection of indelicacy and impropriety, which is so often brought against woman when she addresses a public audience, comes with a very ill-grace from those who encourage, by their attendance, her appearance on the stage, in the concert, or in feats of the circus.

RESOLVED, That woman has too long rested satisfied in the circumscribed limits which corrupt customs and a perverted application of the Scriptures have marked out for her, and that it is time she should move in the enlarged sphere which her great Creator has assigned her.

RESOLVED, That it is the duty of the women of this country to secure to themselves their sacred right to the elective franchise.

RESOLVED, That the equality of human rights results necessarily from the fact of the identity of the race in capabilities and responsibilities.

RESOLVED, *therefore*, That, being invested by the Creator with the same capabilities, and the same consciousness of responsibility for their exercise, it is demonstrably the right and duty of woman, equally with man, to promote every righteous cause by every righteous means; and especially in regard to the great subjects of morals and religion, it is self-evidently her right to participate with her brother in teaching them, both in private and in public, by writing and by speaking, by any instrumentalities proper to be used, and in any assemblies proper to be held; and this being a self-evident truth growing out of the divinely implanted principles of human nature, any custom or authority adverse to it, whether modern or wearing the hoary sanction of antiquity, is to be regarded as a self-evident falsehood, and at war with the interests of mankind.

A daguerreotype portrait of young Boston women, made in the studios of Southworth and Hawes, c. 1850

BIGGER FISH TO FRY

2

The first meeting of Elizabeth Cady Stanton and Susan B. Anthony, in May of 1851, was as anticlimactic as it was momentous. Amelia Bloomer, the editor of *The Lily* and a friend of both women's, introduced them to one another on a street corner in Seneca Falls following a lecture by William Lloyd Garrison. Stanton remembered liking the younger woman— "with her good earnest face and genial smile"—right away, but, preoccupied by "the probable behavior of three mischievous boys who had been busily exploring the premises while I was at the meeting," she failed to invite her home that afternoon.

We know almost nothing of how their friendship developed in the months that immediately followed. Nor, given their upbringing, the contrasting nature of their personalities and the very different conditions under which they lived and worked, is it easy to see how they came to share so much so fast. Yet each seems almost instantly to have recognized special strengths in the other.

Stanton, brimming over with indignation and ideas but pinned down by domestic responsibilities, needed someone to carry her message into the field.

Anthony, unfettered and possessed of almost manic energy, was eager for action, willing to do the kind of arduous logistical work—renting halls, raising funds, running petition campaigns, speaking wherever she could drum up a crowd—that intimidated most women of her time. But she remained unsure of her own rhetorical skills, needed someone to put her own indignation into words.

Anthony in 1852, the year she and Stanton founded their short-lived Women's State Temperance Society in New York

The temperance movement would be their first target. Anthony was growing weary of working under the direction of the male clergymen—"white orthodox male Saints," she came to call them—who controlled the movement's finances, set its agenda, and were dismissive of the opinions of the legion of women like herself whose commitment to the cause was at least the equal of their own. In January of 1852 she was chosen to be a delegate to a statewide convention of the Sons of Temperance at Rochester. No one had worked harder than she had that winter, gathering petitions that called upon the state legislature to pass a law banning the sale and production of liquor, but when, at the convention, she asked

STEP 1.
ss
nd.

STEP 2.
A glass to
keep the
cold out.

STEP 3.
A glass
too
much.

STEP 4.
Drunk
and
riotous.

STEP 5.
The summit attained
Jolly companions
A confirmed drunkard.

STEP 6.
Poverty
and
Disease.

STEP 7.
Forsaken
by
Friends.

STEP 8.
Desperation
and
crime.

STEP 9.
Death
by
suicide.

THE DRUNKARDS PROGRESS.
FROM THE FIRST GLASS TO THE GRAVE.

This cautionary lithograph was published by Nathaniel Currier in 1846. Women and children were believed to be the real victims of what Anthony called "the corrupting influence of the fashionable sippings of wine and brandy" by men.

to be heard, the chairman silenced her. "The sisters were not invited . . . to speak but to listen and learn," he said. Furious, Anthony stalked from the hall. Three or four other women joined her, but most stayed in their seats: for women to act on their anger as Anthony and her supporters had was to risk being considered "bold, meddlesome, disturbers."

Anthony, encouraged by Lucretia Mott and others, had resolved to start a new organization, a Women's State Temperance Society, in which women at long last would run things and men could neither vote nor hold office. Anthony turned to her new friend for help: Would Mrs. Stanton serve as its first president, and would she also write some stirring remarks for Anthony to deliver at their first meeting in April?

She could not have found a more sympathetic ear. The cavalier treatment Anthony had received at the Rochester convention was an all too vivid echo of

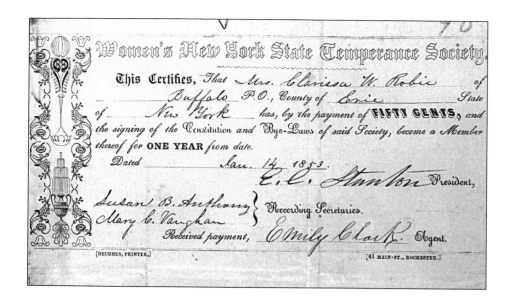

Membership certificate of the Women's New York State Temperance Society, signed by Stanton and Anthony as president and recording secretary

the way women had been rebuffed at the World Anti-Slavery Conference Stanton had attended in London eleven years earlier. "Men and angels give me patience!" she wrote Anthony. "I am at the boiling point! If I do not find some day the use of my tongue on this question . . . I shall die of an intellectual repression, a woman's rights convulsion! . . .

> I will gladly do all in my power to help you. Come and stay with me and I will write the best lecture I can for you. I have no doubt a little practice will make you an admirable speaker. Dress loosely, take a great deal of exercise, be particular about your diet and sleep enough. . . . In your meetings, if attacked, be cool and good-natured, for if you are simple and truth-loving, no sophistry can confound you. As for my own address, if I am to be president it ought perhaps to be sent out with the stamp of the convention. But as anything from my pen is necessarily radical no one may wish to share with me the odium of what I may choose to say. If so, I am ready to stand alone. I never write to please any one. If I do please I am happy, but to proclaim my highest convictions of truth is always my sole object.

The five hundred members of the new society, all of them women, met for the first time in Corinthian Hall at Rochester on April 20, 1852. Anthony was chosen secretary. Stanton was elected president—and in her inaugural address set forth a radical women's-rights program for which few delegates were prepared. Traditional temperance champions had seen alcoholism as a source of men's tyranny over women; Stanton saw it as merely a symptom. If all drinking stopped, she believed, male despotism would stubbornly remain. To eradicate it, statute law and public attitudes alike would have to be changed.

The sole ground for divorce in New York state was adultery; Stanton now proposed that any woman married to an alcoholic be allowed to end her marriage. "Let no woman remain in the relation of wife with a confirmed drunkard," she said. "Let no drunkard be the father of her children." And she also urged women to devote themselves to helping "the poor and suffering around us," rather than support foreign missions or "the building up of a theological aristocracy and gorgeous temples to the unknown God."

Having shaken up the delegates, Stanton hastily retreated to Seneca Falls. Later she would issue a fresh call for woman suffrage as well, "so that woman may vote on this great social and political evil." But she was pregnant again—her fifth child and first girl, named Margaret for Elizabeth's mother, would be born in October—and she was unwilling to make further appearances in public until her baby was born.

Anthony was left to spread the message further—and to face the fury of the opposition. At a Men's Temperance Society meeting at Syracuse in June, she was again refused the right to speak, and a prominent clergyman denounced her and all other women who dared venture out in public. "[W]hen a woman goes out of her sphere," he said, "when she goes miles attended or unattended, to make speeches in Bloomer costume or not, I say she unsexes herself, she is hybrid, and I for one wish to do nothing in approbation."

That September in the same city Anthony attended her very first Woman's Rights Convention, and before the proceedings were fully under way she revealed the remarkable toughness that lay just beneath her quiet Quaker manner. When a fashionable Boston woman, wearing a dress that "left both neck and arms exposed," was nominated for president, Anthony objected on the ground that "nobody who dressed as she did could represent the earnest, solid, hard-working women of the country." Anthony carried the day; her candidate, the suitably modest Lucretia Mott, took the chair.

Anthony was appointed secretary and read aloud a message from Stanton urging that colleges admit women, that women withhold their taxes wherever they were allowed to own property and withdraw from churches that did not treat them equally. She could be heard in every corner of the hall. "Miss Anthony has a capital voice," said the *Syracuse Journal*, "and deserves to be made clerk of the Assembly." She had no patience with women who resisted raising their voices for fear of seeming unladylike; if they couldn't bring themselves to speak up, she said, they should hand their written remarks over to someone who would. "We do not stand up here to be seen," she said, "but to be heard." She also heard for the first time two women who, like herself, had determined not to marry so that they could devote themselves unstintingly to their cause. Antoinette Brown, who would soon become the first American woman to be ordained a minister, demanded women's rights "not as a gift of charity but as an act of justice." Lucy Stone, whose musical voice and unshakable courage had made her the best-known woman orator of her time, declared that "justice and equal rights— the right to vote, the right to our own earnings, equality before the law . . . are the Gibraltar of our cause." Brown and Stone would quickly become Anthony's close allies.

The *Syracuse Star* denounced the gathering as "the Tom- foolery Convention," made up of "brawling women" and "Aunt Nancy men," "frantic and contemptible," but such attacks only strengthened Anthony's growing conviction "that the right which woman needed above every other, the one indeed which would secure to her all others, was the right of suffrage." As she moved from town to town, foster- ing local chapters of the society and collecting signatures, Anthony made that message plain. "Men tell us they vote for us by proxy," she said at Batavia. Women should test that claim by urging their husbands and sons, fathers and brothers, to vote against alcohol; if they failed to do, she urged her listeners to "take the right; march to the ballot box and deposit votes indica- tive of her highest ideas of practical temperance. . . .

[T]o merely relieve the suffering wives and children of drunkards, and vainly labor to reform the drunkard [is] no longer to be called temperance work . . . woman's temperance sentiments [are] not truthfully represented by men at the Ballot Box. . . . Men may prate on but we women are beginning to know that the life and happiness of a woman is of equal value with that of a man; and that for a woman to sacrifice her health, happiness and perchance her earthly existence in the hope of reclaiming a drunken, sensualized man, avails but little.

When she said similar things at Utica, the editor of the *Evening Herald* attacked her directly:

Personally repulsive, she seems to be laboring under feelings of strong hatred towards male men, the effect we assume of jealousy and neglect. . . . With a degree of impiety which was both startling and disgusting, this shrewish maiden counseled the numerous wives and mothers present to separate from their hus- bands whenever they become intemperate, and particularly not to allow the said husbands to add another child to the family. . . . *Think of such advice given in public by one who claims to be a maiden lady.*

Over the next half century, Susan B. Anthony would suffer without complaint hundreds of similar assaults.

———————

Lucy Stone in 1856. A farmer's daughter from Massachusetts, she overcame her family's objections to becoming a teacher, paid for her own education at Oberlin College, and stumped the country speaking against slavery and for women's rights—her plain-speaking and soothing voice a welcome relief from the elaborate thundering oratory of her male colleagues. Anthony once credited a newspaper account of Stone's 1850 address to the first National Woman's Rights Convention at Worcester, Massachusetts, with convert- ing her to the cause.

The Lily, *a temperance journal published at Seneca Falls, reports Stanton's presidential address to the Women's State Temperance Society in June of 1853. Her writings would often fill its columns.*

Stanton and Anthony's enemies were waiting for them when they convened the second annual convention of the Women's State Temperance Society at Rochester, in June of 1853. Conservative women, anxious that no one identify them or their organization with either suffrage or the still more alarming notion of what they called "easy divorce," were determined to refocus the organization exclusively on the struggle against alcohol.

Stanton did her best to change their minds:

> It has been objected that we do not confine ourselves to the subject of temperance, but talk too much about woman's rights, divorce and the church. . . . We have been obliged to preach woman's rights because many, instead of listening have questioned the right of woman to speak on any subject. . . . Let it be clearly understood that we are a Woman's Rights Society; that we believe it is a woman's duty to speak whenever she feels the impression to do so; that it is her right to be present in all the councils of Church and State.

It did not work. The constitution was altered to allow men to vote. The women's-rights program of suffrage and divorce reform was abandoned. Stanton was deposed as president. Anthony had spent some eighteen months building the society into a two thousand–member force, but she felt duty-bound to resign from it nonetheless, in protest against the way her friend had been treated.

This, the first campaign Stanton and Anthony undertook together, set the style for most of those that followed over the next fifty years. Stanton provided

Amelia Bloomer wearing the comfortable costume she publicized in her newspaper, The Lily, *and that came to bear her name. Those who actually wore it called it "the short dress."*

Some of the hostility Elizabeth Cady Stanton engendered among more conventional delegates to the 1852 and 1853 meetings of the Women's State Temperance Society was caused by the clothes she wore while presiding. No matter the weather or the task at hand, women of Stanton's time and class were expected to wear corsets, layered petticoats, and cumbersome floor-length dresses. Stanton appeared onstage instead wearing a loose-fitting skirt that ended just four inches below the knee over capacious "Turkish" trousers. Most men and women found such attire dangerously immodest. Even Stanton's husband worried that when sitting down "ladies will expose their legs somewhat above the knee, to the delight of those gentlemen who are anxious to know whether their lady friends have round and plump legs, or lean and scrawny ones."

The costume had been devised in the autumn of 1850 by Stanton's cousin Elizabeth Smith Miller and its original intent had been simple practicality: "Working in my garden—weeding & transplanting in bedraggled skirts that clung in fettered folds about my feet & ankles," Miller remembered, "I became desperate and resolved on immediate release."

Stanton had been among the first to follow her lead: "To see my cousin with a lamp in one hand and a baby in the other, walk upstairs with ease and grace while, with flowing robes, I pulled myself up with difficulty, lamp and baby out of the question, readily convinced me that there was sore need of reform in women's dress and I promptly donned a similar attire." She came to see in the short dress a useful symbol of the freedom and self-direction she wanted for all women: "Depend upon it," she told Lucretia Mott, "woman can never develop in her present drapery. She is a slave to her rags."

Other workers for women's rights followed Stanton's lead, so many that by the time Stanton persuaded Susan B. Anthony to adopt the short dress in December of 1852, it had become a symbol of the "ultras," the most uncompromising champions of women's rights. Those who dared wear it in public found themselves being followed and jeered at by insulting crowds. Lucy Stone described being surrounded with Anthony on a New York street: "Gradually we noticed that we were being encircled. A wall of men and boys at last shut us in, so that to go back was impossible. There we stood. . . . They laughed at us. They made faces at us. They said impertinent things, and they would not let us out."

Stanton suffered, too. Her husband's political foes chanted about her clothing:

Heigh! Ho! The carrion crow,
Mrs. Stanton's all the go;
Twenty tailors take the stitches,
Mrs. Stanton wears the britches.

Her father forbade her to come home wearing the short dress. Her sons at boarding school begged her to wear something else when she came to visit. "Now why do you wish me to wear what is uncomfortable, inconvenient?" she wrote them. "I'll tell you why. You want me to be like other people. You do not like to have me laughed at. You must learn not to care for what foolish people say."

"Had I counted the cost of the short dress, I would never have put it on," Stanton confessed, "however, I'll never take it off for now it involves a principle of freedom." But by early 1854, even she had had enough, and, having first talked Anthony into adopting the short dress, she determined to talk her out of it.

It was not easy. Once committed to a cause, Anthony found it almost impossible to abandon it; to surrender to fashion violated her belief in every woman's right to live life as she wished. Stanton kept at her. "Let the hem of your dress out today, before tomorrow night's meeting," she told her as Anthony was about to preside over an Albany women's-rights meeting. "The cup of ridicule is greater than you can bear. It is not wise, Susan to use up so much energy in that way."

Anthony agonized over the "rude and vulgar men" who "stared me out of countenance" and said, " 'There comes my bloomer.' Oh, hated name! Oh, I cannot bear it any longer." She held out for months, nonetheless. "Everyone who drops the dress makes the task a harder one for the

The composer of this 1851 tune was careful not to take sides in the battle over bloomers.

few left," she wrote Lucy Stone. "It is hard to stand alone, but no doubt good discipline for us."

Finally, Anthony did surrender, having persuaded herself that her costume was getting in the way of her message. The short dress had become "an intellectual slavery" for her, she wrote. "One never could get rid of thinking of herself, and the important thing is to forget self. The attention of my audiences was fixed upon my clothes instead of my words."

the fiery rationale and served as titular head. Anthony, ostensibly holding a less important office, shouldered full responsibility for both the day-to-day activities of the organization and for carrying what Stanton called her "highest convictions of truth" into the wider—and often unsympathetic—world.

Stanton had failed to radicalize the temperance movement, but she had done something far more important for the future of women's rights: she had helped to radicalize Susan B. Anthony. "In turning the intense earnestness and religious enthusiasm of this great-souled woman into this channel [of women's rights]," she would write, "I soon felt the power of my convert goading me toward a more untiring work."

Compared to the great cause of women's rights, temperance didn't matter much to Stanton, and when Anthony complained bitterly about what had happened to the society she had worked so hard to foster, the older woman was singularly unsympathetic:

You ask me if I am not plunged in grief at my defeat at the recent convention for the presidency of our society. Not at all. I am only too happy in the relief I feel from this additional care. I accomplished all I desired by having the divorce question brought up. . . . Now, Susan, I beg of you to let the past be past, and to waste no powder on the Woman's State Temperance Society. We have other and bigger fish to fry.

That tone, too, would be repeated again and again over the years. Anthony was profoundly affected by defeats and disappointments, but Stanton refused to give in to depression. "I never encourage these moods," she would tell one of her children much later, "but by some active work and practical thinking try to cheat myself into the thought that all is well, grand, glorious, triumphant."

DEEP WATERS

Anthony remained disappointed, but she barely broke stride. Touring New York again that summer, she was astonished to discover that the local temperance societies she had carefully nurtured the previous year had virtually all disappeared. The reason was simple: however zealous local women may have been, they had no funds of their own with which to print pamphlets or hire halls. A Married Woman's Property Act passed in 1848—the first ever enacted—had allowed women to inherit money in their own right, but they still had no right to the moneys they themselves earned, nor any claim to those earned by their husbands.

"Thus," she noted in her journal, "as I passed from town to town was I made to feel the great evil of woman's utter dependence on man for the necessary means to aid reform movements. . . .

Woman must have a purse of her own, and how can this be so long as the law denies to the wife all right to both the individual and the joint earnings? . . . [T]here is no true freedom for woman without the possession of equal property rights, and these can be obtained only through legislation. If this is so, then the sooner the demand is made, the sooner it will be granted. It must be done by petition and this, too, of the next legislature. How can the work be started? We must hold a convention and adopt some plan of united action.

"With her," a friend wrote, "to think was always to act." Determined to hold a women's-rights convention to address the property issue, she persuaded sixty women to help her circulate petitions and in just six weeks managed to harvest six thousand signatures demanding that the legislature expand the Married Woman's Property Act and another four thousand requesting that women be allowed to vote. Then she called upon Stanton to give voice to the women's demands.

Downtown Albany, New York, the city Stanton stirred with her eloquence in 1854

Stanton was reluctant at first. Margaret was not yet five months old. But Anthony and others persisted, and finally, reluctantly, Stanton gave in to her friend as she would do again and again throughout her life.

"I find there is no saying 'no' to you," she wrote Anthony, but she would need help in gathering research material for her speech.

> Women have grievances without number, but I want the exact wording of the most atrocious laws. I can generalize and philosophize by myself, but I have not time to look up statistics. While I am about the house, surrounded by my children, washing dishes, baking, sewing, etc. I can think up many points, but I cannot search books, for my hands as well as my brains would be necessary for that work. . . . Men who can, when they wish to write a document, shut themselves up for days with their thoughts and their books, know little of what difficulties a woman must surmount to get off a tolerable production.

On the evening of February 14, 1854, Elizabeth Cady Stanton stepped to the podium in Albany. (She almost hadn't come: an arrow fired by one of her boys had nearly put out her infant daughter's eye.) She was speaking to the women's-rights convention, but her excoriating words were addressed to the men of the state legislature, in session just a few blocks away:

> How could man ever look thus on woman? She . . . who gave to the world a savior, and witnessed alike the adoration of the Magi and the agonies of the cross.
>
> How could such a being, so blessed and honored, ever become the ignoble, servile, cringing slave. . . . Would to God you could know the burning indignation that fills woman's soul when she turns over the pages of your statute books and sees there how like feudal barons you freemen hold over your women.

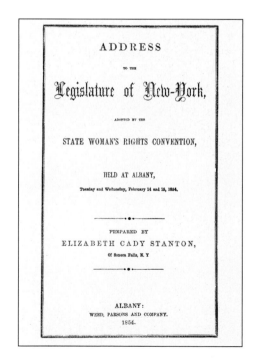

Stanton's "Address to the Legislature of New-York," as printed up and distributed across the state by Anthony

Anthony ordered fifty thousand copies of her friend's remarks printed up, saw that they were scattered across the state "like flakes of snow," and made sure a copy was placed on the desk of every legislator. But it would be a long time before Samuel G. Foote, chairman of the Senate Judiciary Committee, bothered to

Stanton and her sixth child and second daughter, Harriot, in 1856. After Harriot's birth, Stanton promised Anthony that she had borne her last child—but there would be one more.

respond, and when he did, he was ornately contemptuous of the women and their demands.

"The men of the legislature," Foote said, "had studied the women's demands with the experience married life has given them."

> *Thus aided, they are enabled to state that the ladies always have the best place and choicest tid-bit at the table. They have the best seats on the carts, carriage and sleighs. . . . They have their choice on which side of the bed they will lie. . . . [I]f there is any inequality or oppression in the case, the gentlemen are the sufferers. . . . On the whole, the Committee have concluded to recommend no mea-*

The true woman will not be exponent of another, or allow another to be such for her. She will be her own individual self. . . . Stand or fall by her own individual wisdom and strength. . . . She will proclaim the "glad tidings of good news" to all women, that woman equally with man was made for her own individual happiness, to develop . . . every talent given to her by God, in the great work of life.

Susan B. Anthony

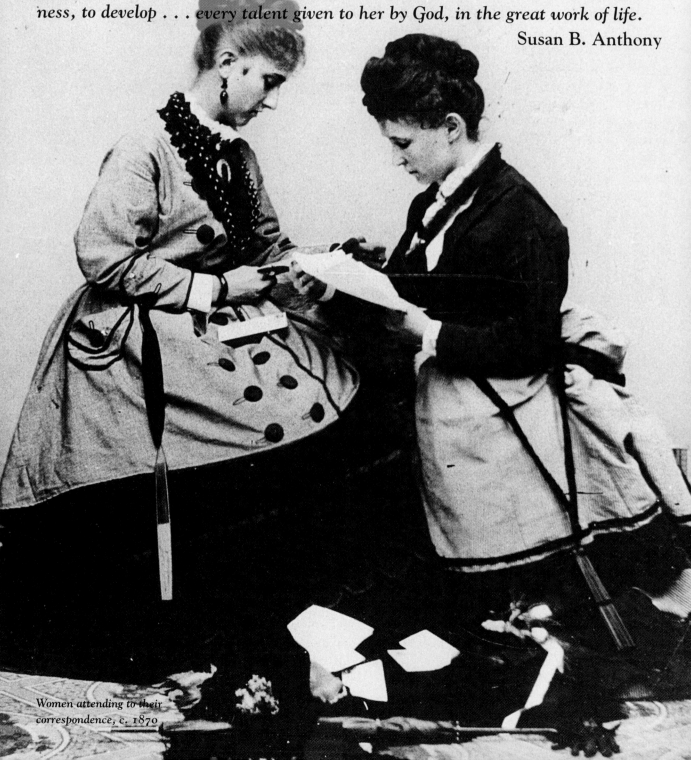

Women attending to their
correspondence, c. 1870

sure, except as they have observed several instances in which husband and wife have signed the same petition. In such case, they would recommend that the parties apply for a law authorizing them to change dresses, that the husband may wear petticoats and the wife the breeches, and thus indicate to their neighbors and the public the relation in which they stand to each other.

Stanton remembered her Albany address as "a great event" in her life. But it also took a great toll, for it further alienated her from the man whose admiration she had always wanted most. Her father had warned her not to appear in Albany: speech-making was unseemly for a wife and mother, an embarrassment to him and his family. If she dared do anything like it again, family legend held that he had told her, he would write her out of his will.

Stanton poured out her misery to Anthony:

My Dear Susan . . .

I wish you to consider this letter strictly confidential. . . .

I passed through a terrible scourging when last at my father's. I cannot tell you how deep the iron entered my soul. I never felt more keenly the degradation of my sex. To think that all in me of which my father would have felt a proper pride had I been a man is deeply mortifying to him because I am a woman. That thought has stung me to a fierce decision—to speak as soon as I can do myself credit. But the pressure on me just now is too great. Henry sides with my friends, who oppose me in all that is dearest to my heart. They are not willing that I should write even on the woman question. . . . Sometimes, Susan, I struggle in deep waters.

As ever your friend, sincere and steadfast.

Elizabeth Cady Stanton

For the next five years, Elizabeth Cady Stanton would continue her work for women's rights—turning out a steady stream of articles, struggling to prepare speeches and letters for Anthony to read aloud at meetings and conventions, but otherwise keeping behind the scenes. "My whole soul is in the work," she wrote, "but my hands belong to my family," and she would find herself living vicariously through the tireless activity of the woman who was now her closest partner. "Through all these years," she wrote, "Miss Anthony was the connecting link between me and the outer world—the reform scout who went to see what was going on in the enemy's camp and returned with maps and observations to plan the mode of attack."

ALMOST EXPIRING

Susan B. Anthony remained close to her own family and continued to weave a network of mostly female friends, but her work, her cause, always came first. On Christmas Day of 1854, she left home, determined to keep up the pressure on the New York state legislature. She would stay on the road for five months straight, canvassing every one of the state's fifty-four counties, jotting down details of her travels in a series of letters to her parents.

[Wendte's Station,] January 14, half past 12 P.M.

Well, well, good folks at home, these surely are the times that try women's souls. After writing you last, the snows fell and the winds blew. . . .

At Olean, not a church or schoolhouse could be obtained for the lecture and it would have had to be abandoned had not the landlord, Mr. Comstock, given us the use of his dining room. . . .

At Angelica, a young methodist minister gave his name for the petition but one of his wealthy parishioners told him he should leave the church unless it was withdrawn. . . .

At Corning, none of the ministers would give notice of our meeting. . . .

She chose to travel in the winter because the fierce cold and deep snows kept farmers at home and there was likely to be little competition from other speakers. She had just a single set of remarks in those early days, she recalled, so she gave half of it in the afternoons to women only and saved the second half for the evenings, when she hoped her daytime listeners would come back and bring with them their husbands and brothers and fathers.

On the road: Anthony at thirty-two.

(Opposite) Canandaigua, one of scores of New York communities Anthony canvassed during the 1850s. "As I passed from town to town," she wrote, "I was made to feel the great evil of woman's utter dependency upon man, for the necessary means to aid any and every reform movement. Though I had long admitted the wrongs, I never until this time, so fully took in the grand idea of pecuniary & personal independence."

She charged a twenty-five-cent entry fee but otherwise often had to use her own savings to buy train tickets and pay for the sleigh and carriage rides that got her to and from the little towns to which no railroad came. The rooms in country inns where she slept were often unheated, she recalled, but "she never omitted" her morning sponge bath, even when she had to break ice in the pitcher.

And everywhere, it seemed, she saw new evidences of women's ill-treatment.

We stopped at a little tavern where the landlady was not yet twenty and had a baby fifteen months old. . . .

When we came to pay our bill, the dolt of a husband took the money and put it in his pocket. He had not lifted a hand to lighten that woman's burdens, but had sat and talked with the men in the bar room, not even caring for the baby, yet the law gives him the right to every dollar she earns. . . .

In spite of this terrible weather, people drive eight and ten miles to our meetings.

Some people turned out to see her merely for the novelty of it: most had never heard a woman speak in public before. But others were drawn to her message. "Susan B. Anthony is in town and spoke . . . this afternoon," one young woman noted in her diary. "She made a special request that all seminary girls should come to hear her as well as all the women and girls in town. She had a large audience and she talked plainly about our rights and how we ought to stand up for them and said the world would never go right until the women had just as much right to vote and rule as men. She asked us all to come up and sign our names who would promise to do all in our power to bring about that glad day. . . . A whole lot of us went up and signed the paper."

A few newspapermen were impressed as well. "While we differ widely with Miss Anthony," said the *Roundout Courier*, "both as regards the propriety of the calling she has assumed, and the notions of which she is an advocate, we cheerfully accord to her credit as a public speaker . . . expressing herself with clearness and many times with elegance and force!"

The *Courier* reporter went on to provide a memorable portrait of Anthony in action:

. . . a lady, unattended and unheralded, quietly glided in and ascended the platform. She was as easy and self-possessed, as a lady should always be when performing a plain duty, even under 600 curious eyes. Her situation would have been trying to a non-self-reliant woman, for there was no volunteer co-operator. The custodian of the hall, with his stereotyped stupidity, had dumped some tracts and papers on the platform. The unfriended Miss Anthony gathered them up composedly, placed them on a table disposedly, put her decorous shawl on one chair and a very exemplary bonnet on another, sat a moment, smoothed her hair discreetly, and then deliberately walked to the table and addressed the audience. She wore a becoming black silk dress, [and has] pleasing rather than pretty features, decidedly expressive countenance, rich brown hair very effectively and not at all elaborately arranged . . . the perfection of common sense physically exhibited. Miss Anthony's oratory is in keeping with all her belongings, her voice well modulated and musical, her enunciation distinct, her style earnest and impressive, her language pure and unexaggerated.

WHY THE SEXES SHOULD BE EDUCATED TOGETHER: *By such education they get true ideas of each other—The College Student associates with only two classes of Women; the kitchen drudge & parlor doll—The Seminary girl . . . gets her idea of man mostly from works of fiction—* Susan B. Anthony

Female students and faculty at the Canandaigua Seminary

Anthony drove herself so hard that winter that she injured her back and had to be carried in and out of one meeting, then was forced to lie on the seat of a sleigh curled up and covered with blankets during the seventeen-mile ride to the next. Her belief that wrapping her injury in sheets soaked in ice water would somehow help only added to her pain, but she kept going. "Every day brings me new conceptions of life and its duties," Anthony told one of her sisters, "and it is my constant desire that I may be strong and fearless, baring my arm to the encounter and pressing cheerfully forward, though the way is rough and thorny."

Anthony's tenacity and fervor so impressed the executive committee of the American Anti-Slavery Society that in 1856 she was asked to become its New York state agent, responsible for arranging speaking tours not only for herself but for a cast of other antislavery speakers as well. She accepted without a moment's hesitation. For the first time in her life she was to be paid at least a little for her reform work—but she was now pursuing two great causes across the state simultaneously.

Her near-infinite capacity for work, her inability to sit still for long or turn down a request for help, were sources of bemused wonder to friends like the antislavery journalist Parker Pillsbury. "Is there work . . . among you for Susan to do?" he asked a mutual friend, his tongue firmly in his cheek:

> *Any shirt-making, cooking, clerking, preaching or teaching, indeed any honest work, just to keep her out of idleness! She seems strangely unemployed—almost expiring for something to do, and I could not resist the inclination to appeal to you . . . that an effort be made in her behalf. At present she has only the Anti-Slavery cause for New York, the Woman's Rights Movement for the world, the Sunday evening lectures for Rochester and other lecturing of her own from Lake Erie to the "Old Man of Franconia" mountains; private cares and home affaires, and the various etceteras of womanity. These are about all so far as appears, to occupy her seven days of twenty-four hours each, as the works rain down to her from Eternal Skies. Do pity and procure work for her if it be possible!*

Antoinette Brown Blackwell and her daughter, Florence, 1859

Lucy Stone (opposite) and her daughter Alice, that same year. She kept her maiden name after marrying Henry Blackwell.

Anthony had few women upon whom she could depend for help. Most women's-rights advocates were, like Stanton, married and preoccupied with home and children. And when first her friend Lucy Stone and then Antoinette Brown announced plans to marry, she felt personally betrayed, just as she had when her own sisters found husbands. She was angry, too. Marriage, she told Stone, was a "defection," evidence that her commitment to women's rights was weaker than her own. She lectured both women on what she insisted was their larger duty

and would eventually even presume to tell them to stop having children. Stanton warned her to "[l]et them rest in peace and quietness . . . do not keep stirring them up or mourning over their repose." But Anthony did not seem able to stop, and her relationship with Lucy Stone would eventually turn cold and bitter, with unfortunate results for the future of women's rights.

Anthony would never abandon her belief that marriage was an obstacle to the movement. Many years later, the African-American journalist and suffragist Ida Wells-Barnett remembered confronting Anthony about her feelings. She had noticed that Anthony, who had always spoken to her with gentle courtesy when she was still single, would "bark out" her married name: "Finally, I said to her, 'Miss Anthony, don't you believe in women getting married?' She said, 'Oh, yes, but not women like you who had a special call for special work. I too might have married but it would have meant dropping the work to which I had set my hand.' "

That work sometimes threatened literally to consume her. Her stream-of-consciousness letters to Stanton, with their pell-mell punctuation, their lists of pledges to be kept and duties to be fulfilled, are evidence both of the prodigious amount of work she routinely performed and of the anxiety that seems to have been her constant companion. The motivation for the letter that follows was her need for help with still another speech, this time championing coeducation for an upcoming teacher's convention at Troy. The fact that Stanton was still nursing her newborn daughter was a matter of little concern to Anthony.

Private
Home getting along toward 12 Oclock
Thursday Evening 5th June [1856]
    And Mrs Stanton, not a word written on that Address for Teachers Con.— This week was to be leisure to me—& lo, our girl, a wife, had a miscarriage on Tuesday,—at eve one Lady Visitor came & to day a man & the mercy only knows when I can get a moment—& what is worse, as the Lord knows full well, is, that if I get all the time the world has—I cant get up a decent document, so for the love of me, & for the sake of the reputation of womanhood, I beg you with one baby on your knee &—another at your feet & four boys whistling buzzing hallooing Ma Ma set your self about the work—it is of but small moment who writes the Address, but of vast moment that it be well done—I promise you to work hard, oh, how hard, & pay you whatever you say for your time & brains—but oh Mrs. Stanton don't say no, nor don't delay it a moment, for I must have it all done & almost commit it to memory.

"I would not object to marriage if it were not that women throw away every plan and purpose of their own life, to conform to the plans and purposes of the man's life. I wonder if it is woman's real, true nature always to abnegate self. There is not one woman left who may be relied on, all have 'first to please their husband' after which there is but little time or energy left to spend in any other direction. I am not complaining or despairing, but facts are stern realities. The twain become one flesh, the woman 'we.' . . . I declare to you that I distrust the power of any woman, even of myself to withstand the mighty matrimonial maelstrom."

Susan B. Anthony

Now let me tell you, Do you write all you think of ready to copy, & then you come out here, or I will come to you & copy—

The Teachers Con. comes the 5 & 6th Aug, the Saratoga [Woman's Rights] Con. the 13 & 14th & probably the Newport the 20 & 21st

During July, I want to speak certainly twice at Avon, Clifton, Sharon, & Ballston Springs & Lake George—Now will you load my gun leaving me only to pull the trigger & let fly the powder & ball—

Don't delay one mail to tell me what you will do—for I must not & will not allow those school masters to say—see these women cant or wont do any thing when we do give them a chance—No, they shant say that, even if I have to get a man to write it—but no man can write from my stand point—nor no woman but you—for all would base their strongest argument on the unlikeness of the sexes— Nette [Antoinette Brown] wrote me that she should, were she to make the Address— & more than any other place does the difference of sex, if there is any, need to be forgotten in the school room. . . .

Now do I pray you give heed to my prayer—those of you who have the talent to do honor to poor oh how poor womanhood, have all given yourselves over to baby making, & left poor brainless me to battle alone—It is a shame,—such a body as I might be spared to rock cradles, but it is a crime for you & Lucy & Nette—I have just engaged to attend a Progressive Meeting in Erie Co. the 1st of Sept. just because there is no other woman to be had, not because I feel in the least competent— . . . how I do wish I could step in to see you & make you feel all my infirmities—mental, I mean. . . .

I haven't half written out the points I have thought of—but will send what I have to stir you up—do get all on fire, and be as cross as you please, you remember Mr. Stanton told how cross you always get in a speech.

Goodby,

Susan B.

Stanton agreed to do her best to help.

Seneca Falls

10 June, 1856

Dear Susan,

Your servant is not dead but liveth. Imagine me, day in and day out, watching, bathing, dressing, nursing and promenading the precious contents of a little crib in the corner of my room. I pace up and down these two chambers of mine like a caged lioness, longing to bring nursing and housekeeping cares to a close. Is your speech to be exclusively on the point of educating the sexes together, or as to the best manner of educating women? Have you Horace Mann on that?

Come here and I will do what I can to help you with your address, if you will hold the baby and make the puddings—Love to Antoinette and Lucy when you write them. Womankind owes them a debt of gratitude for their faithful labors in the past. . . .

You, too, must rest, Susan; let the world alone awhile. We can not bring about a moral revolution in a day or a year. Now that I have two daughters, I feel fresh strength to work for women. It is not in vain that in myself I feel all the wearisome care to which woman even in her best estate is subject.

Good night.

Yours in love,

Elizabeth Cady Stanton

Susan B. Anthony could never leave the world alone even for a moment. Again and again during the late 1850s she would descend upon Seneca Falls, prepared to take over the running of the household while Stanton worked up a speech or public statement.

"Whenever I saw that stately Quaker girl coming across my lawn," Stanton wrote, "I knew that some happy convocation of the sons of Adam was to be set by the ears. . . .

The little portmanteau stuffed with facts was opened and there we had what the Rev. John Smith and Hon. Richard Roe had said: false interpretations of Bible texts, the statistics of women robbed of their property, shut out of some college, half paid for their work, the reports of some disgraceful trial; injustice enough to turn any woman's thoughts from stockings and puddings. . . . We never met without issuing a pronunciamento on some question. . . . Night after night by an old-fashioned fireplace we plotted and planned the coming agitation, how, when and where each entering wedge could be driven, by which woman might be recognized and her rights secured.

Stanton seems always to have welcomed Anthony cordially enough, but her high-spirited children sometimes felt differently. "Her advent was not a matter for rejoicing," Harriot Stanton Blatch remembered, "for it meant that [our] resourceful mother was to retire as mentor and be entirely engrossed in writing a speech for Miss Anthony to deliver . . . while she kept the children out of sight and out of mind." Anthony was also evidently a somewhat severe presence. She "ruled more by compulsion than by attraction," Harriot recalled, and when the boys were small, they believed that her walleye made it possible for her to peer around corners and discover what they were up to; one of them wrote that "Aunt Susan" was the only other person besides his mother who had ever spanked him.

California gathering, 1850s

Quite as many false ideas prevail as to woman's true position in the home as to her status elsewhere. Womanhood is the great fact in her life; wifehood and motherhood are but incidental relations. Governments legislate for men; we do not have one code for bachelors, another for husbands and fathers; neither have the social relations of women any significance in their demands for civil and political rights.   Elizabeth Cady Stanton

At a state teacher's convention the following summer, Anthony introduced a resolution she and Stanton had written together, declaring it "the duty of all our schools, colleges and universities to open their doors to woman and to give her equal and identical educational advantages side by side with her brother man." The proposal was soundly defeated; Charles Davies, professor of mathematics at West Point, denounced coeducation as "a vast social evil . . . a monster of social deformity." Even most of the women present voted against it.

"What an infernal set of fools these school-marms must be!!" Stanton wrote Anthony when she got the news.

> Well, if in order to please men they wish to live on air, let them. The sooner the present generation of women die out the better. We have jackasses enough in the world now without such women propagating any more . . . I glory in your perseverance. Oh, Susan I will do anything to help you on. Courage, Susan, this is my last baby and she will be two years old in January. Two years more and—time will tell what! You and I have the prospect of a good long life. We shall not be in our prime before fifty, and after that we shall be good for twenty years at least.

Such assurances did little to ease Anthony's apprehension or her sense that everything still depended on her. She was often lonely and continued to feel overwhelmed.

> September 29, 1857
> Dear Mrs. Stanton . . .
>
> I have very weak moments—and long to lay my weary head somewhere and nestle my full soul close to that of another in full sympathy—sometimes I fear that I too shall faint by the wayside—and drop out of the ranks of the faithful few. . . .
>
> There is so much, mid all that is so hopeful, to discourage & dishearten—and I feel alone. . . .
>
> How I do long to be with you this very minute, to have one look into your very soul and [hear] one sound from your soul-stirring voice. . . . Oh, Mrs. Stanton, how my soul longs to see you in the great Battlefield. . . . If you come not to the rescue, who shall?
>
> With best love,
> Susan B. Anthony

Stanton's soul longed for the great battlefield, too. She had grown increasingly resentful of remaining at home while her husband busied himself in New York City and Washington with the back-room workings of still another new political organization, the Republican Party. The Stanton marriage had always been turbulent. Elizabeth's boldness had sometimes caused Henry political embarrassment. His inability to earn sufficient income had irritated her. He was away often, and when he did come home, she once wrote, devoted most of his time to "the

A page from one of Anthony's meticulous expense diaries. The train from Boston to Bangor cost $6.50; breakfast was 38 cents, and bonnet strings another 40 cents.

worship of his god, his evening paper." And things may have been further complicated for both of them by the unspoken fact that while he had been the celebrated partner when they first married, her name was now far more widely known than his.

June 4th, 1858
My dear Susan . . .

How rebellious it makes me feel when I see Henry going about where and how he pleases. He can walk at will through the whole wide world or shut himself up alone, if he pleases, within four walls. As I contrast his freedom with my bondage . . . I am fired anew and long to pour forth from my own experience the whole long story of woman's wrongs.

July 4, 1858
My Dear Susan . . .

I have been alone today as the whole family except Hattie [the housekeeper] and myself have been out to celebrate our national birthday. What has woman to do with patriotism? Must not someone watch baby, house and garden? And who is so fitting to perform all these duties, which no one else wishes to do, as she who brought sin into the world and all our woe.

Despite her growing frustration with her marriage, despite her pledge to Susan not to have another baby, she became pregnant again in 1858. Anthony was appalled.

Ah me!!! Alas!! Alas!!!! Mrs. Stanton is embarked on the rolling sea . . . her husband, you know, does not help to make it easy for her. . . . Mr. Stanton will be gone most of the Autumn, full of Political Air Castles. . . . He was gone 7 months last winter. The whole burden of home and children therefore, falls to her, if she leaves the post all is afloat. I only scold now that for a moment's pleasure to herself or her husband she should thus increase the load of cares under which she already groans. But there is no remedy now.

On March 13, 1859, Stanton gave birth to her seventh child, Robert Livingston Stanton. He weighed more than twelve pounds. "I never suffered so much," she admitted to a friend, and she was confined to her bed for a month afterward, depressed and depleted. She was forty-three years old; there would be no more children.

Five months later, John Brown's abortive attempt at leading a slave rebellion ended in his capture at Harpers Ferry, Virginia. To Stanton, he was a hero, a martyr to a sacred cause. Then Gerrit Smith was committed to an insane asylum, convinced that his financial backing for Brown's raid had somehow caused its failure. Finally, on the last day of October, her father died at the age of eighty-six. She had never fully reconciled with him, had never received the unqualified approval for which she had yearned since she was a little girl. In her grief, she turned to Anthony for comfort.

Gerrit Smith in 1862, after his release from the asylum to which he had been sent after John Brown's arrest. He had been "quite deranged" by Brown's raid, according to his physician, "intellectually as well as morally."

> *December 23, 1859—*
>
> *Dear Susan . . .*
>
> *Where are you? Since a week ago last Monday, I have looked for you every day. I had the washing put off, we cooked a turkey, I made a pie in the morning, sent my first-born to the depot and put clean aprons on the children, but lo! you did not come. Nor did you soften the rough angles of our disappointment by one solitary line of excuse. And it would do me such great good to see some reformers just now. The death of my father, the worse than death of my dear cousin Gerrit, the martyrdom of that grand and glorious John Brown— all this conspires to make me regret more than ever my dwarfed womanhood. In times like these, everyone should do the work of a full-grown man.*

TO THE MARROW OF THE BONE

Stanton felt her father's loss deeply, but it also served to liberate her. She was now able to leave her children with her mother and sisters in Johnstown from time to time and speak out on her own. Anthony eagerly arranged for her to deliver three major addresses within three months.

In March of 1860, she addressed—in person this time—the Judiciary Committee and a large mixed audience in the Assembly chamber at Albany. The expanded Married Woman's Property Act for which she and Anthony had fought four years earlier was finally coming up for a vote. In a tough talk entitled "A Slave's Appeal," Stanton dismissed the argument that women would somehow lose men's protection if given the ballot:

> *When you talk, gentlemen, of sheltering woman from the rough minds and revolting scenes of real life, you must be either talking for effect, or be wholly ignorant*

of what the facts of life are. The man, whatever he is, is known to the woman. She is the companion, not only of the statesman, the orator, and the scholar, but the vile, vulgar, brutal man, as his mother, his wife, his sister, his daughter. . . . Gentlemen, such scenes as woman has witnessed at her own fireside, where no eyes save Omnipotence could pity, no strong arm could help, can never be realized at the polls.

The legislature passed the expanded act the following day. New York women now had the right to own property without interference from their husbands, to keep all of their own earnings, to transact business on their own, to sue and be sued in a court of law, and to share custody of their children. It was the first triumph of the women's movement—other states, inspired by New York's example, would soon follow suit—and Stanton was encouraged to press forward on other, more controversial fronts.

On May 8, she spoke again, at Cooper Union in New York City, before the American Anti-Slavery Society. It was "the only organization on God's footstool where the humanity of woman is recognized," she told the delegates, and the men who led it were "the only men who have ever echoed back her cries for justice and equality." But no man could understand the slaves' plight as well as a woman.

Cooper Union in New York City, where Stanton made two of the three controversial addresses that marked her return to public life in the spring of 1860

Eloquently and earnestly as noble men have denounced slavery . . . they have been able to take only an objective view . . . [because as] a privileged class they can never conceive of those who are born to contempt, to inferiority, to degradation. Herein is woman more fully identified with the slave than man can possibly be. . . . She early learns the misfortune of being born an heir to the crown of thorns, to martyrdom, to womanhood. For while the man is born to do whatever he can, for the woman and the negro there is no such privilege.

Three days later, in the same hall but speaking now before the tenth annual National Woman's Rights Convention, Stanton delivered an all-out attack on the institution of marriage itself. As currently constituted, she said, marriage was "nothing more than legalized prostitution. . . . Personal freedom . . . cannot now belong to the relation of wife, to the mistress of the isolated home, to the financial dependent. . . . There is one kind of marriage that has not been tried, and that is a contract made by equal parties to lead an equal life, with equal restraints and privileges on either side. Thus far, we have had *man* marriage and nothing more." She went on to offer a resolution declaring that marriage should be a purely legal contract, which either party should be free to end in case of drunkenness, desertion, or cruelty.

Many of those present had never seen Elizabeth Cady Stanton before—she had remained almost entirely at home for the past six years—though all were familiar with her name. Nothing had prepared them for this, and even some of her oldest allies were stunned. Lucy Stone had tried to keep the whole issue of divorce reform off the agenda. She agreed that it was essential but believed it must not be called part of women's rights because it "concerns men just as much." The Reverend Antoinette Brown Blackwell insisted that marriage was ordained by God—permanent and indissoluble. "All divorce," she insisted, "is naturally and morally impossible." Wendell Phillips called for Stanton's resolution to be expunged from the record. "This convention is no *Marriage* Convention," he said. "I as a man, have exactly equal interest in the essential question of marriage as a woman has."

Anthony rose to defend her friend:

Marriage has ever and always will be a one-sided matter, resting most unequally upon the sexes. By it, man gains all—woman loses all; tyrant law and lust remain supreme with him—meek submission, and cheerful, ready obedience, alone befit her. Woman has never been consulted. . . . By law, public sentiment and religion, from the time of Moses down to the present day, woman has never been thought of other than as a piece of property, to be disposed of at the will and pleasure of man.

Bride and bridesmaid, 1870s

Marriage is not all of life to man. His resources for amuse-ment and occupation are boundless. He has the whole world for his home. . . . But to women, marriage is all and every thing; her sole object in life,—that for which she is educated—the subject of all her sleeping and waking dreams. . . . In the present undeveloped condi-tion of woman, it is only through our fathers, brothers, husbands, sons, that we feel the pulsations of the great outer world.

ELIZABETH CADY STANTON

The delegates allowed the debate over Stanton's resolution to remain in the record, but they adjourned without voting on it, and the press seized upon the radical tone of her address to further tar the women's-rights movement. The meeting had been "infidel and licentious," said the *New York Observer*, corrupted by sentiments "which no true woman could listen to without turning scarlet . . . unblushingly read and advocated by a person in woman's attire, named in the programme as Elizabeth Cady Stanton." To turn marriage into a mere business contract "would turn the whole world into one vast brothel."

As always, Stanton returned to Seneca Falls unshaken in her conviction that she had been right: "This marriage question," she insisted to Anthony, "lies at the very foundation of all progress," and nothing her critics inside or outside the movement could say would shake that belief:

> [T]hat which is of the very being must stand forever. Nothing, nobody could abate the all-absorbing, agonizing interest I feel in the redemption of woman. I could not wash my hands of woman's rights, for they are dyed clear through to the marrow of the bone.
>
> Those sad-faced women who struggled up to press my hand, who were speechless with emotion, know better than the greatest of our masculine speakers and

editors who has struck the blow for them in the right place. I shall trust my instinct and my reason until some masculine logic meets mine better than it has yet done.

In December of that year, the fresh gulf between Stanton and Anthony and a good many of their old antislavery allies widened further. A heavily veiled Massachusetts woman named Phoebe Harris Phelps sought out Anthony and begged for help: she was in hiding from her husband, a Republican state senator, who had beaten her, seized her property, had her locked up in an asylum, and refused to allow her to see her three children—all because after years of abuse she had dared threaten to expose his many infidelities. Desperate, she had finally stolen away her thirteen-year-old daughter and fled to New York state in search of refuge. Anthony found her temporary sanctuary in Manhattan, then refused to divulge her whereabouts to her pursuers. Wendell Phillips and William Lloyd Garrison insisted that she give them up. Phillips urged that "our movement's repute for good sense . . . not be compromised" by defying Massachusetts law, which, Garrison pointed out, gave complete guardianship of children to their fathers.

That Garrison and Phillips should insist on carrying out an unjust law was more than Anthony could bear. The law also required that fugitive slaves be returned to their owners, she reminded them, yet "[y]ou would die before you would deliver a slave to his master, and I will die before I will give up that child to its father." She did not betray the fugitives, though eventually both Phelps and her daughter were returned to Massachusetts, where the father was given full custody of the child. But the Phelps case was further disturbing evidence that the men alongside whom she had fought slavery for so long did not share fully in her convictions about women.

"Very many abolitionists," she noted in her diary, "have yet to learn the ABCs of woman's rights." Their further education would be delayed by the crisis that now convulsed the country.

North Carolina women, 1860s

LET NONE
STAND IDLE

3

I n November of 1860, Abraham Lincoln had
been elected president, pledged to halt slavery's
westward spread but convinced he had no constitutional power to move against it where it
already existed. Abolitionists mounted a campaign
aimed at forcing him to commit himself to immediate emancipation. Anthony, assigned the task of organizing a "No Compromise with Slavery" tour of
upstate New York towns, assembled what she proudly
called "a tremendous force of speakers": Lucretia
Mott, Martha Wright, Gerrit Smith, Frederick Douglass, Stephen Foster—and Elizabeth Cady Stanton.
It was Stanton's first extended trip away from home
in years. She had craved excitement during her time
at the hearthside and would not be disappointed.

Democrats and Republicans may have differed
among themselves about slavery, but in the winter
of 1861 most were united in their dislike of the abolitionists, whose uncompromising zeal they believed
had precipitated the crisis that was tearing the country apart. In Buffalo, a jeering bipartisan mob prevented the speakers from being heard at all. At
Rochester, Stanton was drowned out and driven from
the platform; Anthony refused to leave until the chief
of police jumped onstage and adjourned the meeting. In Utica, management refused to open the doors
of Mechanics Hall even though Anthony had paid
sixty dollars to rent it for the evening, and when the
mayor arrived to escort her to safety, she denounced
him as a coward for failing to guarantee her right of
free speech. At Rome, the Republican newspaper
denounced the speakers as "pestiferous fanatics." A

Syracuse mob pelted them with eggs and burned Anthony in effigy. Serious violence was averted at Albany only because the mayor of that city accompanied the speakers onstage and sat throughout their presentation with a revolver prominently displayed on his lap.

Henry Stanton pleaded with his wife to go home. He was in Washington, trying to arrange a patronage job for himself with the new Republican administration. "I think you risk your lives, . . ." he wrote. "[T]he mobocrats would as soon kill you as not. . . . I advise you, & Susan, & all friends to keep quiet & let the Revolution go on. . . . Stand out of the way & let the current run." When Henry Stanton was courting the young woman who became his wife, he had been celebrated for his fearlessness. Now he was just one of thousands of political job seekers, issuing words of caution while she faced down the mobs.

By the time the Civil War began, in April of 1861, Anthony had already made all the arrangements for the annual National Woman's Rights Convention at New York in May, but in the swell of patriotic fervor that followed Fort Sumter, every other cause seemed to shrink in significance. The American Anti-Slavery Society canceled its convention, and Stanton was just one of the chorus of suffragists who advised Anthony to call off the Woman's Rights Convention as well. If women wholeheartedly supported the Union, Stanton and most of her allies thought, the grateful Republican Party would reward them with the vote they'd been demanding for thirteen years once victory was won.

Anthony was aghast. She had been raised a Quaker pacifist and remained deeply distrustful of Abraham Lincoln, whom she believed "weak and trembling," nothing more than a timid prairie politician. By canceling their agitation, she believed, by cooperating with a government whose Constitution still permitted slavery, the abolitionists were acting like mere politicians, out of "expediency, not principle." "All of our reformers seem suddenly to have grown politic," Anthony complained to a friend. "All alike say, 'Have no convention at this crisis!' Garrison, Phillips, Mrs. Mott . . . Mrs. Stanton, etc. say, 'Wait until the war excitement abates.' I am sick at heart but I cannot carry the world against the wish and will of our best friends."

Having no faith whatsoever in what she scornfully called "man's sense of justice," she especially feared that any gains women had made would be reversed once their champions relaxed their vigilance. She would soon be proved right:

Henry B. Stanton and a newspaper account of one of the antiabolitionist riots that made him beg his wife to abandon speech-making in January 1861

Once the Civil War began, the nascent women's-rights movement slowed as Northerners—like these Manhattan members of the Women's Central Associ-ation for Relief tallying shipments to the field in their office at Cooper Union—devoted their energies to supporting the Union cause.

in 1862 the New York legislature repealed the provision of the Married Woman's Property Act that gave mothers equal guardianship of their children, part of the expanded act for which she had labored so long.

Anthony returned to the family farm, where, the pages of her journal suggest, she found enforced inaction almost unendurable:

Tried to interest myself in a sewing society; but little intelligence among them. . . .

Attended Progressive Friends Meeting; too much namby-pambyism. . . .

Went to colored church to hear [Frederick] Douglass. He seems without solid basis. Speaks only popular truths. . . .

Quilted all day but sewing no longer seems to be my calling.

I stained and varnished the library bookcase today, and superintended the plowing of the orchard.

Washed every window in the house today. . . .

Fitted out a fugitive slave for Canada with the help of Harriet Tubman. . . .

I wish the Government would move quickly, proclaim freedom to every slave and call on every able-bodied negro to enlist in the Union army. How not to do it seems the whole study at Washington. . . . To forever blot out slavery is the only possible compensation for this merciless war.

The all-alone feeling will creep over me. It is such a fast after the feast of great presences to which I have been so long accustomed.

Meanwhile, the Stantons had left Seneca Falls for Manhattan, where Henry had talked himself into a job as deputy collector at the Customs House. In early January of 1863 he sent Anthony a proposal. Lincoln had finally issued his Emancipation Proclamation, which freed the slaves in the rebellious states but said nothing about those residing within the Union. The war was still going badly for the North, and while Republican senator Charles Sumner of Massachusetts had introduced a constitutional amendment freeing all slaves everywhere, it was by no means clear that the amendment had enough public support to produce the two-thirds majority in both houses necessary to send it on to the states for ratification. Northern women, Henry Stanton suggested, could make all the difference by rallying the North. "Here then is work. Susan, put on your armor and go forth!"

Anthony needed little urging. By late February she was living in the Stantons' home, working on an appeal to the women of the North.

At this hour the best word and work of every man and woman are imperatively demanded. To man, by common consent, is assigned the forum, the camp and field. What is woman's legitimate work, and how she may best accomplish it, is worthy of our earnest counsel with one another. . . . Woman is equally interested and responsible with man in the settlement of this final problem of self-government; therefore, let none stand idle spectators now.

Then, with the help of Lucy Stone and others, she and Stanton formed the Women's National Loyal League. Stanton was president. Anthony served as secretary and—fueled each day by precisely the same spartan thirteen-cent lunch of milk, strawberries, and two tea rusks—supervised the work of two thousand volunteers across the country.

Stanton, Anthony, Lucy Stone, and other suffrage leaders created the Women's National Loyal League in 1863 for the purpose of collecting a million signatures on petitions like the one opposite, calling for the total emancipation of all slaves everywhere in the United States. To finance their work, they sold the badge below for three dollars in solid silver, and a third of that price in Britannia metal. Stanton especially liked its design, she said, because it showed a slave rising to his feet, not still on his knees.

WOMEN'S EMANCIPATION PETITION.

☞ Put no signatures on the back of the Petition.
☞ When this sheet is full, paste another at the bottom.
☞ If possible, send us contributions to help pay the heavy expenses incurred at this office.
☞ Do not copy the names—return the original signatures; no matter if the paper is worn or soiled.
☞ When your district is thoroughly canvassed, return the petitions and donations to this office.
☞ Address SUSAN B. ANTHONY, Secretary, Women's National League, Room 20, Cooper Institute, New York.

To the Senate and House of Representatives of the United States:

The Undersigned, Women of the United States above the age of eighteen years, earnestly pray that your Honorable Body will pass, at the earliest practicable day, an Act emancipating all persons of African descent held to involuntary service or labor in the United States.

NAME.	RESIDENCE.
Eliza Williams	Seneca Nemeha Co Kansas
Rhoda W. Metcalf	Turecreek Nemeha Co Kansas
Ellen Irvine	
Lizzie L. Fuller	Seneca Nemeha Co Kansas
W. C. Peckham	"
H. A. Flower	"
Lizzie W. Pelton	"
Mary A. Barnes	"
Amanda M. Lappin	"
C. E. Sampson	"

We have undertaken to canvass the nation for freedom. Women, you can not vote or fight for your country. Your only way to be a power in the government is through the exercise of this one sacred, constitutional right of "petition" and we ask you to use it now to the utmost.

On February 9, 1864, Sumner presented to the Senate the first one hundred thousand signatures gathered by the volunteers. By the time the Loyal League disbanded that summer, its representatives had amassed three hundred thousand more, and the amendment was on its way to passage. The petition campaign had been the largest in history up to that time, and Senator Sumner lavished praise on the women who had labored so hard to rally the North for freedom. The signatures they had gathered came from the "heart" of the country, he said; gathering them had been "noble work."

Both Stanton and Anthony suffered tragedy during the Civil War. Anthony's father, whose support for her every assertion of independence had meant everything to her, died suddenly of what the doctors diagnosed only as "neuralgia of the stomach." And Henry Stanton was driven from his Customs House post in disgrace after his eldest son, Daniel, was found to have forged his signature to steal government bonds from his office, a humiliation so great that for a time the Stantons considered moving to Kansas and starting over.

Still, at the war's end, the future of women's rights seemed brighter than ever before. For seventeen years Stanton and Anthony had made common cause with the abolitionists, had eagerly gathered their petitions and often deferred to their male leaders—who always professed to share completely their belief in the political equality of men and women as well as blacks and whites. Now, with talk everywhere of building a more just Union, with the Republicans in control of both houses of Congress, and with their old abolitionist allies no longer outsiders but closely allied with that party's radical wing, the vote for former slaves seemed a real and immediate possibility. Surely now, the women and their allies reasoned, the Republicans they had so loyally served during the war would reward that loyalty by also granting *women* the vote they had been asking for since 1848. "The millennium is on the way," the abolitionist editor Theodore Tilton wrote Anthony. "Three cheers for God!"

THE NEGRO'S HOUR

Stanton, Anthony, and their allies in the women's-rights movement were about to run head-on into cold political reality. In May of 1865 the American Anti-Slavery Society met to decide whether or not it had a future in a country no longer corrupted by the hideous institution against which they had fought so hard. William Lloyd Garrison argued that the society's great work was done and that it should dissolve. But Wendell Phillips, one of Stanton and Anthony's oldest allies—Anthony called him "dear ever-glorious Phillips"—insisted that the society still had work to do: black freedom could never be "beyond peril" unless the former slaves had the vote. He proposed that the society now focus on passage of a fourteenth amendment to the Constitution, enfranchising the roughly two million freedmen living in the former Confederacy.

Stanton was among Phillips's most ardent supporters and was delighted when he won and accepted the presidency of a newly energized Anti-Slavery Society. But she was appalled by his inaugural address. Winning the vote for former slaves would not be easy, Phillips maintained; millions of Democrats and conservative Republicans—all of them male—would have to be won over. The burden of simultaneously persuading those same men that women be given the vote as well was simply too heavy to bear. Votes for women, he said, would have to wait. "[T]his hour

After the Civil War, African-Americans in Richmond celebrate Emancipation—and the Emancipator: Republican enthusiasm for black male suffrage was in part due to the expectation that hundreds of thousands of southern freedmen like these would remain faithful to the "party of Lincoln."

A PETITION
FOR
UNIVERSAL SUFFRAGE.

To the Senate and House of Representatives:

The undersigned, Women of the United States, respectfully ask an amendment of the Constitution that shall prohibit the several States from disfranchising any of their citizens on the ground of sex.

In making our demand for Suffrage, we would call your attention to the fact that we represent fifteen million people—one half the entire population of the country—intelligent, virtuous, native-born American citizens; and yet stand outside the pale of political recognition.

The Constitution classes us as "free people," and counts us whole persons in the basis of representation; and yet are we governed without our consent, compelled to pay taxes without appeal, and punished for violations of law without choice of judge or juror.

The experience of all ages, the Declarations of the Fathers, the Statute Laws of our own day, and the fearful revolution through which we have just passed, all prove the uncertain tenure of life, liberty and property so long as the ballot—the only weapon of self-protection—is not in the hand of every citizen.

Therefore, as you are now amending the Constitution, and, in harmony with advancing civilization, placing new safeguards round the individual rights of four millions of emancipated slaves, we ask that you extend the right of Suffrage to Woman—the only remaining class of disfranchised citizens—and thus fulfil your Constitutional obligation "to Guarantee to every State in the Union a Republican form of Government."

As all partial application of Republican principles must ever breed a complicated legislation as well as a discontented people, we would pray your Honorable Body, in order to simplify the machinery of government and ensure domestic tranquillity, that you legislate hereafter for persons, citizens, tax-payers, and not for class or caste.

For justice and equality your petitioners will ever pray.

NAMES.	RESIDENCE.
Elizabeth Cady Stanton,	New York
Susan B. Anthony,	Rochester—N.Y.
Antoinette Brown Blackwell,	New York
	Newark N. Jersey
Joanna S. Moore	48 Livingston. Brooklyn
Ernestine L. Rose	New York
Harriet E. Eaton	6. West 14th Street N. Y
Catharine C. Wilkeson	83 Clinton Place New York

Petition for universal suffrage signed by Stanton, Anthony, Antoinette Brown Blackwell, and Lucy Stone but only reluctantly submitted to the House of Representatives by Thaddeus Stevens of Pennsylvania in 1866

belongs to the negro," Phillips told the gathering. "As Abraham Lincoln said, 'One war at a time'; so I say, 'One question at a time.' This is the negro's hour."

Elizabeth Cady Stanton felt betrayed. "May I ask just one question based on the apparent opposition in which you place the negro and the woman?" she remembered writing Phillips a few days later. "My question is this: Do you believe the African race is composed entirely of males?"

For Stanton, to defer rights for women was to violate basic principles. "The struggle of the last thirty years has not been merely on the black man as such, but on the broader ground of his humanity," she argued. Either men and women—all men and all women, black as well as white—were equal or they were not. The vote was a citizen's natural right. To grant suffrage to one group of citizens at the expense of another was to betray the conviction that had been the mainspring of the movement since 1848, argued with equal vehemence by men and women alike. To abandon it was to accept an "aristocracy of sex."

There were also practical reasons for Stanton's concern. Two million newly enfranchised black men offered the party in power the possibility of building a Republican South. Woman suffrage carried with it no such glittering prize. If votes for slaves and women were not pushed through together now—if, as Stanton put it, "when the constitutional door is open" women were not able to "avail ourselves of the strong arm and blue uniform of the black soldier to walk in by his side"—votes for women could be delayed for decades.

Anthony was in Kansas that summer, visiting her brother Daniel and working for the relief of the freedmen living there, when she received a letter from Stanton: "I have argued constantly with the whole fraternity, but I fear one and all will favor enfranchising the negro without us. Woman's cause is in deep water. . . . Come back and help. There will be a room for you. I seem to stand alone."

Anthony soon boarded the train for New York. Together, she and Stanton orchestrated a petition campaign that collected ten thousand signatures pleading with Congress to include woman suffrage in the Fourteenth Amendment. Charles Sumner dismissed them as "most inopportune" and Radical Republicans refused even to present them to Congress. The women's frustration grew. Not only did the proposed amendment say nothing about votes for women; it also explicitly designated as voters "male citizens." For the first time, the United States Constitution was to include a sexual distinction. "If that word 'male' be inserted as now proposed," Stanton confided to Gerrit Smith, "it will take us a century to get it out again." "I would sooner cut off my right hand," Anthony told Wendell Phillips, "than ask the ballot for the black man and not the woman." Abolitionists were not happy with the Fourteenth Amendment either: it did not explicitly guarantee freedmen the right to vote; rather, it promised them only equal protection under their state laws and provided for a reduction of representation for any state that denied the vote to male citizens. But abolitionists felt they had no choice but to support it—and to close ranks behind the Republican Party when it made the amendment part of its 1866 platform.

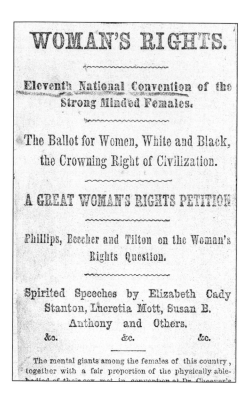

The New York Herald *reports the 1866 convention at which the American Equal Rights Association was founded.*

In May of that year, at the first women's-rights convention since before the war, the leaders of the women's movement invited members of the Anti-Slavery Society to join them in forming a new American Equal Rights Association so that both causes could go forward together. The time had come, Stanton said, "to bury the black man and the woman in the citizen, and our two organizations in the broader work of reconstruction."

THE SPIRIT OF THE AGE

One month after the American Equal Rights Association was founded, Congress passed the Fourteenth Amendment without change and sent it on to the states to be ratified. That summer white mobs attacked freedmen so viciously in so many places in the South that the Radical Republicans began to argue that if black suffrage were to become a reality, a fifteenth amendment would eventually be necessary, explicitly barring the states from discriminating against freedmen at the polls. If women couldn't create a groundswell of support for their cause they would likely be asked to wait again.

Eighteen sixty-seven seemed to offer Stanton, Anthony, and the AERA two opportunities to do just that. In June, New York was to hold a constitutional convention, which they hoped would win votes for women in the state. And in Kansas, in November, for the first time anywhere in the United States, male citizens were to vote on woman suffrage as well as votes for blacks.

No country ever has had or ever will have peace until every citizen has a voice in the government. Now let us try universal suffrage. We cannot tell its dangers or delights until we make the experiment. Elizabeth Cady Stanton

Black and white teachers who worked together to educate freedmen

While Lucy Stone and her husband, Henry Black-well, hurried west to launch a suffrage campaign in Kansas, Stanton and Anthony mounted a massive petition drive in New York. "The spirit of the age impels an onward step," they said, ". . . the lifting of the entire nation into the practical realization of our republican Idea." All sixty counties were canvassed, and more than twenty-eight thousand petitions by women attesting to their personal desire to vote were formally presented to the committee that was to report on suffrage.

It had no impact. Horace Greeley, the committee chairman and an early friend of women's rights, professed to be unimpressed. "However defensible in theory," he said, "we are satisfied that public sentiment does not demand and would not sustain an innovation so revolutionary and sweeping." Stanton and Anthony were furious, and a vengeful Stanton so humiliated Greeley when she announced in public session that one of the petitions had been signed by his own wife, that he—and his influential *Tribune*—would remain hostile to her and her cause for the rest of his life.

The prospects for woman suffrage in Kansas, too, now seemed dim. By the time Stanton and Anthony got there in September, they saw betrayal everywhere. The state Republican Party refused to endorse votes for women, and some party leaders were campaigning actively against it. Old abolitionist friends balked at coming to Kansas to campaign for woman suffrage, citing the greater urgency of enfranchising blacks. The antislavery press was silent on the issue. So was Greeley's *Tribune*. And Wendell Phillips, who administered a fund meant in part to finance woman suffrage, refused to release any of the money for the movement in Kansas.

Anthony took over suffrage headquarters in Lawrence while Stanton headed out on the road. For Stanton, who had occupied comfortable homes all her life, it was a baptism by fire. She traveled on the "very verge of civilization," she remembered, speaking in log cabins, barns, one-room schoolhouses. She endured fleas and bedbugs; had her sleep disrupted by rooting hogs; subsisted on tinned herring, crackers, and greasy bacon. "Oh . . . !" Stanton wrote to her cousin Elizabeth Smith Miller, "the dirt, the food!" but at least in retrospect, she loved it all. "It gave me added self-respect," she said, "to know that I could endure such hardships and fatigue with a great deal of cheerfulness."

Little cheerfulness was evident at the time. Without funds, infuriated by the desertion of Republican leaders and old antislavery allies, and desperate to corral Democratic votes to make up for massive Republican defections, Stanton and Anthony felt abandoned by "the liberal men" who had always been their comrades. And when an offer of help came from a flamboyantly illiberal man, they took it—to the astonishment of many of their oldest friends.

George Francis Train was a maverick Democrat, a wartime copperhead who liked to call himself the "Champion Crank," an eccentric millionaire, fond of pastel waistcoats, lavender gloves, and the sound of his own voice. He dreamed of being elected president on a platform that included freedom for Ireland, the eight-hour workday, paper currency, women's rights—and racist arguments against black suffrage. Train offered to come to Kansas at his own expense to help win the vote for women.

Unsteady allies: Horace Greeley (left), who backed away from women's rights, and George Francis Train (above) whose advocacy of those rights was tainted with racism

Lawrence, Kansas, head-quarters of Stanton and Anthony's 1867 campaign for woman suffrage in that state

During the final two weeks of the campaign, Anthony crisscrossed the state at Train's side, speaking first at every appearance, then sitting in uncharacteristic silence while he launched into remarks laced with the crudest kind of bigotry. Some of it came in the form of epigrams.

Let your corrupt politicians dance their double clogged jig,
As a bid for the suffrage of the poor Kansas Nig,
For our women will vote while the base plot thickens,
Before barbers, bootblacks, melons and chickens.

And

Woman votes the black to save,
The black he votes to make the woman slave,
Hence, when blacks and "Rads" unite to enslave the whites,
'Tis time the Democrats championed woman's rights.

Train made crude remarks about Anthony, too. "She commenced the campaign four-fifths negro and one-fifth woman," he would shout as the crowd laughed; "now she is four-fifths woman and one-fifth negro." Then, holding his nose, he went on: "Keep your nose twenty years on a negro and you will have hard work to smell a white man again."

Whatever Anthony may have thought privately of such remarks, she never made the slightest public protest. Train was for woman suffrage. Besides, he had promised her and Stanton financial backing for a newspaper of their own, to be called *The Revolution.* Anthony had spent years hurrying from newspaper office to newspaper office in cities and towns all across the country, imploring the usually skeptical men who ran them to give her cause a fair hearing. Now, she wrote, women would finally have a paper "through which we can make our own claim in our own time."

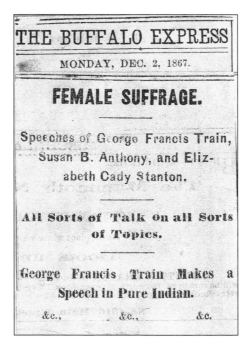

On their way home from Kansas, Stanton and Anthony accompanied George Francis Train on a tour of eastern cities, including Buffalo, New York, where they spoke at Corinthian Hall on December 2, 1867.

Mr. and Mrs. L. N. Beager exchange wedding vows on the open prairie north of West Union, Nebraska, in 1889.

Home life to the best of us has its shadows and sorrows, and because of our ignorance this must needs be. . . . The day is breaking. It is something to know that life's ills are not showered down upon us by the Good Father from a kind of Pandora's box, but are the results of causes that we have the power to control.

ELIZABETH CADY STANTON

Train's commitment to women's rights and his pledge of financial support were evidently enough to make her close her eyes to twenty years of her own work for the rights of slaves and former slaves. Train, Anthony now wrote, was "*a man terribly in earnest—one who never fails—who takes woman . . . as the only salvation for man.*" He was the only man she ever met, she told a friend, who could "*move mountains.*"

He proved less good at moving voters: in the end, votes for both blacks and women lost roughly three to one in Kansas. Over the next half-century, suffragists would find themselves forced to mount 479 assaults on state legislatures, aimed at giving male voters the opportunity to vote on whether or not to grant the ballot to women, as well as 56 full-scale statewide campaigns. Almost all of them would end in defeat. More remarkable even than the unshakable determination of the women who undertook those grueling campaigns would be the implacable resistance they encountered from most American men.

Stanton, Anthony, and their closest allies claimed their defeat in Kansas had really been a victory. "With all the obstacles which the dominant party could throw in our way; without organization, without money, without political rewards to offer, we gained one-third of all the votes!" said Olympia Brown. "Surely it was a great triumph of principle."

But to a good many others, fellow veterans of the struggle against slavery, Stanton and Anthony's decision to ally themselves with George Francis Train seemed startling evidence of their willingness to abandon principle altogether. Anthony's old friend Lucy Stone now privately denounced her for "making a spectacle of herself. It seems to me that she is hardly less crazy than he is."

When Stanton and Anthony got back to New York, the executive committee of the AERA demanded to know why Anthony had placed advertisements in the newspapers supporting Train and using the names of Lucy Stone and other members without their permission. Anthony lashed back at her questioners. "I AM the Equal Rights Association," she said, according to Stone. "Not one of you amounts to shucks except for me." Then she added

This list of tracts published by Anthony and including a pamphlet setting forth the erratic views of George Francis Train angered many of her old associates in the antislavery movement because it seemed to imply approval by the Equal Rights Association.

TRACTS published at the Office of the American Equal Rights Association:

ENFRANCHISEMENT OF WOMEN,
BY Mrs. JOHN STUART MILL.

Suffrage For Women,
BY JOHN STUART MILL, M. P.

FREEDOM FOR WOMEN,
BY WENDELL PHILLIPS.

PUBLIC FUNCTION OF WOMAN,
BY THEODORE PARKER.

WOMAN AND HER WISHES,
BY COL. T. W. HIGGINSON.

RESPONSIBILITIES OF WOMEN,
BY Mrs. C. I. H. NICHOLS.

Woman's Duty to Vote,
BY HENRY WARD BEECHER.

UNIVERSAL SUFFRAGE,
BY ELISABETH CADY STANTON.

The Mortality of Nations,
BY PARKER PILLSBURY.

EQUAL RIGHTS FOR WOMEN,
BY GEORGE WILLIAM CURTIS.

SHOULD WOMEN VOTE?
AFFIRMATIVE TESTIMONIALS OF SUNDRY PERSONS.
Price, per Single Copy, 10 Cents; per Hundred Copies, $5; per Thousand Copies, $30.

GEO. FRANCIS TRAIN'S KANSAS CAMPAIGN FOR WOMAN'S SUFFRAGE.
Price 25 Cents per Copy.
Orders should be addressed to
SUSAN B. ANTHONY,
Secretary American E. R. Association,
37 PARK ROW, (Room 17), NEW YORK CITY.

insult to injury: "I know what is the matter with you. It is envy, and spleen, and hate, because I have a paper and you have not."

And when William Lloyd Garrison complained that Train continued to raise racial fears by crying, "nigger, nigger, nigger," Stanton also refused to back down: "So long as Mr. Train speaks nobly for the woman, why should we repudiate his services, even if he does ring the changes 'nigger, nigger, nigger'?" Train's views, she wrote elsewhere, compared favorably with the "invective and denunciations and anathemas" of some of the odder early abolitionists she remembered, with "their tattered coat-tails . . . besmeared with rotten eggs."

The old alliance between abolitionists and the Stanton-Anthony wing of the woman-suffrage movement was coming apart. "The year goes out," Anthony noted in her diary as 1867 ended, "and never did one depart that had been so filled with earnest and effective work . . . 9,000 votes for woman in Kansas and a newspaper started." Then she added: "All the old friends, with scarce an exception, are sure we are wrong. Only time can tell, but I believe we are right and hence bound to succeed."

THE REVOLUTION

"If I were to draw up a set of rules for the guidance of reformers," Elizabeth Cady Stanton wrote late in her life, "I should put at the head of the list: Do all you can to get people to think on your reform, and then, if the reform is good, it will come out in due season."

She would edit and write for *The Revolution* in that defiant, optimistic spirit from the very first issue, which appeared on January 8, 1868. Its slogan was "Principle, Not Policy. Justice, Not Favors—Men, Their Rights and Nothing More. Women, Their Rights and Nothing Less." Susan B. Anthony was the sixteen-page weekly's tireless proprietor, tending to everything from fulfilling subscriptions and tracking down advertisers to coming up with the office rent each month. Parker Pillsbury, one of the handful of male abolitionists who stuck by women's

The masthead of The Revolution

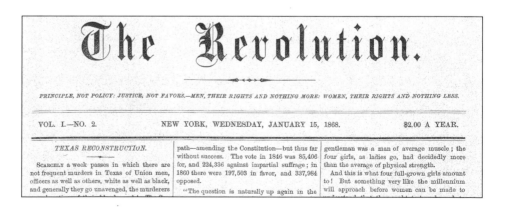

rights after the war, acted as coeditor with Stanton. And freelance contributors kept subscribers up to date on women's achievements all around the world—a Swiss who had outshot all her male competitors in a rifle contest; a French girl who saved fifteen sailors from drowning; two Indiana sisters who ran their father's gristmill; a new postmistress appointed in Bowling Green, Kentucky. But it was Stanton's voice—powerful, sometimes imperious, but always fearless—that caused the *New York Times* to characterize *The Revolution* as "charged to the muzzle with literary nitroglycerin." Stanton routinely lashed the Republican Party for what she believed was its utter faithlessness to equal rights. She discussed openly topics at which most middle-class women still blushed: abortion, infanticide, prostitution.

Stanton's views were bold; her rhetoric was still bolder.

The male element is a destructive force, stern, selfish, aggrandizing, loving war, violence, conquest, acquisition, breeding in the material and moral world alike discord, disorder, disease, and death. . . . The idea strengthens at every step, that woman was created for no higher purpose than to gratify the lust of man. . . . Society as organized today is one grand rape of womanhood under the man power.

She championed labor's right to strike, too, called for equal pay for equal work, and encouraged Anthony's efforts at building a coalition with organized labor. Anthony became a full-fledged delegate to a loose coalition of unions called the National Labor Union and organized two female chapters, but she could not persuade the men in charge to come out for woman suffrage and was eventually driven out because, in her zeal to improve the plight of female workers, she urged woman typographical workers to apply for the jobs of men who were out on strike. Stanton saw her ouster as evidence "that the worst enemies of woman's suffrage will ever be the laboring class of men."

"We are now in the midst of a serious quarrel with Miss Anthony and Mrs. Stanton and the Train admixture," wrote Lucy Stone. To Stone and many of Stanton and Anthony's old suffrage allies, *The Revolution* was a hideous embarrassment, filled with radical opinions certain to offend their Republican supporters and to deflect attention from the single issue of woman suffrage. In the autumn of 1868 Stone and other Boston-based suffragists—including Antoinette Brown Blackwell, Frederick Douglass, and Stephen Foster and his wife, Abby Kelley Foster—formed an organization of their own, the New England Woman Suffrage Association. "The strength of Mrs. Stanton's and Miss Anthony's position is that they are acting zealously and constantly," wrote another of its founders, Thomas Wentworth Higginson. "What we ought to do is 'criticize by superior action.'"

Parker Pillsbury, coeditor of The Revolution.

(Opposite) Printing House Square in New York City in 1868: Anthony rented an office for her paper on the third floor of the building on the far right.

The ferocity of Stanton's opposition to the Fifteenth Amendment, the final element in the Radical Republicans' program of Reconstruction, further alienated the New Englanders. The amendment was meant to protect the rights of freedmen by preventing the states from barring anyone from voting on the basis of "race, color or previous condition of servitude." Once again, women were expected to wait for rights they believed should have been theirs by birth. The Fifteenth Amendment would do nothing to remedy the cruel paradox spelled out by a young suffragist from Missouri: "Every intelligent virtuous woman is the inferior of every ignorant man."

The Boston circle regretted that black and woman suffrage were not being pushed through together, but they also continued to see no alternative to working through the Republican Party, and believed that granting universal manhood suffrage represented a giant step toward true democracy. Women would again have to be patient.

Stanton and Anthony had no patience. They sensed that time was running out on Reconstruction, that it might be years before Congress would again be in the mood to alter the Constitution. "ALL WISE WOMEN WILL OPPOSE THE FIFTEENTH AMENDMENT," said *The Revolution*. Stanton denounced the Republicans as hypocrites, and the principle of manhood suffrage as the most "base proposition" since "God first called light out of darkness and order out of

Make up your minds to take the "lean" with the "fat," and be early and late at the case, precisely as men are. I do not demand equal pay for any woman save those who do equal work in value. Scorn to be coddled by your employers; make them understand that you are in their service as workers, not as women.

Susan B. Anthony

Kansas typesetters, 1883

chaos." To grant black and immigrant men the vote while denying it to women, she said, was to "exalt ignorance above education, vice above virtue, brutality and barbarism above refinement and religion."

No one had been a more eloquent voice for absolute equality than Elizabeth Cady Stanton. She had been especially caustic in 1865 when dismissing the notion that there should be property or educational requirements for would-be voters. "Where does the aristocrat get his authority to forbid poor men, ignorant men, and black men, the exercise of their rights?" she had asked then.

> All this talk about education and property qualification is the narrow assumption of a rotten aristocracy. How can we grade wealth and education?
> Shall a man . . . be disfranchised because he never had time to learn the signs of Cadmus, or because by the statute laws of his State he was forbidden to read and write, or amass property in his own name?

But faced with the prospect of seeing black men enfranchised while white women continued to be kept from the polls, Stanton shifted her ground. Now, she argued, woman's claim to the ballot should have precedence over that of the former slave, precisely *because* he—along with the immigrant—was uneducated.

> The Republican Party today congratulates itself on having carried the Fifteenth Amendment of the Constitution, thus securing "manhood suffrage" and establishing an aristocracy of sex on this continent. . . . The lower orders of men . . . the slaves of yesterday are the lawmakers of today. . . . The legislation of the ignorant African . . . in whose eyes woman is simply the being of man's lust . . . must culminate in fearful outrages on womanhood, especially in the Southern states.
> Think of Patrick and Sambo and Hans and Yung Tung, who do not know the difference between a monarchy and a republic, who cannot read the Declaration of Independence or Webster's spelling book, making laws for . . . the daughters of Adams and Jefferson . . . women of wealth and education. . . . Shall American statesmen, claiming to be liberal, so amend their constitutions as to make their wives and mothers the political inferiors of unlettered and unwashed ditch-diggers, bootblacks, butchers and barbers, fresh from the slave plantations of the South . . . to establish an aristocracy based on sex alone?

A fresh strain of hauteur was evident, too. In the old world, Stanton said, "women of rank have certain hereditary rights which raise them above a majority of men, certain honors not granted to serfs and peasants," while in the United States "women of wealth and education"—women like herself and her readers—were "thrust outside the pale of political consideration with minors, paupers, lunatics, traitors, idiots."

From now on, Stanton would argue that women deserved the vote not because they were equal to men but because they were superior to them. "Men need refin-

"The Age of Brass, or The Triumphs of Woman's Rights," an 1869 Currier & Ives lithograph, includes a caricature of Anthony, second from right.

ing," Stanton wrote in *The Revolution*. "Let woman fulfill her God-like mission. She is nobler, purer, better than man."

Once the Fifteenth Amendment had passed the House and Senate and gone to the states in early 1869, Stanton and Anthony headed for the Midwest, hoping to rally women to oppose its ratification—and to support a sixteenth amendment granting woman suffrage at the same time. Moving from Illinois to Missouri, then on to Wisconsin and Ohio, they found enthusiastic audiences. Their presence "was like a match to the kindling," one Ohio woman remembered. Women established local societies and declared themselves wholeheartedly in favor of a sixteenth amendment. But again and again they also refused to oppose the Fifteenth. Most suffrage women, even in the Midwest, proved sympathetic to the Republicans and willing to wait their turn for the vote.

THE SHOWDOWN

The lonely campaign against the Fifteenth Amendment was clearly failing. Even Stanton and Anthony saw that a shift in tactics was needed. Anthony called for the annual meeting of the deeply divided American Equal Rights Association to be held in New York City in May of 1869, hoping that the old differences between them and the New England group might be forgotten in the greater cause of winning passage of a sixteenth amendment on which all could agree. Stanton declared a moratorium on all "sarcasm and ridicule," all "unkind acts and words." She now desired, she said, "to sink all petty considerations in the one united effort to secure woman suffrage."

It was too late. Hostile feelings had long since hardened, and a large, unruly crowd pushed its way into Steinway Hall, eager to be present for the showdown. Stanton presided over the meeting as first vice president, and there was trouble almost as soon as she opened the first session.

Stephen S. Foster of Massachusetts, who had known Anthony since her first tentative forays into temperance and antislavery work, rose to demand that both she and Stanton withdraw immediately from the organization. By refusing to repudiate the racism of George Francis Train, he charged, by using *The Revolution*'s pages to "ridicule the negro," espouse educated rather than universal suffrage, and pronounce the Fifteenth Amendment "infamous," they had publicly repudiated the principles of the society. Beyond that, he implied that Anthony had been less than forthcoming about AERA moneys she had spent during the Kansas campaign.

Anthony, frugal to a fault and a lifelong keeper of meticulous accounts, was indignant. "That is false!" she shouted. As for Train, he had "almost been sent by God" to start *The Revolution*.

Lucy Stone's husband, Henry Blackwell, did his best to smooth things over. Train had long since withdrawn from *The Revolution* and was therefore no longer a legitimate issue, he said; no one could seriously question Stanton or Anthony's commitment to equal rights, and the executive committee had been fully satisfied as to Anthony's record-keeping.

Stanton called for a vote of confidence from the convention and got it.

But tempers remained high. Frederick Douglass asked to be heard. His eloquence had helped Stanton win support for the woman-suffrage resolution at Seneca Falls in 1848, and they had been friends since she had lived in Boston with her husband. He still admired her, he said, but her views as reported in *The Revolution* had deeply wounded him: "The employment of certain names such as

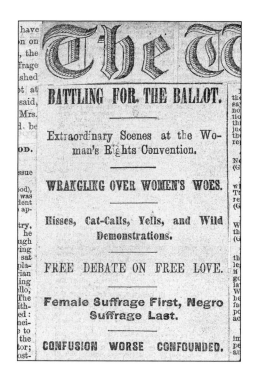

The New York World *reports on the angry debate at Steinway Hall that resulted in a schism in the women's movement, May 14, 1869.*

'Sambo' . . . and 'the boot black,' and 'the daughters of Jefferson and Adams' and all the rest, *that* I can not coincide with. I have asked what difference there is between the daughters of Jefferson and Washington and other daughters? . . ."

> *I must say that I do not see how any one can pretend that there is the same urgency in giving the ballot to woman as to the negro. With us, the matter is a question of life and death, at least in fifteen States of the Union. When women, because they are women, are hunted down through the cities of New York and New Orleans; when they are dragged from their houses and hung upon lamp-posts; when their children are torn from their arms, and their brains dashed out upon the pavement; when they are objects of insult and outrage at every turn; when they are in danger of having their homes burnt down over their heads; when their children are not allowed to enter schools; then they will have an urgency to obtain the ballot equal to our own. [Great applause.]*
>
> *A voice: Is that not all true about black women?*
>
> *Douglass: Yes, yes, yes; it is true of the black woman, but not because she is a woman, but because she is black. [Applause] Julia Ward Howe, at the conclusion of her great speech delivered at the convention in Boston last year, said: "I am willing that the negro shall get the ballot before me." [Applause] Woman! Why, she has 10,000 modes of grappling with her difficulties. . . .*

Then, evidently anxious to avoid an open break with the woman who had been his friend for so many years, he paused to pay tribute to Stanton.

> *Let me tell you that when there were few houses in which the black man could have put his head this wooly head of mine found refuge in the house of Mrs. Elizabeth Cady Stanton, and if I had been blacker than sixteen midnights, without a single star, it would have been the same. There is no name greater than [hers] in the matter of woman's rights and equal rights.*
>
> *Anthony: If Mr. Douglass had noticed who applauded when he said "black men first and white women afterwards," he would have seen that it was only the men. When he tells us that the case of black men is so perilous, I tell him that even outraged as they are by the hateful prejudice against color, he himself would not today exchange his sex and color with Elizabeth Cady Stanton.*
>
> *Douglass: Will you allow me a question?*
>
> *Anthony: Yes, anything for a fight today.*
>
> *Douglass: I want to inquire whether granting to woman the right of suffrage will change the nature of our sexes? [Great laughter.]*

Anthony: It will change the nature of one thing very much, & that is the pecuniary position of woman. It will place her in a position in which she can earn her own bread, so that she can go out into the world on equal competition in the struggle for life, so that she shall not be compelled to take such positions as men choose to accord her . . . & then take such pay as men choose to give her. . . .

Battle lines were drawn as Anthony offered two resolutions: one calling for opposition to the Fifteenth Amendment, the other demanding educated suffrage.

The amendment would "not mean equal rights," Anthony said; "it [would] put 2,000,000 colored men in the position of tyrants over 2,000,000 colored women, who until now had at least been the equals of the men at their side." If "you will not give the whole loaf of justice to the entire people," she continued, "if you are determined to extend the suffrage piece by piece, then give it first to women, to the most intelligent & capable portion of the women at least, because in the present state of government it is intelligence, it is morality which is needed."

Lucy Stone now tried to calm the storm:

Mrs. Stanton will, of course, advocate the precedence for her sex, and Mr. Douglass will strive for the first position for his, and both are perhaps right. . . . [But we] are lost if we turn away from the middle principle and argue for one class. . . . Woman has an ocean of wrongs too deep for any plummet, and the negro too has an ocean of wrongs that cannot be fathomed. There are two great oceans; in the one is the black man, and in the other is the woman. But I thank God for the Fifteenth Amendment, and hope that it will be adopted in every State. I will be thankful in my soul if any body can get out of the terrible pit.

The debate only intensified. Paulina Davis, an old ally of Stanton and Anthony's, alleged that enfranchising black men would enslave black women. "Take any class that have been slaves," she said, "and you will find that they are the worst when free and become the hardest masters."

Stanton agreed. The official record summarized her sentiments: "Not another man should be enfranchised until enough women were admitted to the polls to outweigh those already there. She did not believe in allowing ignorant negroes and foreigners to make laws for her to obey."

Frances Watkins Harper, a poet and novelist and one of the very few black suffragists present, could keep silent no longer. She regretted the fact that the nation could not seem to handle more than one question at a time, but since it was a fact, she said, she would not "have the black woman put a single straw in the way, if only the men of the race could obtain what they wanted."

In the end, Stanton and Anthony were beaten. The convention voted against educated suffrage, expressed only its "profound regret" that Congress had not sub-

Anthony and Stanton about the time they found themselves isolated from almost all their former allies. "So closely interwoven have been our lives, our purposes and experiences," Stanton wrote, "that, separated, we have a feeling of incompleteness— united, such strength of self-assertion that no ordinary obstacles, difficulties, or dangers ever appear to us insurmountable."

mitted a Sixteenth Amendment—and overwhelmingly approved ratification of the Fifteenth.

Discouraged and still further isolated from their old allies, the two women now formed a new organization, the National Woman Suffrage Association. It would have a broad agenda: continued opposition to ratification of the Fifteenth Amendment, a sixteenth amendment that would specifically recognize a woman's right to vote, an eight-hour workday and equal pay for working women, and divorce reform that would obliterate forever the notion that wives "belonged" to their husbands.

Stanton was chosen president. No man was to be permitted to hold office in the new organization. After 1869, Stanton remembered, she and Anthony "repudiated man's counsels forevermore; and solemnly vowed that there should never be another season of silence until woman had the same rights everywhere on this green earth, as man . . . woman must lead the way to her own salvation with a hopeful courage and determination that knows no fear nor trembling. She must not put her trust in man in this transition period, since, while regarded as his subject, his inferior, his slave, their interests must be antagonistic."

In response, the leaders of the New England Woman Suffrage Association met in Cleveland in November and formed a new group, the *American* Woman Suffrage Association. "I think we need two national associations for woman suffrage,"

The Rev. Henry Ward Beecher (left), first president of the rival American Woman Suffrage Association; and Henry Blackwell, Lucy Stone's husband and one of its most prominent male members wrote Lucy Stone, "so that those who do not oppose the Fifteenth Amendment, or take the tone of *The Revolution,* may yet have an organization with which they can work in harmony." Men were actively encouraged to join—the Reverend Henry Ward Beecher became the American's first president—and every effort was to be made to work for suffrage, and suffrage alone, on the state level and within the Republican Party. "No side issues" were to be taken up. The American was to be a haven, Lucy Stone said, for "those who cannot use the methods which Mrs. Stanton and Susan use."

Anthony made an unwanted appearance at the American's inaugural meeting and issued a grudging promise to cooperate, "though it nullify completely the national Association . . . [and *The Revolution*] for which I have struggled as never man or woman struggled before." But mutual suspicion now ran too deep for reconciliation. Neither Stanton nor Anthony would hear of reuniting with the men and women Stanton denounced as "the Boston malcontents." "The American," said Anthony, "was organized by persons who ignored the two persons, Stanton & Anthony, who had stood in the front ranks of the suffrage army (if not its acting generals). . . . They are persons who are either new converts or new workers, or old ones who had been comparatively silent, out of the public field for the last ten or fifteen years. . . . [T]o make proposals of peace to them & theirs . . . would prove just as futile as . . . overtures to Jeff Davis and his compeers."

For her part, Lucy Stone agreed that cooperation was impossible. It was best, she told one of her allies, not to "strike hands" with Stanton or Anthony or any of the others in charge of the National. When she and Julia Ward Howe launched the American's weekly, *The Woman's Journal,* they made a point of doing so on January 8, 1870—the second anniversary of *The Revolution's* debut.

The woman-suffrage movement was split in two. On the surface, all the wasted energy involved, all the backbiting and apparent duplication of effort, would seem likely to have damaged the cause in which both groups believed so passionately. But whether the division actually slowed or accelerated votes for women remains a matter of debate. "I hope that you will see it as I do," Lucy Stone told Stanton when the split occurred, "that with two societies, each in harmony with itself . . . we shall secure the hearty active cooperation of *all* the friends better than either could do alone. The radical abolitionists and the Republicans could never have worked together but in separate organizations both did good service. There are just as distinctly two parties to the woman movement."

She may have been right. It is hard to see how Stanton and Anthony would have been able to function if they'd had to wait for the approval of Stone and her allies, and equally difficult to imagine how Stone could have held on to her conservative allies if she had remained formally linked with the two radical women whom they considered an embarrassment. In any case, the woman-suffrage movement would remain divided for more than twenty years.

Homes of Single Women

Susan B. Anthony wrote this speech during a brief 1887 stopover in Denver. Her hope was that by hearing about women who had successfully combined economic independence with domesticity, other wage-earning single women would be encouraged to own homes of their own. Anthony herself did not have such a home until she was seventy.

A home of one's own is the want, the necessity of every human being, the one thing above all others longed for, worked for. Whether the humblest cottage or the proudest palace, a home of our own is the soul's dream of rest, the one hope that will not die until we have reached the very portals of the everlasting home.

Probably none of us will attempt to question the superiority of the time-honored plan of making a home by the union of one man and one woman in marriage. But in a country like ours where such considerable numbers of men, from choice or necessity, fail to establish matrimonial homes, there is no way of escape; vast numbers of women must make homes for themselves, or forego them altogether. In Massachusetts, alone, there are, to-day, 70,000 more women than men, wives and sisters of soldiers and sailors, miners and stockmen, lumber-men and mountain-men, who in their search for wealth have forgotten the loved of their youth. To these deserted women, necessity has proved the mother of invention. And as you pass from village to village, you will see lovely white cottages, wreathed in vines, nestled midst gardens of vegetables and flowers, fruit and shade trees, each a little Paradise save the presence of the historic Adam before whom woman reverently says, "God thy law, thou mine!!" For homes like these, the passer-by is wont to heave a pitying sigh, as there rises before him the sad panorama of crushed affections, blighted hopes, bereaved hearts. But these are homes of exceeding joy and gladness, compared with the myriads of ill-assorted marriage homes, where existence, by night and by day, is but a living death!!

It has been said that the man of the nineteenth century insists upon having for a wife a woman of the seventeenth century. It is perhaps nearer the truth to say that he demands the spirit of the two centuries combined in one woman: the activity and liberality of thought which characterize the present era, with the submission to authority which belonged to the past. . . . In woman's transition from the position of subject to sovereign, there must needs be an era of self-sustained self-supported homes, where her freedom and equality shall be unquestioned. As young women become educated in the industries of the world, thereby learning the sweetness of independent bread, it will be more and more impossible for them to accept the Blackstone marriage limitation that "husband and wife are one, and that one the husband. . . ."

Even when man's intellectual convictions shall be sincerely and fully on the side of Freedom and equality to woman, the force of long existing customs and laws will impel him to exert authority over her, which will be distasteful to the self-sustained, self-respectful woman. The habit of the ages cannot, at once, be changed. Not even amended constitutions and laws can revolutionize the practical relations of men and women, immediately, any more than did the Constitutional freedom and franchise

Anthony's parlor in Rochester. The circular table at the right is the one on which Stanton and her earliest allies were said to have written the Declaration of Sentiments at Seneca Falls in 1848.

of Black men, transform white men into practical recognition of the civil and political rights of those who were but yesterday their legal slaves. Constitutional equality only gives to all the aid and protection of the law, while they educate and develop themselves, while they grow into the full stature of freemen. It simply allows equality of *chances to establish equality.*

Not until women shall have practically demonstrated their claim to equality in the world of work, in agriculture, manufactures, mechanics, inventions, the arts and sciences, not until they shall have established themselves in education, literature and politics and are in actual possession of the highest places of honor and emolument, by the industry of their own hands and brains, and by election or appointment; not until they shall have actually won equality at every point, morally, intellectually, physically, politically, will the superior sex really accept the fact and lay aside all assumptions, dogmatic or autocratic.

Meanwhile, "the logic of events" points, inevitably, to an *epoch of single women.* If women will not accept

marriage *with subjection,* nor men proffer it *without,* there is, there can be, *no alternative.* The women who will *not be ruled* must live without marriage. And during this transition period, wherever, for the maintenance of self-respect on the one side, and education into recognition of equality on the other, single women make comfortable and attractive homes for themselves, they furnish the best and most efficient object lessons for men.

Fanny Fem, in her inimitable way, pictures the Modern "Old Maid" thus: "No, sir, she don't shuffle round in skimpy raiments, awkward shoes, cotton gloves, with horn side-combs fastening six hairs to her temples. She don't . . . keep a cat, a snuff box, or go to bed at dark, or scowl at little children, or gather catnip, not a bit of it. She wears nicely fitting dresses and becoming bits of color in her hair; and she goes to concerts and parties and suppers and lectures, and

The Anthony home in Rochester, c. 1895. Stanton and Anthony are seated on the lawn.

she don't go alone, either! She lives in a good house earned by herself, and she gives nice, little teas in it. She don't work for no wages and bare toleration, day and night; no sir. If she has no money, she teaches or she lectures or she writes books or poems, or she is a book-keeper, or she sets type, or she does anything but depend on somebody else's husband; and she feels well and independent, in consequence, and holds up her head with the best, and asks no favor, and woman's rights has done it. . . ."

Mary Clemmer very truly says, "The secret of the rare material success which attended the Cary sisters is to be found in the fact that from the first they began to make a home." . . . The sisters were deeply interested in the cause of equal rights to all; and the subject of woman's enfranchisement was frequently the topic of conversation. While at that time Mr. [Horace] Greeley, almost always present, advocated warmly the right of women to equal educational and industrial advantages, he stoutly opposed their demand for suffrage. It was his habit to say, "The best women I know do not want to vote." The charming Alice would as often put the question to each of the distinguished women at her table, "Do you want to vote, Miss Booth?" "Yes," and "Do you want to vote, Mrs. Allen?" "Yes." "Do you want to vote, Miss Dickenson?" "Yes." And each and every one as invariably replied, "Yes." Yet at the very next reception, Mr. Greeley would again repeat his stereotype "settler" of the question. . . . He died in the delusion that "the best women do not want to vote." . . .

Another delightful home of women alone is that of Mary L. Booth, the successful editor of *Harper's Bazaar,* and Mrs. Wright, in a beautiful four story brown front on 59th Street. . . . Of this co-partnership, Miss Booth is so purely a woman of literary pursuits and outside affairs, that she gives over all domestic details, and largely too all those of her own wardrobe, to the care of Mrs. Wright, whom the world would call more feminine in her character. Yet, I have been told that she was the wife of a Captain of a ship, and

that once, when on a voyage with her husband, he was taken very ill, and his mates and other officers proving inefficient, she bravely took command, and brought the vessel safely into port. . . .

A woman's home all must love and honor is that of the President of the National Woman Suffrage Association, Dr. Clemence S. Lozier, a very mother in Israel to every woman struggling for an honest subsistence. For twenty and more years, her house has been the home of one or more poor young women studying medicine at the College she herself founded, and in the maintenance of which she has invested between fifteen and twenty thousand dollars of her own earnings. . . . She is often heard to say, in public and in private, "All my success, professionally, and financially, I owe to the 'Woman's Rights Movement.' It is but my duty, therefore, to help it, and thereby help all other women who shall come after me."

The marriage of Dr. Lozier's youth was a very happy, but brief one, her husband dying early, leaving her the mother of one child. Her second experiment was exceedingly unfortunate; the man not only leaving her to support herself and young son, by sewing and teaching and nursing, but he himself *fed* on the scanty earnings of her hands. . . . Mrs. Lozier's eye chanced to rest on a letter of Elizabeth Cady Stanton's read at the first New York State Women's Temperance Convention, held at Albany in 1852, urging the right of divorce for drunkenness, and clearly setting forth the crime of the mother who stamped her child with the drunkard's appetite for rum. That letter shocked Mrs. Lozier into her first thought, not only of her right, but her solemn duty to cease to be the *wife* of such a man. She quickly obtained a legal separation from bed and board, which was all the laws of New York, then or now, allow for drunkenness, [and] set about studying medicine. . . .

What numbers of the wayfaring advocates of reform, will with me bear grateful testimony to that haven of rest, that coziest home of the Mott sisters, in Albany, New York. . . . For thirty years and more,

Anthony's attic heaped with some of the scrapbooks and papers from which Ida Husted Harper wrote her authorized biography

in that stolidly conservative old Dutch City, those two women stood almost the *sole* representatives of the then unpopular movements for Temperance, Peace, AntiSlavery, and Woman's Rights. At different periods during those years, those sisters earned their living by teaching, boardinghouse keeping, and skirt-manufacturing. They were the most self respecting women I ever knew, always ennobling whatever work they laid their hands on. . . .

Do any of you Gentlemen and Ladies doubt the truth of my picturings of the homes of unmarried women? Do any of you still cling to the old theory, that single women, women's rights women, professional women, have no home instincts? . . . All this is done from pure love of home; no spurious second-hand domesticity affected for the praise of some man, or conscientiously maintained for the comfort of the one who furnishes the money; nor because she has nothing else to busy herself about, but her one impelling motive is from the true womanly home instinct, unsurpassed by that of any of the women who "have all the rights they want."

. . . The charm of all these women's homes is that their owners are "settled" in life; that the men, young or old, who visit them, no more count their hostesses' chances in the matrimonial market, than when guests in the homes of the most happily married women. Men go to these homes as they do to their gentlemen's clubs, to talk of art, science, politics, religion and reform. . . . They go to meet their equals in the proud domain of intellect, laying aside for the time being at least, all of their conventional "small talk for the ladies."

But, say you, all these beautiful homes are made by exceptional women; the few women of superior intellect, rare genius, or masculine executive ability, that enables them to rise above the environments of sex, to lean on themselves for support and protection, to amass wealth, to win honors and emoluments. They are not halves, needing complements, as are the masses of women; but evenly balanced well rounded characters; therefore are they models to be reached by the average women we everyday meet. . . .

Mother and daughter in a Wyoming wheat field, 1893

Under Such Fire

B y the spring of 1870, *The Revolution* was in trouble. George Francis Train had long since withdrawn his financial backing. The paper had never had more than three thousand subscribers, and *The Woman's Journal*, well-financed and nonconfrontational, was eating into those. Anthony did everything she could think of to keep her paper afloat. She raised subscription rates, borrowed from members of her family, canvassed friends, exhausted first her own savings and then those of her sister Mary. Harriet Beecher Stowe and her sister, Isabella Beecher Hooker, offered to help, provided the paper's name was changed to something less threatening, *The True Republic*, perhaps.

Stanton would not hear of it. "There could not be a better name" than *The Revolution*, she told Anthony.

> *The establishing of woman on her rightful throne is the greatest revolution the world has ever known or ever will know. You and I have not forgotten the conflict of the last twenty years—the ridicule, persecution, denunciation, detraction, the unmixed bitterness of our cup for the past two years when even friends crucified us. A journal called the Rosebud might answer for those who come with kid gloves and perfumes to place immortal wreaths on the monuments which in sweat and tears others have hewn and built, but for us . . . there is no name like the* Revolution!

And as if to prove it, Stanton hurled herself into the heart of the notorious McFarland case. A half-mad

THE WOMAN'S JOURNAL.

A WEEKLY PAPER, FOUNDED 1870.

Devoted to Women's Interests, and especially to Woman Suffrage.

EDITORS:

LUCY STONE.   HENRY B. BLACKWELL.   ALICE STONE BLACKWELL.

Mothers, Sisters, Daughters.

FOR news concerning Women, their advancement and successes in all countries, read THE WOMAN'S JOURNAL. Among our corps of contributors we not only number eminent women, but bright unknown writers gain an audience, and we gather fresh enthusiasm from the record of their vigorous work. Our editors are familiar forms on Boston streets, and their voices are always to be heard in behalf of the oppressed.

"The best source of information upon the woman question that I know."—*Clara Barton.*

"The best woman's paper in the United States, or in the world."—*Englishwomen's Review.*

"It is so much the best of the woman suffrage papers that no comparison is possible."—*Rev. Anna H. Shaw, National Superintendent of Franchise, W. C. T. U.*

"I would give up my daily paper sooner than THE WOMAN'S JOURNAL."—*Maria Mitchell.*

"It is an exceedingly bright paper, and, what is far better, a just one. I could not do without it."—*"Josiah Allen's Wife," (Marietta Holley).*

"It is able, genial and irreproachable—an armory of weapons to all who are battling for the rights of humanity."—*Mary A. Livermore.*

"I never forget to recommend THE WOMAN'S JOURNAL. I deem it the best journal published for our work in this line (the woman question)."—*Mrs. Helen M. Gougar.*

"THE WOMAN'S JOURNAL has long been my outlook upon the great and widening world of woman's work, worth and victory. It has no peer in this noble office and ministry. Its style is pure and its spirit exalted."—*Frances E. Willard.*

"It is the most reliable and extensive source of information regarding what women are doing, what they can do, and what they should do. It is the oldest of the women's papers now in existence, and has built up for itself a solid and unblemished reputation."—*Julia Ward Howe.*

Three weeks on trial, FREE. One year on trial to new subscribers, $1.50. Regular price per year, $2.50. To libraries and reading-rooms, half-price. Address,

THE WOMAN'S JOURNAL,

3 Park Street, Boston, Mass.

THE · WOMAN'S · COLUMN.

A SMALL WEEKLY PAPER

FOR THE MILLION.

EDITED BY ALICE STONE BLACKWELL, No. 3 PARK STREET, BOSTON, MASS.

It gives every week the news of the movement, together with short articles, arguments, and answers to objections.

PRICE, 25 CENTS A YEAR.

More genteel, more single-minded, but no less committed to suffrage than The Revolution, The Woman's Journal *helped put Anthony's paper out of business.*

alcoholic named Daniel McFarland, separated from the wife whom he had brutalized for years, shot and killed a well-known journalist named Albert D. Richardson, who had become her lover and protector. The New York City press was unanimous in condemning the battered wife and her murdered protector. (So were the courts, which eventually found McFarland innocent by reason of insanity and then promptly awarded him total custody of his twelve-year-old son.)

Stanton could not allow such injustice to go unchallenged:

I rejoice over every slave that escapes from a discordant marriage. With the education and evolution of women we shall have a mighty sundering of the unholy ties that hold men and women together who despise each other. Such marriages are a crime against both the individual and the State. . . . One would really suppose that a man owned his wife as the master the slave, and that this was simply an affair between Richardson and McFarland, fighting like two dogs over one bone. . . . This wholesale shooting of wives' paramours should be stopped. . . . Suppose women should shoot their husband's mistresses, what a wholesale slaughter of innocents we should have of it!

Disappointed that Stanton and Anthony would not change their paper's name and put off by Stanton's mordant tone and enthusiasm for divorce, Harriet Beecher Stowe and her sister withdrew their offer of help for *The Revolution.*

By the spring of 1870, it was clear the paper would have to be sold. It was deeply disappointing to Anthony—"like signing my own death warrant," she noted in her diary—but she had no choice except to sell it for the consideration of one dollar to a wealthy sympathizer who turned it into an inoffensive literary and society journal. "I feel a great calm sadness," she wrote, "like that of a mother binding out a dear child that she could not support. . . . But I have the joy of knowing that I showed the thing possible—to publish a live out-and-out woman's paper, taught other women to invest, to enter in and reap where I had sown—sown in faith, too, such as no canting priest or echoing follower ever dreamed of."

Stanton refused to mourn. "You know when I drop anything," she told Anthony, "I drop it absolutely. You cannot imagine what a deep gulf lies between me and the past."

Anthony did not have the same luxury. The newspaper left her saddled with a debt of ten thousand dollars, with which Stanton was either unable or unwilling to help. Friends urged her to declare bankruptcy, but she would not hear of it. "My pride for women, to say nothing of my conscience," she insisted, "says no." It would take her six years, but she'd pay back every penny.

The news of their newspaper's demise produced press speculation that the two women had had a falling-out.

> *June 27th, 1870*
> *Dearest Susan*
> *The New York "Sun" has an article about you and me "having dissolved partnership." Have you been getting a divorce . . . without notifying me? I should like to know my present status. I shall not allow any such proceedings. I consider that our relations are to last for life; so make the best of it. . . .*
> *Do not feel depressed, my dear friend. What is good in us is immortal, and if the sore trials we have endured for . . . years are sifting out pride and selfishness, we shall not have suffered in vain. How I long to see my blessed Susan!*

Anthony replied that her love for Stanton was "unchanged, undimmed by time and friction." But there really was beginning to be trouble now between them. Elizabeth Cady Stanton was as devoted to woman suffrage as she had ever been, but she had wearied of the infighting and intrigue of suffrage politics. "Don't speak to me of conventions," she told Anthony. "I can't bear having to hold my tongue for fear of offending someone." And she only sporadically bothered to attend her own organization's meetings, sending along manifestos for Anthony to read out for her instead.

Anthony was profoundly irritated by what she saw as her friend's willful inconstancy to their cause: "To my mind there was never such a suicidal letting go as has been yours these last two years," she scolded when Stanton passed up the National convention in January 1871. "How you can excuse yourself is more than I can understand."

Stanton did have an excuse. Her husband's earnings as a lawyer and journalist were insufficient to pay for the college educations they both wanted all their

Anthony in 1870. "Among all the company," wrote Mary Clemmer in the Independent, "'Susan' is the most violently and unjustly abused. To be sure, she can be very provocative. But this is only. . . . a very small side of Susan Anthony. A man, and more than a man—a woman who can deny herself, ignore herself, for a principle, for what she believes to be the truth, whether we believe it or not, is at least entitled to our respect."

Stanton in 1870. "Of all their speakers," wrote Grace Greenwood in the Philadelphia Press, "she seemed to me to have the most weight. . . . Mrs. Stanton has the best arts of the politician and the training of the jurist, added to the fiery, unresting spirit of the reformer. She has a rare talent for affairs, management, and mastership. Yet she is in an eminent degree womanly, having an almost regal pride of sex."

children to have. To come up with the money—and also perhaps to satisfy her own fondness for appearing in public—she had become an eagerly sought-after lecturer on the lyceum circuit. In her first seven months, she proudly told Gerrit Smith, she cleared two thousand dollars "besides stirring up the women generally to rebellion." She would keep stirring up the women, eight months out of every twelve, for the next eleven years.

In June, the two women joined forces on a train trip from Chicago to California, lecturing along the way. It was a rare opportunity for them to spend some relatively quiet time together. "We have a drawing room all to ourselves," Anthony noted, "and here we are just as cozy and happy as lovers. We look at the prairie schooners slowly moving along with ox-teams or notice the lone cabin light on the endless plains, and Mrs. Stanton will say: 'In all that there is real bliss, if only the two are perfect equals, two loving people, neither assuming to control the other.' "

But as soon as they got to San Francisco their friendship underwent more stress. The city was gripped by a sensational murder case. An alleged prostitute named Laura Fair had stabbed her lover, a prominent attorney, and the press was calling for stern punishment. Concerned as always to hear the woman's side of things, Stanton and Anthony visited Fair in prison. Newspapers attacked them for daring to do so, and when Anthony appeared to give her standard lecture on "The Power of the Ballot" the following evening, a large crowd had gathered to denounce her. With characteristic bluntness, she attacked male hypocrisy head-on. Men claimed to be the protectors of women, she charged, yet "if all men had protected all women as they would have their own wives and daughters protected, you would have no Laura Fair in your jail tonight." The audience drowned her out with boos and hisses. She waited till they fell silent, said precisely the same words, was shouted down again, repeated them defiantly a third time, and finally won cheers for her courage if not her sentiments.

But the next morning, all the city's newspapers attacked her for seeming to approve of prostitution and condone murder. Speaking engagements were canceled all over the state. "Never in all my hard experience," she noted in her diary, "have I been under such fire," and her unhappiness was compounded when Stan-

Stanton and Anthony took their message west to women like these, meeting at the corner of Cutler and Water Streets in Helena, Montana, sometime during the 1870s

ton chose to say nothing publicly in her defense. Again and again over the years, Anthony had risen to defend her outspoken friend for saying things that angered one element or another of their constituency. Now, Stanton was leaving her alone to fend for herself, just as she had been left alone with *The Revolution's* debt: "[S]he could do so much," Anthony noted in her journal, "to put Editors right to what I say & do."

Stanton soon returned to the East, where her mother was now confined to her bed with what turned out to be her final illness. Anthony continued on alone, determined to bring the women's-rights message to the people of Oregon and Washington Territories—and to whittle away at *The Revolution's* debt with her lecture fees. She traveled by stagecoach,

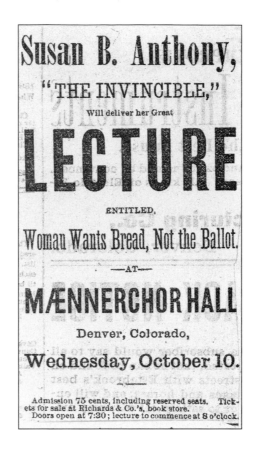

Anthony delivered her provocatively titled lecture, "Woman Wants Bread, Not the Ballot," scores, perhaps hundreds, of times during the 1870s and 1880s. In it she argued that the popular notion that "a woman wants nothing but a home with her daily needs supplied" was utterly false; that in fact "the only possibility of her securing bread and a home for herself is to give her the ballot."

often riding outside, next to the driver, rather than endure the cramped, dust-filled interior. She bemoaned the rutted roads and the "horrid" food prepared by "Chinamen or any other men. I am really making up my mind that cooking is out of man's sphere for he does set before us such villainous compounds." And she admitted to her journal that even after all her years on the road, she was still sometimes made "very blue" by the hostility with which she was received: "Boys," she noted, cleared one hall by pouring cayenne pepper onto the red-hot stove.

Newspapermen were by turns condescending and hostile. "We could not help thinking," wrote the editor of the *Oregon City Weekly Enterprise,* "what a fine looking and useful woman she would have been had she got married years ago. . . . We wish she had been more fortunate in her younger days." Anthony's lectures, said the *Portland Herald,* were "a devilish contrivance to poison the morals of . . . wives, mothers and daughters." The editor of the *Seattle Territorial Dispatch* agreed: her whole message was "coarse, sensual . . . the worst phase of French infidelity and communism."

Such attacks from men were to be expected. More annoying were the assaults of an antisuffrage lecturer named Jennett Blakesley Frost, who followed her from town to town. "I never could see," Frost said of Anthony, "how it was that an Old

Maid who had neglected to fill the office in society for which God in his providence had wisely created her, should essay to lecture married women upon child-rearing, maternity, and other kindred topics when, as a Miss who was never married, she is supposed to be innocently ignorant of all such matters." Mrs. Frost, Anthony noted in her diary, was "the weakest silliest acting and talking woman I ever saw—fairly dirty in her insinuations."

Still, Anthony admired the northwestern landscape, took some pleasure in the battle, and could not resist telling her sister Mary how much she enjoyed being on her own, out from under the shadow of her celebrated friend.

I miss Mrs. Stanton, still I cannot but enjoy the feeling that the people call on me, and the fact that I have an opportunity to sharpen my wits a little by answering questions during the chatting, instead of sitting merely a lay figure and listening to the brilliant scintillations as they emanate from her never-exhausted magazine. There is no alternative—whoever goes into a parlor or before an audience with that woman does it at the cost of a fearful overshadowing, a price which I have paid for the last ten years, and that cheerfully, because I felt that our cause was most profited by her being seen and heard, and my best work was making the way clear for her.

GONE & DONE IT!!

In 1869, a St. Louis lawyer named Francis Minor and his suffragist wife, Virginia, had developed an argument for woman suffrage so novel that it became known as "the new departure." American women already *had* the right to vote under the Fourteenth and Fifteenth Amendments, the Minors reasoned; since women were citizens and since they came in all races and colors, the states could not bar them from the polls.

Stanton and Anthony were newly energized. If the courts would uphold the new departure, there would be no further need for either a constitutional amendment or state-by-state campaigns. They urged women all over the country to go to the polls in 1872 and attempt to vote. The long, maddening wait for simple justice might be nearing its end.

Anthony herself would lead the way. On Friday, November 1, she and her three sisters appeared at the Rochester barbershop in which three registrars sat waiting to sign up voters. Anthony insisted on being registered, and when the men nervously refused—they were young enough to be her sons, she remembered—she vowed personally to pay their fines if the government prosecuted them.

Two out of three of the registrars gave in: the women's names—along with those of ten more women—were added to the voter rolls of Rochester's Eighth Ward. On Election Day, Anthony and six other women turned out again and cast their ballots for U. S. Grant and the Republicans because that party had included

On January 11, 1871—for the first time in American history—a woman was allowed to address a committee of Congress. The speaker was not Elizabeth Cady Stanton or Susan B. Anthony, but a charismatic newcomer to the women's movement—Victoria Claflin Woodhull. Like Francis and Virginia Minor, she argued that women already had the right to vote under the Fourteenth and Fifteenth Amendments. There was no need for a new amendment, she said, so long as Congress passed a Declaratory Act to enable women's rights.

The House Judiciary Committee denied it had any such power, but Stanton and Anthony were so impressed that they invited Woodhull to appear before the annual convention of the National to deliver it again. The following year, Anthony asked Woodhull back again, and she gave a fiery speech calling openly for revolution if women's demands were not met. "We mean treason," she told the delegates, "We mean secession, and on a scale a thousand times greater than was that of the South. We are plotting revolution; we will . . . [overthrow] this bogus Republic and plant a government of Righteousness in its stead."

Stanton and Anthony, who had not heard such stirring rhetoric since their antislavery days, led the enthusiastic applause.

Woodhull had her own ambitious agenda—the formation of a new "People's Party" followed by a run for President. But there had always been rumors about her character, rumors that now grew alongside her reputation. Two marriages, numerous lovers, stints as a tent-show spiritualist, and sometime prostitute—it was hard to tell truth from fiction. Conservative reformers, including some leaders of the American Woman Suffrage Association, denounced her for practicing "free love." She defiantly pled guilty to the charge: "Yes, I am a free lover!" she told a stunned New York audience. "I have an inalienable, constitutional and natural right to love whom I may love, to love as long, or as short a period as I can, to change that love every day if I please!"

Such candor only endeared her to Elizabeth Cady Stanton. "We have had women enough sacrificed to this sentimental, hypocritical prating about purity," she told Lucretia

Victoria Woodhull, spiritualist, stockbroker, suffragist, free lover, presidential candidate—and nemesis of Susan B. Anthony

Mott. "This is one of man's most effective engines for our division and subjugation. He creates the public sentiment, builds the gallows, and then makes us hangman for our sex. Women have crucified the Mary Wollstonecrafts, the Fanny Wrights, . . . the Lucretia Motts of all ages. . . . Let us end this ignoble record and henceforth stand by womanhood. If Victoria Woodhull must be crucified, let men drive the spikes and plait the crown of thorns."

Anthony admired Woodhull's forthrightness, too, but she was wary. She had not liked it when the newspapers referred to the 1872 suffrage meeting as "The Woodhull Convention," and feared that the controversy that seemed always to surround Woodhull would distract attention from the sacred cause of woman suffrage. She was furious

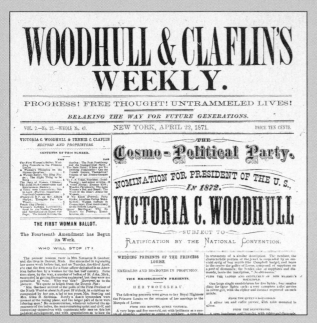

Woodhull & Claflin's Weekly, *published by the presidential candidate and her sister, Virginia Claflin, sets forth Woodhull's presidential platform while, in* Harper's Weekly, *the cartoonist Thomas Nast portrays her as "Mrs. Satan," whose blandishments are resisted by a burdened wife who says, "I'd rather tread the hardest path of matrimony than follow your footsteps."*

when Stanton permitted her name to be used in a notice promising that Woodhull's new "People's Party" would be launched at the June meeting of the National at Steinway Hall in New York. Anthony demanded her name be withdrawn: "I do not believe in any of us women, the majority of whom do not even own our own bodies to say nothing of our purses—forming a *political party*," she told Stanton. Besides, Woodhull "persistently means to run our craft into her port and no other." Anthony was not interested in becoming "a mere sail-hoister for her"; let her hire her own hall.

Stanton angrily accused Anthony of being "narrow minded and domineering," and refused to preside over the meeting.

Anthony took her place as president pro tem. On the first day, when Woodhull tried to speak, she ruled her out of order; when Woodhull's supporters noisily objected,

Anthony ordered them out of Steinway Hall. The following evening, Woodhull appeared again to move that the convention adjourn to a nearby hall to form the People's Party. Anthony again ruled her out of order—and when she persisted in speaking stalked backstage, found the janitor, and ordered him to turn out the gaslights. The bewildered delegates groped their way out onto the street. The crisis passed; Susan B. Anthony was still in charge.

Woodhull's candidacy went nowhere. By election day, she would be in jail for mailing allegedly obscene material in her newspaper. But before then she had threatened to expose those in the suffrage movement who "preach against free love openly, [but] practice it secretly," a reference to an adulterous affair involving the Rev. Henry Ward Beecher, first president of the American Woman Suffrage Association. The scandal that followed tainted the whole suffrage movement.

"There was never such a foolish muddle," Anthony confided to her diary, "I never was so hurt by the folly of Stanton. . . . Our movement as such is so demoralized by the letting go of the helm of the ship to Woodhull—though we rescued it—It was by a hair breadth escape."

a plank—Stanton dismissed it as a mere "splinter"—that at least promised that women's demands would be given a respectful hearing.

"Well I have been & gone & done it!!" Anthony exulted to Stanton. "Positively *voted* the Republican ticket—straight—this AM at 7 o'clock and *swore my vote in at that*—fifteen other women followed suit in this ward. . . . So we are in for a fine agitation in Rochester. . . . I hope you voted too."

Anthony's daring made headlines, but for almost three weeks, the government did nothing. Then, on Thanksgiving Day, a United States marshal came to Susan B. Anthony's house at 17 Madison Street in Rochester. He had a warrant:

> *Without having a lawful right to vote in said election district the said Susan B. Anthony, being then and there a person of the female sex, as she, the said Susan B. Anthony, then and there well known contrary to the statute of the United States of America in such cases made and provided, and against the peace of the United States of America . . . did knowingly, wrongfully and unlawfully vote.*

The marshal was elaborately polite. There was no hurry, he said, but when Miss Anthony had a moment, the United States Commissioner would be grateful if she would come by his office. "Is this your usual method of serving a warrant?" Anthony asked. She would not hear of any special treatment, insisted that she

Anthony announces to Stanton that she has "gone & done it"— cast a vote for President, November 5, 1872.

Justice Ward Hunt (left), who set bail for Anthony at one thousand dollars; and Anthony's attorney, Henry Selden, who foolishly paid it—and thereby ruined his client's case.

be formally arrested, even held out her wrists, demanding to be handcuffed. The marshal refused to put on the cuffs; he didn't want to draw any more attention than he could help to this distasteful duty.

The two boarded a horse-drawn trolley for the trip downtown. When the conductor asked for her fare, Anthony spoke loudly enough so that everyone on board could hear: "I am traveling at the expense of the government," she said, pointing to her escort. "Ask him for my fare."

All fifteen of the women who had voted in the Eighth District—along with the hapless registrars who had allowed them to do so—were held guilty by the U.S. commissioner. Bail was fixed at five hundred dollars each.

Everyone but Anthony paid. She applied instead for a writ of habeas corpus, aimed at getting her case before the United States Supreme Court. When her attorney, Henry Selden, a former judge and longtime friend, failed to persuade the U.S. district judge at Albany to issue her a writ, and the judge, in turn, raised her bail to one thousand dollars, Anthony again refused to pay, declaring that she would rather be imprisoned than recognize the right of the courts to interfere with her sacred right to vote.

Her lawyer then told her there were times when a client must be guided by her counsel, and he put up the money from his own bank account. It was not until they had left the courthouse together that she realized that by allowing her bail to be paid, she had lost her chance to get her case taken to the Supreme Court. Shaken, she asked her lawyer if he'd realized that when he'd written out his check.

The United States Court-house at Canandaigua, New York, the scene of Anthony's trial for the crime of voting

"Yes," Selden said, "but I could not see a lady I respected put in jail." Misplaced male gallantry had ruined her constitutional case.

Anthony's trial was set for the following June, a long enough delay for her to fit into her customarily relentless speaking schedule an exhaustive tour of the county in which she was to be tried. She appeared in all of its twenty-nine towns and villages to deliver a lecture entitled "Is It a Crime for a Citizen of the United States to Vote?" She convinced so many of her listeners that voting should not be a crime that, for fear no neutral jurors could be found, the prosecution obtained an order removing her case to the United States Circuit Court at Canandaigua.

Anthony's trial finally began there on June 17, 1873, before Justice Ward Hunt, whom Stanton described as "punctilious in manner, scrupulous in attire, conscientious in trivialities, and obtuse on great principles." He was also brand-new to his job—the Anthony case was the very first he'd ever heard from the federal bench—and eager to please his powerful political mentor, Senator Roscoe Conkling, an adamant foe of woman suffrage. Anthony never had a chance: Hunt had written out his opinion before a shred of evidence was presented, refused to permit Anthony to testify on her own behalf—women were incompetent to do so, he ruled—and would not permit the all-male jury even to deliberate, directing them instead to find Anthony guilty as charged.

Before he pronounced sentence, Hunt asked Anthony if she had anything to say. He would regret having asked:

Anthony: Yes, your honor, I have many things to say; for in your ordered verdict of guilty you have trampled under foot every vital principle of our government. My natural rights, my civil rights, my political rights, my judicial rights are all alike ignored. Robbed of the fundamental privilege of citizenship, I am degraded from the status of a citizen to that of a subject; and not only myself individually but all of my sex are, by your honor's verdict, doomed to political subjection under this so-called republican form of government.

Hunt: The Court can not listen to a rehearsal of arguments which the prisoner's counsel has already consumed three hours in presenting.

Anthony: May it please your honor, I am not arguing the question, but simply stating the reasons why sentence can not, in justice, be pronounced against me. Your denial of my citizen's right to vote, is the denial of my right of consent as one of the governed, the denial of my right to representation as one of the taxed, the denial of my right to a trial by a jury of my peers as an offender against law; therefore, the denial of my sacred right to life, liberty, property and . . .

Hunt: The Court can not allow the prisoner to go on.

Anthony: But your honor will not deny me this one and only poor privilege of protest against this high-handed outrage upon my citizen's rights. May it please the Court to remember that, since the day of my arrest last November, this is the first time that either myself or any person of my disfranchised class has been allowed a word of defense before judge or jury

Hunt: The prisoner must sit down—the Court can not allow it.

Anthony: Of all my prosecutors, from the corner grocery politician who entered the complaint, to the United States marshal, commissioner, district attorney, district judge, your honor on the bench—not one is my peer, but each and all are my political sovereigns; and had your honor submitted my case to the jury, as was clearly your duty, even then I should have had just cause of protest, for not one of those men was my peer; but, native or foreign born, white or black, rich or poor, educated or ignorant, sober or drunk, each and every man of them was my political superior; hence, in no sense, my peer. Under such circumstances a commoner of England, tried before a jury of Lords, would have far less cause to complain than have I, a woman, tried before a jury of men. Even my counsel, Hon. Henry R. Selden, who has argued my cause so ably, so earnestly, so unanswerably before your honor, is my political sovereign. Precisely as no disfranchised per-

son is entitled to sit upon a jury, and no woman is entitled to the franchise, so none but a regularly admitted lawyer is allowed to practice in the courts, and no woman can gain admission to the bar—hence, jury, judge, counsel, all must be of the superior class.

Hunt: The Court must insist [that] the prisoner has been tried according to the established forms of law.

Anthony: Yes, your honor, but by forms of law all made by men, interpreted by men, administered by men, in favor of men and against women, and hence your honor's ordered verdict of guilty, against a United States citizen for the exercise of the "citizen's right to vote," simply because that citizen was a woman and not a man. But yesterday, the same man-made forms of law declared it a crime punishable with $1,000 fine and six months' imprisonment to give a cup of cold water, a crust of bread or a night's shelter to a panting fugitive tracking his way to Canada; and every man or woman in whose veins coursed a drop of human sympathy violated that wicked law, reckless of consequences, and was justified in so doing. As then the slaves who got their freedom had to take it over or under or through the unjust forms of law, precisely so now must women take it to get their right to a voice in this government; and I have taken mine, and mean to take it at every opportunity.

Hunt: The Court orders the prisoner to sit down. It will not allow another word.

Anthony: When I was brought before your honor for trial, I hoped for a broad and liberal interpretation of the Constitution and its recent amendments, which should declare all United States citizens under its protecting aegis—which should declare equality of rights the national guarantee to all persons born or naturalized in the United States. But failing to get this justice, failing even, to get a trial by a jury not of my peers—I ask not leniency at your hands but rather the full rigor of the law.

THE WOMAN WHO DARED.

Close of the Trial of Susan B. Anthony.

OPINION AND DECISION OF JUDGE HUNT.

The Fourteenth Amendment Gives No Right to a Woman to Vote.

MISS ANTHONY'S ACT A VIOLATION OF LAW.

Exhaustive Opinion on the Force and Scope of the Amendments.

A VERDICT OF GUILTY.

The Champion of Woman's Rights Awaiting Sentence and Martyrdom.

CANANDAIGUA, N. Y., June 18, 1873.

The court room was again thronged this morning at the hour of opening by an attentive audience as spectators in the further progress of the trial of Miss Anthony.

In the aftermath of her trial, Anthony saw publicity of any kind—even attacks like this brutal caricature from the New York Graphic, "The Woman Who Dared" (opposite)—as ultimately helpful to her cause.

Hunt: The Court must insist— [Here the prisoner sat down.] The prisoner will stand up. [Here Miss Anthony rose again.] The sentence of the Court is that you pay a fine of $100 and the costs of the prosecution.

Anthony: May it please your honor, I will never pay a dollar of your unjust penalty. All the stock in trade I possess is a debt of $10,000, incurred by publishing my paper, The Revolution, *the sole object of which was to educate all women to do precisely as I have done, rebel against your man-made, unjust, unconstitutional forms of law, which tax, fine, imprison and hang women, while denying them the right of representation in the government; and I will work on with might and main to pay every dollar of that honest debt, but not a penny shall go to this unjust claim. And I shall earnestly and persistently continue to urge all women to the practical recognition of the old Revolutionary maxim, "Resistance to tyranny is obedience to God."*

Hunt: Madam, the Court will not order you to stand committed until the fine is paid.

"The greatest judicial outrage history ever recorded!" Anthony wrote in her diary that evening. "We were convicted before we had a hearing and the trial was a mere farce." The trial had indeed been a farce, but Anthony knew that it had also

Anthony, Stanton, and their friend and ally Matilda Joslyn Gage signed this petition to Congress calling for legislation to "protect women citizens in the several states of the Union in their right to vote" on behalf of the National Woman Suffrage Association in 1873. The Minor v. Happersett *decision handed down the following year rendered this and similar appeals moot.*

exposed the government's case for what it was, and she arranged to have three thousand copies of the court transcript of the exchange between herself and the judge printed up and distributed across the country. "If it is a mere question of who has got the best of it, Miss Anthony is still ahead," said one upstate New York paper; "she has voted and the American constitution has survived the shock. Fining her one hundred dollars does not rule out the fact that . . . women voted, and went home, and the world jogged on as before."

Some 150 women had attempted to vote in 1872. Anthony's case was the most celebrated, its course the most widely followed, but because her attorney had put up bail, it had no legal impact. But in St. Louis, Virginia Minor, who, with her husband, Francis, had devised "the new departure," had also tried to register to vote. Unlike Anthony, she had been turned away and was therefore free—provided she did so in partnership with her husband—to sue the registrar, a man named Reese Happersett.

It took three years, but *Minor* v. *Happersett* finally reached the United States Supreme Court in 1875. The justices unanimously decided against Minor: citizenship merely meant "membership in a nation and nothing more." Furthermore, the Constitution recognized the right of each individual state to decide who could—and who could *not*—vote within its borders.

Minor v. *Happersett* helped justify the Southern states in passing laws designed to ensure white supremacy by imposing literacy and property-owning requirements to keep former slaves from the polls. Anthony had seen it all coming: "If we once establish the false principle that United States citizenship does not carry with it the right to vote in every state in this union," she wrote, "there is no end to the petty freaks and cunning devices that [will] be resorted to to exclude one and another class of citizens from the right of suffrage."

She and Stanton now abandoned hope of winning the vote through the courts. As the American Woman Suffrage Association redoubled its efforts to obtain the vote state by state, the National would work to persuade Congress, and the American people, of the rightness of their cause, would have to renew their efforts to amend the Constitution.

MAKING HISTORY

Eighteen seventy-six marked America's centenary. To Stanton and Anthony there seemed very little for women to celebrate. The *Minor* decision had dashed their hopes of swift justice; it was as disastrous for women, Stanton said, as the *Dred Scott* decision had been for the slave nearly two decades earlier. Some suffragists withheld their taxes in protest. The leaders of the National toyed with the notion of encouraging women to drape themselves in black on July Fourth and parade through cities and towns carrying banners that read, TAXATION WITHOUT REPRESENTATION IS TYRANNY. In the end, they decided instead to do all that they could to make their presence felt in Philadelphia, birthplace of the Declaration of Independence and site that summer of a vast Centennial Exhibition.

They first rented headquarters near the fairgrounds so that visitors could pick up literature and sign petitions. As the sole single woman among the National's leaders—and therefore the only one who could legally enter into a business contract—Anthony rented the rooms in her own name; the others would have needed their husbands' signatures.

Then, together with their friend the suffragist writer and organizer Matilda Joslyn Gage, Anthony and Stanton set about writing a new Declaration of Rights for Women. This document differed from the Declaration of Sentiments Stanton had written almost thirty years earlier. Gone were the calls for equal educa-

tion, for the right to write and speak in public and earn a living, because real
progress had been made on all those fronts since 1848. Nor were men per se now
the oppressors. Rather, it was the government that "deserved to be impeached"
for keeping women from enjoying "the broad principles of human rights proclaimed in 1776": "We protest against this government of the United States as
an oligarchy of sex, and not a true republic; and we protest against calling this a
centennial celebration of the independence of the United States."

Having written their Declaration, the women had to figure out a way to get it
included in the program of the official Fourth of July ceremony, to be held in Independence Hall.

Stanton wrote to General Joseph Roswell Hawley of Connecticut, the president of the Centennial Commission, requesting fifty seats for the officers of the
National. General Hawley, a Republican politician determined that nothing be
allowed to disturb the centennial's relentlessly self-satisfied tone, politely refused—
there was no room even for his wife, he said. Stanton then asked to be allowed
simply to present the women's declaration to the president of the United States
"as an historical part of the proceedings." Too late, answered the general. All the
arrangements had been made. The programs were printed. The general's unwill-
ingness to bend only proved her point, Stanton told him: men had "run this government for one hundred years without consulting the women of the United
States." The answer was still no, said Hawley. "We propose to celebrate what we
have done the last hundred years," he said, "not what we have failed to do."

Picnickers overlooking the Centennial Exhibition

Looking over these twenty-eight years [since the 1848 Declaration of Sentiments] I feel that what we have achieved, as yet, bears no proportion to what we have suffered in the daily humiliation of spirit from the cruel distinctions based on sex. . . . [The] undercurrent of popular thought, as seen in our social habits, theological dogmas, and political theories still reflects the same customs, creeds and codes that degrade women in the effete civilizations of the old world.

EIZABETH CADY STANTON

Meanwhile, Anthony obtained a press pass for herself through her brother's Kansas newspaper. Hawley finally did come up with four more seats, a concession Stanton thought so grudging that she and Lucretia Mott refused to attend, arranging for a separate and simultaneous women's-rights meeting to be held in a nearby Unitarian church. But Anthony gave them to four coworkers. She was determined that their Declaration would be part of the ceremony no matter what General Hawley might say.

The Fourth of July was hot and muggy in Philadelphia, and it was especially stifling inside Independence Hall. As the speech-making inched along, the discomfort only added to the five women's nervousness. One remembered trembling "with suppressed emotion" as Richard Henry Lee of Virginia, a descendant of one of the signers, began reading aloud the Declaration of Independence. "Mr. Lee's voice was inaudible," another of Anthony's companions remembered, "but at last I could make out the words 'our sacred honor.'"

That was Anthony's cue. She and her companions left their seats and began moving rapidly up the aisle toward the stage. Anthony was in the lead, on her face, one of the women remembered, "a look of intense pain, yet historic determination."

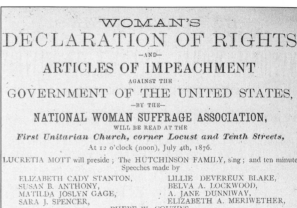

Protest: the press pass Anthony used to get past the guards at the Fourth of July ceremony in Independence Hall (top), and a notice of the meeting Stanton and Lucretia Mott organized to coincide with the official observance

The acting vice president of the United States, Michigan senator Thomas W. Ferry, was at the podium—and stunned to see Anthony approaching. She stopped just below him and, "with fitting words," handed him a rolled-up parchment copy of the Woman's Declaration tied with ribbon. Ferry accepted it, bowing low. Then Anthony turned and strode back up the aisle. Her friends followed, handing out copies of the Declaration to anyone who reached out for one. Some men climbed onto their chairs to get them. Meanwhile, General Hawley banged his gavel and shouted, "Order! Order!" over and over again.

Once outside, in Independence Square, Anthony commandeered a bandstand that had been set up for an evening concert, and while Matilda Joslyn Gage held up an umbrella to shield her from the merciless sun, she read aloud the Declaration of Rights for Women. "Woman has shown equal devotion with man to the cause of freedom and has stood firmly by his side in its defense," Anthony told the big, curious crowd that gathered around to hear her.

And now, at the close of a hundred years, as the hour-hand of the great clock that marks the centuries points to 1876, we declare our faith in the principle of self-government, our full equality with man in natural rights; that woman was made first for her own happiness, with the absolute right to herself—to all the opportunities and advantages life affords for her complete development; and we deny that dogma of the centuries, incorporated in the codes of all nations—that woman was made for man—her best interests . . . to be sacrificed to his will. We ask our rulers, at this hour, no special favors, no special privileges. . . . We ask justice, we ask equality, we ask that all civil and political rights that belong to the citizens of the United States be guaranteed to us and to our daughters forever.

Posterity was on the women's mind that centennial summer. Within weeks of the Philadelphia events, Stanton and Anthony were ensconced in the house in Tenafly, New Jersey, that Stanton had purchased with an inheritance from her father shortly after the Civil War. They were hard at work on another, far more demanding writing task, a full-scale chronicle of their movement, *The History of Woman Suffrage*.

"Men have been faithful in noting every heroic act of their half of the race," Anthony wrote, "and now it should be the duty as well as the pleasure, of women to make for future generations a record of the heroic deeds of the other half." Anthony saw to the business side of things: she found a publisher, arranged for distribution to schools and libraries. Stanton did the editing and much of the

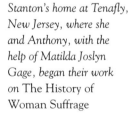

Stanton's home at Tenafly, New Jersey, where she and Anthony, with the help of Matilda Joslyn Gage, began their work on The History of Woman Suffrage

writing. The women worked surrounded by heaps of old letters and newspaper clippings. "It makes me sad and tired to read them over," Anthony wrote, "to see the terrible strain I was under every minute then, have been since, am now and shall be for the rest of my life."

Every paragraph stirred memories, and some sparked arguments, as Stanton's eldest daughter, Margaret, wrote:

*Advertisement for
the first three volumes
of* The History of
Woman Suffrage

It is as good as a comedy to watch these two souls from day to day. They start off pretty well in the morning, fresh and amiable. They write page after page with alacrity, they laugh and talk, poke the fire by turn, and admire the flowers on their desk. . . . Everything is harmonious for a season but after straining their eyes over the most illegible, disorderly manuscripts . . . suddenly the whole sky is overspread with dark and threatening clouds. . . . Susan is punctilious on dates, mother on philosophy, but each contends as stoutly in the other's domain as if equally strong on both points. Sometimes these disputes run so high that down go the pens, one sails out one door and one out the other, walking in opposite directions around the estate and just as I have made up my mind that this beautiful friendship of forty years has at last terminated, I see them walking down the hill, arm in arm. . . . When they return they go straight to work where they left off, as if nothing had ever happened. . . . The one that was unquestionably right assumes it, and the other silently concedes the fact. They never explain, nor apologize, nor shed tears, nor make up, as other people do.

Stanton and Anthony would work together on their *History,* off and on, for the next ten years, producing three massive volumes—an invaluable, exhaustive, often elegantly written record of the whole movement. (There would eventually be three more volumes, written without Stanton's help.) Anthony's belief in the importance of the project never wavered, but she hated every minute of the work itself. It was "a perfect prison," she told her diary. "O, how I long to be in the midst of the fray and here I am, bound hand and foot"; it made her "growly all the time. . . . No war horse ever panted for the rush of battle more than I for outside work. I love to make history but hate to write it."

WANDERING, WANDERING

On January 10, 1878, Senator Arlen A. Sargent of California rose in the Senate to introduce a newly worded sixteenth amendment to the Constitution: "The right of citizens to vote," it said, "shall not be denied or abridged by the United States or by any State on account of sex."

When Stanton testified in support of it before the Senate Committee on Privileges and Elections, she was met with languid derision:

> *In the whole course of our struggle . . . I never felt more exasperated . . . standing before a committee of men many years my junior, all comfortably seated in armchairs. . . . The particularly aggravating feature . . . was the studied inattention and contempt of the chairman, Senator [Benjamin] Wadleigh of New Hampshire . . . [who] alternately looked over . . . manuscripts and newspapers . . . jumped up and down to open or close a door or a window . . . stretched, yawned, gazed at the ceiling, cut his nails, sharpened his pencil. . . . It was with difficulty that I restrained the impulse . . . to hurl my manuscript at his head.*

The amendment never even made it out of committee that year. It would not be voted on by the full Senate until 1887 (when it lost 34 to 16, with twenty-five members not thinking the topic important enough even to turn up for the roll call) and would have to be reintroduced in every session of Congress for the next forty-two years.

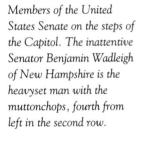

Members of the United States Senate on the steps of the Capitol. The inattentive Senator Benjamin Wadleigh of New Hampshire is the heavyset man with the muttonchops, fourth from left in the second row.

To oversee that effort, Anthony saw to it that the National Woman Suffrage Association held its convention in Washington every winter. Members offered petitions, called on congressmen and senators, testified before legislative committees—and followed the orders of Susan B. Anthony. "The members of Congress always knew when Miss Anthony had arrived in Washington," her friend and first biographer remembered. "Other women accepted their word that they were going to do something and waited patiently at home. Miss Anthony followed them up and saw that they did it. If she could not find them at the Capitol, she went to their homes. If they promised to introduce a certain measure on a certain day, she was in the gallery, looking them squarely in the face."

No detail of the annual meeting was too small to escape her attention. "Can you give us a flag or two over the platform," she asked the proprietor of one hall, "& make [it] *wear a lady-like* appearance generally—for though we are *strong-minded* we do not wish to have things about us look *Manish*."

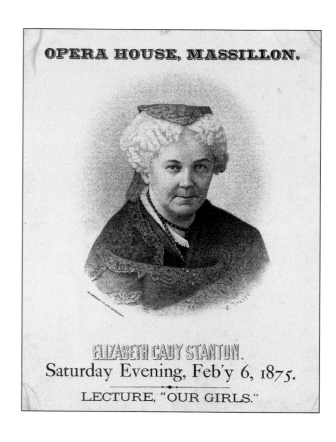

OPERA HOUSE, MASSILLON.

ELIZABETH CADY STANTON.
Saturday Evening, Feb'y 6, 1875.
LECTURE, "OUR GIRLS."

A deceptively demure poster for a Stanton appearance at Massillon, Ohio, in 1875

Anthony's return to Washington year after year helped make her the living symbol of woman suffrage, so familiar a visitor that even the red shawl that was the brightest spot of color in her wardrobe became celebrated. Once when she appeared onstage in the capital wearing a new white one, veteran reporters sent her a note: "No red shawl," it said, "no report."

She laughed. "All right boys," she said, "I'll send to the hotel for it." As she wrapped the red shawl around her shoulders the audience burst into applause, and reporters picked up their pencils.

Elizabeth Cady Stanton was a less frequent presence in Washington. She disliked the drudgery of lobbying—found it hard to hold her tongue in the presence of legislators she was quite sure were less able and intelligent than she was—and she was still spending eight months a year on the lecture circuit.

Her talks often had deceptively tranquil titles—"Our Boys," "Home Life," "Our Girls"—and her grandmotherly appearance further belied her often revolutionary message. She was portly now—of "robust proportion," she liked to say—and her elaborate curls had turned snow white. "Surely Mrs. Stanton has secured much immunity," wrote one newspaperwoman, "by a comfortable look of motherliness

*These splendid people are
hungry, hungry. Oh, for more
power to give out the truth!*
Elizabeth Cady Stanton

Women of Echo City, Wyoming Territory

Emma G. Gibbs, center, surrounded by satisfied customers in front of her millinery and needlework shop in Reno, Nevada, 1880

and a sly benignancy in her smiling eyes, even though her arguments have been bayonet thrusts and her words gun shots."

In the afternoons, she often held meetings for women only, focused around what she called "the new science of marriage and maternity": birth control. These informal talks sometimes went on for three hours, she told a friend, "and then they hunger still. The new gospel of fewer children and a healthy, happy maternity is gladly received."

Her visits to the homes of small-town women who prepared elaborate dinners for her were gladly received, too.

> I often saw weary little women coming to the table after most exhausting labors, and large, bumptious husbands spreading out their hands and thanking the Lord for the meals that the dear women had prepared as if the whole came down like manna from Heaven. So I preached a sermon in the blessing I gave. You will notice that it has three heresies in it: "Heavenly Father and Mother, make us thankful for the blessings of this life, and make us ever mindful of the patient hands that oft in weariness spread out tables and prepare our daily food. For humanity's sake, Amen."

Male hecklers got the back of her hand. At one appearance in Nebraska, a small, angry man interrupted her talk. "Don't you think that the best thing a woman can do is perform well her part in the role of wife and mother?" he asked. "My wife has presented me with eight beautiful children; is not this a better life-work than that of exercising the right of suffrage?" Stanton slowly looked him up and down. "Frankly, sir," she said, "I know of few men worth repeating eight times."

Stanton rarely passed up an opportunity to deliver her message:

> Crossing the Mississippi at McGregor, Iowa, we were icebound in the middle of the river. The boat was crowded with people, hungry, tired, and cross with the delay. Some gentlemen, with whom we had been talking on the cars, started the cry, "Speech on Woman's Suffrage!" Accordingly, in the middle of the Mississippi river . . . we presented our claims to political representation, and debated the question of universal suffrage till we landed. Our voyagers were quite thankful that we had shortened the many hours, and we equally so at having made many converts and held a convention on the very bosom of the great "Mother of Waters."

Applause and adulation invariably bolstered her spirits. "You would laugh," she wrote her daughter Harriot, "to see how everywhere the girls flock around me for a kiss, a curl, an autograph." (Her signatures often came with a political postscript: "I am a citizen and demand the right to vote.") Several years later, when she was warmly received at a convention in St. Louis, she could not contain her glee: "All the . . . papers have given more space to me than to all the others put together . . . ," she told her son Gerrit, "and what they say has been very com-

Harriot Stanton, right, and classmates at Vassar, c. 1875. Although her mother favored coeducation, Stanton's conservative older sisters—who helped pay Harriot's tuition—insisted she attend a women's college.

plimentary. . . . I spoke in the largest Methodist Church in the city. . . . As we walked slowly up the center aisle, I heard those in the pews whisper, 'There she is,' 'There she is,' which made me put as much life into my steps as possible, though on such occasions I begin to feel that age is upon me."

By the late 1870s, even Stanton was growing weary of the lecture circuit. "I have been wandering, wandering . . . ," she told her cousin Elizabeth Smith Miller:

Up early and late; sleepy and disgusted with my profession, as there is no rest from the time the season begins until it ends. Two months more, containing sixty-one days, still stretch their long length before me. I must pack and unpack my trunk sixty-one times; pull out the black silk train and don it; puff my hair and pin on the illusion ruffling round my spacious throat, sixty-one more times; rehearse "Our Boys," "Our Girls," or "Home Life," sixty-one times; eat 183 more miserable meals; sleep between cotton sheets under these detestable things called "comforters"— tormentors would be a more fitting name—sixty-one more nights; shake hands with sixty-one more committees, smile, try to look intelligent and interested in everyone who approaches me, while I feel like a squeezed sponge; and endeavor to affect a little spring and briskness in my gait on landing in each town in order to avoid giving an impression that I am seventy, when in reality I feel more like crawling than walking.

In 1881, at the age of sixty-six, she gave up lecturing altogether and returned to Tenafly. "I do not believe," she confided to her diary, "there ever was a woman who esteemed it such a privilege to stay at home."

But she found burdensome work to be done there, too. She and Anthony and Matilda Joslyn Gage were all supposed to be working together on the second volume of their *History of Woman Suffrage*, but Gage was often ill and Anthony on the road, so the bulk of the editorial burden fell on Stanton. She worked so hard that when Harriot came home from studying in France in the spring of 1882, she feared for her mother's health and determined to take her back to Europe with her just as soon as the manuscript was finished.

Volume two was to cover the period of the 1869 schism in the suffrage movement, and the bitterness that had brought about the break had only deepened over the years. Anthony wished no mention whatsoever made of the American Woman Suffrage Association in their chronicle. Lucy Stone didn't want it mentioned there either; she did not trust her rivals to deal fairly with her or her organization.

There matters stood until Harriot proposed that she be allowed to try her hand at writing an account of the American. "I contended that since the two associations were and had been in an internecine war," she remembered, "it would certainly do credit to the authors if they rose above the roar of battle and gave space for a record of the work of their antagonists." It proved a thankless task: Anthony agreed to pay her for the completed chapter, Harriot remembered, only because her mother insisted that she do so.

On May 27, when the last proofs had been read, Harriot and her exhausted mother sailed for Europe. This sojourn would mark a new era in Stanton's relationship with the suffrage movement—and with Susan B. Anthony.

In the practical world of suffrage politics, there had already seemed less and less room for Stanton's explosive ideas, her sweeping agenda, her blistering rhetoric. She was frankly bored with the dreary business of building a suffrage organization, disliked the endless round of conventions and petition campaigns and testifying before mostly heedless legislators, and was eager to meet new people, investigate new issues.

Stanton would spend nearly half of the next nine years abroad, living part of the time with her son Theodore and his family in Paris, the rest with Harriot and her husband, William Henry Blatch, in England. (Henry Stanton's death in 1887 further loosened her ties to America.) She kept up as best she could with the struggle back home, writing letters and offering resolutions for conventions when she could not attend them, but she also explored Fabian socialism and British secularism. Above all, she enjoyed relaxing in the heart of her family. "This is the first time in my life," she noted in her diary, "that I have had uninterrupted leisure for reading, free from all care of home, servants, and children."

Ann D. Gordon

Taking Possession of the Country

"The *West* is crazy over her, commanding her *second* appearance everywhere—" Susan B. Anthony wrote of Elizabeth Cady Stanton on January 1, 1870. At fifty-four Stanton had launched her career as a popular lecturer six weeks earlier, heading out from Tenafly, New Jersey, to meet engagements in towns from Ohio to Minnesota, south to Missouri, and through Kentucky to Indiana and Michigan. She was enthralled by her reception: "$75. a night and perfect jams of audiences & *private ovations* as well as public." Just before she fell victim to pneumonia, the bane of nineteenth-century lecturers, Stanton herself boasted: "I have made $2000 above all expenses since the middle of November beside stirring up the women generally to *rebellion*." She was hooked, and it was work that would occupy her for the next eleven years.

Susan B. Anthony soon joined her on the circuit, recording her first check for seventy-five dollars, paid her at Uniontown, Pennsylvania, on March 1, 1870. She was the more seasoned traveler of the two. Modeling herself on the abolitionists, who mapped out a territory and saturated it with their propaganda, Anthony set the pace for political travel in the 1850s. She had then accompanied more practiced lecturers to make the arrangements, and now still doubted her ability to be the main attraction. A diary entry written after Uniontown, just before a lecture in Pittsburgh, reads: "If I can only give the people what they shall feel worthy, as I seemed to at Uniontown, is the burden of my hope." Confident or not, Anthony soon mastered the demands of this new work. At the end of 1871, while she was snowed in aboard an eastbound train in the Rockies, she counted up the lectures and miles she had logged in just twelve months:

171 lectures, 13,000 miles traveled, and gross receipts of $4,318. For Anthony, this was work for the rest of her life.

No reformers—indeed, no politicians—rivaled the miles logged by Stanton and Anthony as they crisscrossed the country in the decade after 1869 to take their case for woman suffrage to the people. Leaving home in October or November, with trunk, portmanteau, and several lectures ready for the season, they stayed on the road until spring. With their lives centered somewhere in the Midwest, they adapted to the discomforts of strange beds, dirt, sleeping on trains, and schedules that conceded nothing to ill health. When Anthony boarded the Michigan South Railroad one evening in Ohio, "there sat Mrs. Stanton all curled up—gray curls sticking out—fast asleep—." The travelers talked until the time came to change trains for their next destinations.

When Stanton and Anthony headed west, they knew that suffrage activists were scattered across the country all the way to the Pacific Coast. Their decision to lecture coincided with widespread discussion of woman suffrage and the beginnings of serious political support for it. Since the war, state politicians, prodded by petitions, had debated and voted on woman suffrage in Ohio, Michigan, Missouri, Kansas, Wisconsin, Minnesota, and Wyoming, and that list continued to grow after 1869. Every session of Congress beginning in January 1866 received petitions in support of woman suffrage, arriving from places like Faribault, Minnesota; Portage, Wisconsin; Neoga, Illinois; and Waterloo, Indiana. Though the justice of woman suffrage was widely conceded, it lacked political urgency. Senator Charles Sumner, the avatar of equal rights among men, envisaged a glacial pace.

Woman suffrage was, he told the Senate in 1866, the "great question of the future," not the present; it would be "easily settled, whenever the women in any considerable proportion insist that it shall be settled." As leaders of the cause, Stanton and Anthony needed to produce that "considerable proportion," with new converts and better coordination among the pockets of activism.

To reach a national audience, Stanton and Anthony each signed up with several lecture bureaus and agencies. Lecture agents identified promising talent for the entertainment and edification of audiences in towns and cities of all sizes, advertised their roster of speakers to local lecture committees, scheduled each speaker's tours, and more or less mapped out the transportation. In return, the agency received a percentage of the gate at each engagement. So long as the speakers met local expectations for entertainment (and on Sundays delivered speeches with high moral purpose), they were free to select their own topics. Competing agencies deemed Stanton and Anthony to be profitable additions to their lists, while Stanton and Anthony seized the political opportunity that the lecture circuit offered.

Lecture circuits took advantage of the boom in postwar construction of railroads. For weeks at a time the lecturer might be scheduled to travel every day and speak every night. The new transportation made it possible to tour on a national scale, but it did not make the task easy. It was an era of spectacular train wrecks, causing extensive delays for passengers lucky enough to be on the next train. A major line might carry passengers before it had laid all its track or built its bridges, filling in with stagecoaches and rafts. Imperfect technologies for clearing snow from the tracks sometimes left passengers in the Western mountains snowbound for days on end.

This was grueling work. As fast as the railroads extended their reach, Stanton and Anthony traveled the new lines, reaching California just two years after the transcontinental line opened. Stanton lec-

tured in Texas in 1870, and in 1871 Anthony toured the Pacific Northwest and went into British Columbia. At the termini of rail traffic, they hopped aboard sleighs, boats, stages, and horses to journey farther into the country. They made an enormous sweep across the continent and returned time and again to many towns throughout the decade.

Elizabeth Cady Stanton left a record of the experience that was, nearly all of it, written for publication while she traveled, or later as reminiscences. Its pride in her accomplishments contrasts with the more immediate record of exhaustion and satisfaction jotted in Susan B. Anthony's diaries. The differences in the sources, in the tones of voice, reinforce the stereotypes of each woman's personality: a fearless Stanton who responded to adversity by taking the offensive, and an Anthony who felt every punch but soldiered on. In the details, however, they described similar experiences. Stanton reported back to her newspaper, *The Revolution*, about trying to navigate around Iowa, where the railroads "run generally in parallel lines, never looking at or shaking hands with each other," and any crossroad that exists "never runs with the slightest reference to the main road." It was not fair, she opined, to say "Just like a woman" when she missed an engagement; "Please remember, dear sirs," men alone, without one word from women, designed the railroads, stages, and bridges. At the western end of these same parallel lines, Anthony told her diary about anxious hours spent waiting to cross the Missouri River, because four major railroads wanted to reach Omaha at the same hour but all their passengers needed to cross the river on one temporary bridge in transfer cars.

Stanton was the heroine of her own tales, who triumphed against the trials of misdirected trunks, lost manuscripts, unheated halls, crying babies, and inept agents. No one, she recalled, thought to schedule "eating, sleeping or resting, so that you step on the platform at the appointed hour, fresh and smiling, charged with enough magnitude to hold the audi-

Stagecoach on the way from Silverton to Ouray, Colorado

ence. You speak from one to two hours, shake hands with friends for half an hour, then hurry to your hotel, don your traveling attire, repack your platform dress, then chat with friends until it's time for the midnight train." From the vantage point of retirement, she made it sound rather jolly.

The immediacy of the details in Anthony's diary bring life to Stanton's broad strokes. The entries for a few December days in Wisconsin in 1877 provide a representative glimpse. On a Sunday, after speaking in Milwaukee in the afternoon, she caught the midnight train for Green Bay, spoke there on Monday, and traveled six hours by train and stage on Tuesday to lecture at Stevens Point. On Wednesday, she wrote: "Left [Stevens] Point at 8 a.m.—carriage to Plover—mud and slush—five miles—then freight to New London—and then freight to Appleton arriving 4 p.m.—and lo my trunk had been set off at Hortonville—so I had to get my beefsteak—go to bed—but couldn't sleep—and go to Platform in my travelling gear—was introduced by Prof. Sawyer—of the Lawrence University here—had splendid audience but didn't feel at home in my mohair gray travelling dress." Despite a cold that reached "the

sneezing stage" and roads of "mud without precedent," she kept up this pace, setting off on Christmas Eve to keep a similar schedule in Minnesota.

It was the splendid audiences, as Anthony repeatedly described them, that rewarded their labors. Public lectures drew large and curious crowds whose members did not necessarily share the ideas they came to hear. Indeed, a certain pleasure might come of hearing dangerous doctrine straight from the devil's own mouth, or from "that disgusting old *female* Cady Stanton," as one woman wrote from Mt. Carroll, Illinois. "Notwithstanding my detestation of her theories on free-love, and so forth," she continued, "I shall go to hear her out of curiosity, she is one of the notorieties in an age full of shams." Her excuse for listening to Elizabeth Cady Stanton stir up rebellion mattered less than her willingness to satisfy her curiosity. Lecturers survived, according to one wit, because the public paid "twenty-five cents to hear them lecture, with the privilege of looking at them for an hour and criticizing them for a week." When Susan B. Anthony debated a local college professor in Bloom-

Temperance women hold
their ground outside a
Minnesota saloon in 1878
despite the pitcher of water
the owner's indignant wife
has poured down upon them
from an upstairs window.

The railroad depot and restaurant at Arrow, Colorado

ington, Illinois, streetcars and the various railroads delivered large crowds from adjoining towns until Schroder's Opera House "filled to its capacity," according to the city's newspaper. Anticipating the curiosity of readers who had missed the event, the paper published the debate verbatim as well.

Each season Stanton and Anthony offered at least one lecture that laid out their basic arguments for woman suffrage and the current strategy for obtaining it. In the 1870 season, Stanton listed a lecture entitled "The Sixteenth Amendment," in which she made the case for completing the constitutional reforms of Reconstruction with one more federal amendment to establish universal suffrage. A year later she offered "The New Departure," spreading the new idea that women already enjoyed the right to vote as citizens, protected by the Fourteenth Amendment. That lecture remained in her repertoire until the Supreme Court ruled to the contrary in the case of *Minor* v. *Happersett* in 1875. In the season of 1879–80, Susan B. Anthony lectured on "United States vs. States Rights," delivering a critique of the Republican Party's retreat from federal

protection of civil and political rights and a plea for national citizenship.

Although neither Stanton nor Anthony resorted to such stock items of the lecturer's trade as travelogues or historical compositions, they did move off the center of their political message to speak more generally about women in contemporary society. Anthony seldom risked speaking about the intimate angles of womanhood because she could not defeat the social taboo against a maiden mentioning sexuality. Even her efforts to lecture on laws about prostitution raised a storm in the press. When she did venture beyond the political talk, it was to examine new aspects of women's lives, such as their paid labor, range of occupations, and opportunities to live single outside the family structure.

Sanctioned by her marriage and motherhood to speak on sexuality and family life, Stanton drew large crowds to hear advice on raising daughters, as well as more controversial lectures on "Marriage and Divorce" and "Marriage and Maternity (to ladies alone)." The press rarely accorded these lectures the space they allowed for political topics, but Stanton hit a nerve with her audiences. "I shall be a reservoir of sorrow!" she once told a friend. "O! the experiences women pour into my ears!"

By 1880, Stanton and Anthony had popularized woman suffrage beyond their own circle of reformers and beyond the reach of any organized movement. They had touched a great many lives. Mary Newbury Adams, of Dubuque, Iowa, insisted that she first heard Stanton and Anthony only because a newspaper paid her to report the event. Had she not been there as a reporter, she assured her sister, she would have mounted the stage to give some arguments against the cause. But Mrs. Stanton was so delightful, "[m]y pail full of arguments against is getting emptied and the pail for arguments for is filling up." The experience turned Mary Adams into a local suffrage leader.

Sometimes the lecturers simply helped a very private life. In 1873, Elizabeth Yates Richmond heard Elizabeth Cady Stanton lecture on maternity in Appleton, Wisconsin. Seven years later, she answered a public call for women to let the Republican Party know that they wanted to vote. Addressing her letter to Stanton, she testified to her desire to vote and went on to recall their earlier encounter. "I am glad of a chance to thank you personally for the grand lecture which you delivered . . . & for the earnest helpful words you left to us mothers." In the interval, while Stanton exercised "far-reaching influence," Elizabeth Richmond had raised daughters "who will I trust be fully qualified to enter upon the duties of American citizenship when the day comes."

Their lecture audiences had uncovered activists, and those activists had built a political structure of local, state, and national suffrage associations. To Anthony, this evidence of the movement's coming-of-age signaled a time for organization and leadership of a more traditional kind. She continued to

travel until her death at eighty-six, in 1906, helping to meet the needs of an era no longer concerned with popular entertainment and preliminary discussion of the issues, but engaged in tough political campaigns to change federal or state law. When she campaigned for constitutional amendments in South Dakota, Kansas, or California at the end of the century, she relied on the suffrage movement to produce the schedule, publicity, and audiences that lecture bureaus once delivered. Stanton was tired out by the end of the 1870s. She went west only once after 1881, making a stately pilgrimage through Cleveland, Chicago, and Omaha. Still in the public eye, she provided leadership to the national suffrage movement and was much sought after by the press as a commentator on everything from women on bicycles to the taxation of church property. Syndicated news services took the place of lecture bureaus.

Stanton and Anthony had also demonstrated their staying power and perseverance as politicians, gaining the recognition of elected officials as well as of women. Their lecture tours brought them into the neighborhoods of state politicians, who heard them speak and then extended invitations to address legislatures. It happened on Susan B. Anthony's trip to Olympia, in Washington Territory, in 1871. She traveled to the capital to deliver a public lecture, and the legislature voted that she be asked to address them in session on the following day, to inform their debate on a measure for woman suffrage. It happened, too, in Wisconsin, Michigan, Ohio, and Nebraska. The presidential candidates of 1880 acknowledged this new stature of the movement and its leaders in a backhanded way when they took the trouble to explain in great detail their refusals to endorse woman suffrage and did so in private meetings with the movement's leaders. For women who began the seventies with neither organization nor political party committed to gaining their rights, it was quite an achievement.

Clubwomen in Oklahoma, 1890s

THE ONE &
SOLE POINT

S usan B. Anthony had no time for leisure. As early as 1875, she had urged Matilda Joslyn Gage to focus all her efforts on *"the one & sole point of women disfranchised—* separate & alone—and not mixed up with—or one of 19 *other points of protest*—all of the 19 good & proper perchance . . . however we must keep our claim first and most important overshadowing every other . . . just woman & her disfranchised—leaving the other 19 demands of the *Old* Liberty to wait our emancipation."

That single-minded view had steadily intensified with the changing postwar world in which American women found themselves. The birthrate was steadily declining, leaving middle-class women with more time on their hands than ever before. New technology—and an influx of young immigrants who could provide cheap household help—further encouraged those same women to develop interests outside the home. Women were more likely to have attended college now, and more eager to join the women's clubs that were fast proliferating in cities and towns all across the country. Many of these focused exclusively on "self-improvement," a few were devoted to reform, but all of them, by encouraging women to take up leadership positions, to organize and speak and travel from town to town, helped foster a new generation of potential leaders who had never been jeered at for simply demanding the right to be heard. They were more conservative than their predecessors on the whole and more conventional, but

Anthony knew that if suffrage was ever to be won, large numbers of them would have to be attracted to her cause.

She set out to build bridges to as many organizations as she could. The Women's Division of the Knights of Labor, the Ladies of the Grand Army of the Republic, the Women's Conference of the Unitarian Association, the Universal Peace Union, the Daughters of the American Revolution, the National Association of Colored Women—Anthony would eventually reach out to them all.

None was as powerful as the Woman's Christian Temperance Union. Its president was Frances Willard, an educator whose drive and organizational skills were a match for Anthony's own. Willard had single-handedly transformed a small Ohio-based Protestant benevolent society into a dynamic national movement that would boast 150,000 members by 1890. (By contrast, Anthony's organization then still had fewer than 13,000.) Its program—Willard called it a "Do-Everything Policy"—called for dozens of reforms ranging from prohibition and prosecution for authors of obscene literature to prison reform and a federal law designating Sunday as a day of rest. All were aimed at preserving the sanctity of the home, and in 1882 Willard persuaded her membership to support woman suffrage in the interest of bringing them all about.

"My one source of gratification in the present club-engrossment of our women is that they cannot work far in any direction without finding themselves crippled in their efforts by the lack of political force. It is good to have woman's moral influence on the right side of every question, but it would be better if to this she could add political power, for then she would be able not only to crystallize moral sentiments into laws but to enforce these laws after they were enacted."

Susan B. Anthony

Colored Women's League of Washington, D.C., 1894

(Overleaf) Leaders of the Woman's Christian Temperance Union at Minneapolis in 1886

Anthony liked and admired Willard and welcomed help from her rank-and-file members—whom she once privately called "dear religious bigots"—so long as their target was the vote. But in doing so, she also earned the enmity of the powerful liquor lobby, which henceforth identified votes for women with an end to its profits and poured hundreds of thousands of dollars into opposing them.

Stanton, suspicious of organized religion since her school days, warned Anthony and her allies not to be "dazzled by the promise of a sudden acquisition of numbers to our platforms with the wide-spread influence of the Church behind them, if with all this comes a religious proscription that will undermine the secular nature of our government."

She was growing increasingly unsettled by Anthony's single-minded focus on suffrage. "For over thirty years," she wrote, "some people have said from time to time that I have injured the suffrage movement beyond redemption; but it still lives. Train killed it, Victoria Woodhull killed it, the *Revolution* killed it . . . Susan dealt us a death blow at various times. But with each death it put on new life. . . . Reforms are not made of blown glass to be broken to pieces with the first adverse wind."

National Woman's Christian Temperance
13th Annual Convention, October 22 = 28

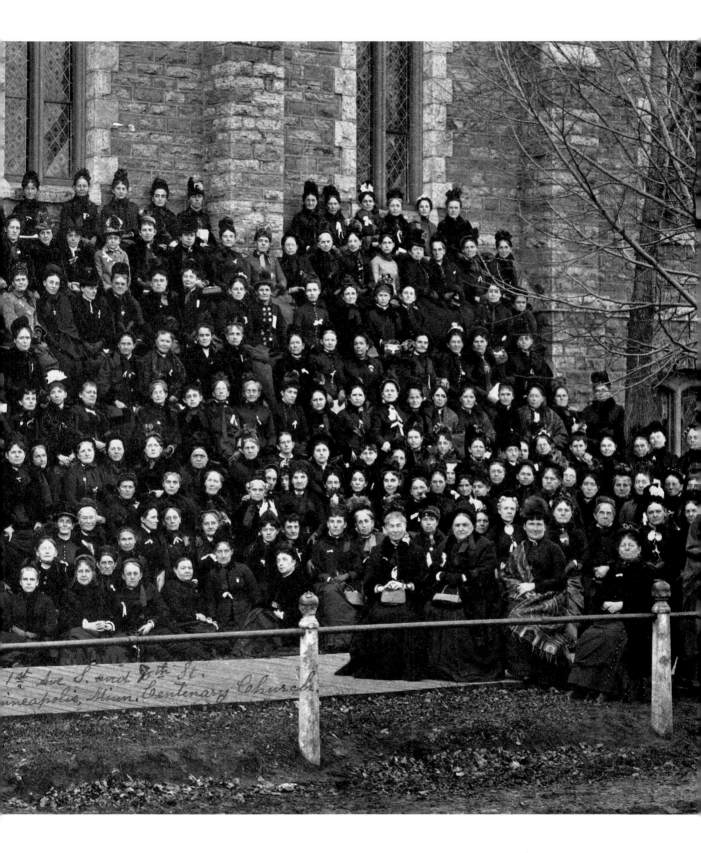

A Weapon of Protection

Even Susan B. Anthony recognized that Frances Willard, not she or Elizabeth Cady Stanton, was the greatest mobilizer of middle-class American women in the nineteenth century. In the nearly seventeen years of Willard's dynamic leadership, the Woman's Christian Temperance Union grew from 27,000 dues-paying members to 150,000—more than one hundred times the membership of the National American Woman Suffrage Association.

The WCTU was the outgrowth of a remarkable temperance uprising that swept Ohio and western New York towns in the winter of 1873–74. Small bands of singing, praying, beseeching women managed to shame some three thousand saloon-keepers into closing. Most eventually reopened, however, and when temperance women went to court or state legislators for help in closing them down again they found themselves ignored or ridiculed. Without the vote they had no power. The women of the WCTU had "a lever," Anthony told a reporter, but "no fulcrum on which to place it."

Frances Willard, recording secretary of the new organization, resolved to try to provide that fulcrum. Like Anthony, she was unmarried and had pursued a career in education before turning to reform. While praying alone in 1876, she remembered, God told her "to speak for woman's ballot as a weapon of protection to her home . . . from the tyranny of drink." For her, voting was less a right than a religious duty.

It took Willard only three years to unseat the organization's conservative president, and once in office she lost little time in transforming the WCTU into something altogether new. She had two mottoes: "Do Everything" and "Woman Will Bless and Brighten Every Place She Enters, *and She Will Enter Every Place*." To make them a reality she reorganized the WCTU into thirty-eight separate "departments," each with its own program, such as kindergartens, prison reform, prostitution, child care—

and the franchise. Soon, the white ribbon traditionally worn by WCTU members to symbolize the purity of the True Woman was intertwined with a yellow ribbon that stood for woman suffrage.

Anthony was delighted; Willard would bring thousands of new recruits to the cause. At first, Stanton saw no danger in it, either: neither Willard nor the WCTU "harms us a particle," she wrote in 1880. But as the years passed, the WCTU and its leaders joined other religious conservatives in pressing Congress to declare Christianity America's official faith, urging the strict enforcement of Sunday blue laws and demanding religious instruction in the public schools. Stanton rebelled, and in 1881, with her old ally Matilda Joslyn Gage—who believed Willard "the most dangerous person on the American continent today"—wrote a public letter in which she took Anthony to task for working too closely with organizations she believed inimical to women's long-term interests.

Anthony, deeply wounded, expressed her feelings in a letter to Willard:

I am more vexed than I can tell you. . . . They, to my face, charge me with having become weak & truckling not only to the Church Women—but also to Society Women!—They say I am eaten up with desire to make our movement popular *&c . . .*

Of one thing I feel pretty sure—and that is that I shall not allow myself to act the bigot *and persecute women who don't believe about God, or Christ, or heaven or earth as I do—The trouble with so many is that they can't see that so called Liberals are likely to become as bigoted and narrow as are the bigots of the various religions of the past or present—Let's you & I—my dear—stick together on this point—*

In fact, Anthony rarely allowed her admiration for Willard to overcome her shrewd tactical sense. Suffrage always

The post–Civil War temperance movement that began in Ohio in the winter of 1873–74 inspired Currier & Ives to issue the lithograph (at right) entitled "Woman's Holy War: Grand Charge on the Enemy's Works." Some six years later, temperance agitation had spread to downtown Devil's Lake, North Dakota (above), where marchers vowed to sweep the streets clean of alcohol.

came first. She was glad to have WCTU help during the grueling South Dakota suffrage campaign in 1890, but refused to join Willard in backing a new Prohibition Party because she did not feel she could turn her back on members of other parties who supported suffrage. And when campaigning in California in 1896, she talked Willard into moving her annual convention from San Francisco to St. Louis so that voters would not confuse the suffrage and temperance causes.

Willard was just fifty-eight when she died in 1898. Anthony never forgot her or her impact. "She was a bunch of magnetism possessing . . . occult force," she recalled. "I never approached her but what I felt my nerves tingle from this magnetism."

That view was no longer fully shared by Susan B. Anthony. In 1884, Frederick Douglass married a white woman named Helen Pitts. Many admirers, both black and white, were sharply critical. Not Elizabeth Cady Stanton, who wrote Douglass a warm note of encouragement from England, then sent Anthony the draft of an open letter for them both to sign, declaring their wholehearted support for his marriage, along with a request to have him speak at the upcoming National convention.

In earlier times, when Anthony criticized her fellow abolitionists for acting like "mere politicians" whenever they showed the slightest willingness to temper their rhetoric, she might well have signed the letter and issued the invitation. But not anymore, not if by so doing she would further complicate the struggle toward what was now her sole objective.

Frederick Douglass and his second wife, Helen Pitts Douglass, at Niagara Falls on their honeymoon, 1884

I do hope you won't put your foot into the question of intermarriage of the races. It has no place on our platform, any more than the question of no marriage at all, or of polygamy, and, so far as I can prevent it, shall not be brought there. I beg you therefore not to congratulate him publicly. Our intention at this convention is to make every one who hears or reads believe in the grand principle of equality of rights and chances for women, and if they see on our program the name of Douglass every thought will be turned toward the subject of amalgamation and away from that of woman and her disfranchised. Neither you nor I have the right thus to complicate or compromise our question, and if we take the bits in our teeth in one direction we must expect our compeers to do the same in others. You very well know that if you plunge in, as your letter proposes, your endorsement will be charged upon me and the whole association. Do not throw around that marriage the halo of a pure and lofty duty to break down race lines. Your sympathy has run away with your judgment.

Lovingly and fearfully yours
Susan

By the late 1880s, it was clear that neither the National's focus on persuading Congress to pass a constitutional amendment nor the American's emphasis on state-by-state campaigning was working. Thousands had been converted to the cause, and women had won the vote in school-board and municipal elections here and there across the country, but just two states—Utah and Wyoming—had fully enfranchised women. The younger generation of suffrage leaders—Stanton dismissed them as "the children"; to Anthony, they were her "nieces"—had no firsthand memories of the bitter personal strife that had helped divide the suffrage movement in 1869. And the substantive differences between the two organizations had largely disappeared with time as the sweeping agenda once set by Stanton for the National was soft-pedaled in the interest of suffrage and suffrage alone.

"Lucy [Stone] and Susan alike see suffrage only," Stanton told a friend. "They do not see woman's religious and social bondage. Neither do the young women in either association, hence they may as well combine for they have one mind and purpose." Even with one mind and purpose it took more than two years of wary negotiation for the Anthony and Stone factions finally to agree to join forces, and it still might not have happened had Stone's daughter, Alice Stone Blackwell, and one of Anthony's favorite "nieces," Rachel Foster Avery, not determined that it would. "The elders," Alice Blackwell remembered, "were not keen for it on either side."

In February of 1890, the two organizations merged at last into the National American Woman Suffrage Association. Lucy Stone, now ailing, had withdrawn her name from consideration as its first president. Stanton and Anthony were both nominated for the job. Many of the more conservative delegates now favored Anthony because, while their relationship with her in the past had often been stormy, they thought she could now at least be counted upon to stick to the one subject on which they could all agree: woman suffrage.

But Anthony recoiled from running against the woman who had brought her into the movement, and even though her own star had long since eclipsed the Stanton's, she could not bring herself to compete with her. "I never expect to know any joy in this world," she said toward the end of her life, "equal to that of

Rachel Foster Avery (left), one of Anthony's best-loved "nieces"

(Right) Alice Stone Blackwell and Anna Howard Shaw

Delegates to the first International Council of Women, held in Washington, D.C., in 1888 to celebrate the fortieth anniversary of the Seneca Falls Declaration and, in Anthony's words, "impress the important lesson that the position of women anywhere affects their position everywhere." Anthony and Stanton, second and fourth from the left, are surrounded by representatives of Canada, Norway, England, Ireland, Scotland, France, and Finland. The woman to the right of Stanton is her old friend and collaborator Matilda Joslyn Gage.

Norwegian-born serving women in a Black River Falls, Wisconsin, hotel, c. 1890

Whether our feet are compressed in iron shoes, our faces hidden with veils and masks; whether yoked with cows to draw the plow through its furrows, or classed with idiots, lunatics and criminals in the laws and constitutions of the State, the principle is the same; for the humiliations of spirit are as real as the visible badges of servitude.

ELIZABETH CADY STANTON

going up and down the land, getting good editorials written, engaging halls, and circulating Mrs. Stanton's speeches."

Anthony begged the delegates to vote for Stanton instead of her. "When the division was made twenty-two years ago," she told them, "it was because our platform was too broad, because Mrs. Stanton was too radical. A more conservative association was wanted. And now if we divide and Mrs. Stanton shall be deposed from the presidency you virtually degrade her."

Stanton won. Anthony became vice president at large. Lucy Stone agreed to chair the executive committee.

Stanton was planning to head back to England the day after the convention, and so her inaugural address was also something of a farewell. She considered it "a greater honor to go to England as President of this Association," she said, "than would be the case if I were sent as Minister Plenipotentiary to any court in Europe."

But in the rest of her address she evidenced not the slightest willingness to modify her remarks in deference to the conservative delegates who were now at least nominally among her constituents. She called for complete equality for women within all of America's churches, warned male legislators not to enact further divorce legislation until women had the power to vote on it, and explicitly opposed the Woman's Christian Temperance Union's campaign to "introduce the name of God into the Constitution."

The National American Woman Suffrage Association, she said, should oppose "all Union of Church and State" and remain open to the views of any woman who wished to speak before them: "We do not want to limit our platform to bare suffrage and nothing more. . . . Wherever a woman is wronged her voice should be heard."

As their new president made her slow, stately way off the platform, the delegates stood as one and waved their handkerchiefs. Some were cheering her gallantry and her sentiments. Others must have been relieved just to see her go.

"INNER GROAN OF MY SOUL"

In August of 1891, Elizabeth Cady Stanton sailed home again for America. She was seventy-six years old. Her mind was still keen, but her body was failing. "I have one melancholy fact to state," she had recently told a friend, "which I do with sorrow and humiliation. I was weighed yesterday and brought the scales down to 240, just the speed of a trotting horse, and yet I cannot trot 100 feet without puffing." She now had difficulty simply crossing her stateroom, had to be helped around the deck by a paid companion. It was a pity "that such mental powers must be hampered with such a *clumsy* body," Anthony wrote to a friend. "If we could only give her elasticity of limbs—and locomotive powers."

Since her husband's death, Stanton had been without a permanent home, preferring to make her regal way from one to another of her children's homes. Now

(Overleaf) Anthony and Anna Howard Shaw waiting to speak at an 1894 rally in Lillydale, New York, during their last, losing campaign to win votes for women in that state

WELCOME

With malice toward none and charity for all

The Black Struggle for Suffrage

A series of Supreme Court decisions handed down during the 1890s legitimated segregation in nearly every aspect of American life—including indirectly even the woman-suffrage movement. Its leaders, many of them veterans of the struggles against slavery and for equal rights, now began to back away from their former allies, fearing that if they welcomed black suffragists to their ranks, southern white women and southern white legislators alike would abandon their cause and doom the constitutional amendment for which they had struggled so long.

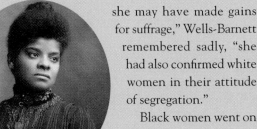

Ida B. Wells-Barnett

In 1894, Susan B. Anthony herself rejected a plea from a group of African-American women who wanted to form their own chapter of the National American Woman Suffrage Association and was chastised for it by her friend, the black suffragist, journalist, and antilynching crusader, Ida B. Wells-Barnett. "Although she may have made gains for suffrage," Wells-Barnett remembered sadly, "she had also confirmed white women in their attitude of segregation."

Black women went on to build their own separate suffrage movement, but leaders like Wells-Barnett never abandoned their belief in integration. In 1913, when Wells-Barnett attended the National American Suffrage Parade in Washington, D.C., as a delegate from her own all-black Alpha Suffrage Club of Chicago, she was told she could not march with other suffragists from Illinois for fear of alienating white southerners. Blacks were expected to march together at the end of the parade. Wells-Barnett would have none of it; she waited on the sidewalk until the Illinois delegation came into view, then slipped between two white women and marched with them up Pennsylvania Avenue toward the Capitol.

she moved permanently into a Manhattan apartment with her widowed daughter, Margaret, and her unmarried son, Robert.

Anthony, who had herself been traveling without letup for half a century, had settled down a little, too, moving in with her sister Mary into her old family home in Rochester. Anthony delighted in having her own home at last. "The girl was washing and I got the dinner alone," she wrote one evening: "broiled steak, potatoes, sweet corn, tomatoes and peach pudding, with a cup of tea. All said it was good and I enjoyed it hugely. How I love to receive in my own home and at my own table!"

"I rejoice that you are going to housekeeping . . . ," Stanton wrote to her when she heard of it. "My advice to you, Susan, is to keep some spot you can call your own; where you can live and die in peace and be cremated in your own oven if you desire."

But Anthony had something else in mind. Now that she had a home of her own, she saw no reason why Stanton shouldn't come and live with her. For the first time in more than forty years of friendship, she thought, they would be able to work steadily in tandem.

Stanton wouldn't hear of it. She loved and admired Susan B. Anthony, but she did not want to live every day under her lash, could not abide the thought of being subject to her every call for help.

Anthony could not hide her disappointment:

Well, I hope you will do and be as seemeth best unto yourself. . . . Still, I cannot help sending you this inner groan of my soul. . . .

[My] constant thought was that you would come here, where are the documents necessary to our work, and stay for as long . . . as we must be together to put your writings into systematic shape to go down to posterity. I have no writings to go down to posterity, so my ambition is not for myself, but it is for one by the side of whom I have wrought these forty years.

Anthony may have had a home, but she spent precious little time there. New York amended its constitution again in 1894, and Anthony, at seventy-four, spoke for suffrage in all sixty counties, only to see it defeated once again. It was "the bitterest disappointment of my life," she told her first biographer. But she wasted little time in grieving, hurrying west instead, to Kansas, where the Republicans—in order to appeal to what she called "lager beer foreigners and whiskey Democrats"—went back on their word to support suffrage just as they had twenty-seven years earlier. In 1896, she would spend eight more months campaigning all-out in California, sometimes speaking three times a day—in soldiers' homes, military encampments, farmers' picnics, even poolrooms. In the end, the men of California, too, would vote against giving their wives and daughters the right to vote.

"I am as deeply and keenly interested in the many reforms in city, state & National government as any one can possibly be," Anthony said in 1894, "but knowing that no right solution of any great question can be reached until the whole people have a voice in it—I give all of myself to the getting of the whole people inside the body politick."

Anthony at seventy-five, fifth from the left (opposite, above), riding through Yosemite in 1895, just before launching the statewide California suffrage campaign that took her to the San Diego rally and picnic (opposite, below). "Oh no! I don't want to die just as long as I can work," she told the journalist Nellie Bly that year. "The minute I can't I want to go. I dread the thought of being enfeebled. I find the older I get the greater power I have to help the world. I am like a snowball—the further I am rolled, the more I gain."

Anthony was now instantly recognizable in every community in the country, including San Francisco's Chinatown, where her 1896 visits were reported in the local press.

Giving all of herself to that single goal sometimes led Anthony to make expedient choices that would have been unimaginable in her early days. Her private belief in racial equality never wavered, and she spoke out publicly against the wave of lynchings that accompanied the imposition of Jim Crow on the post-Reconstruction South, but she also went along with younger suffrage leaders who made it clear that black chapters were not welcome in the National American. In 1895, she personally asked Frederick Douglass not to attend a convention in Atlanta for fear his presence would alienate white Southerners; and in 1899, she would help table a motion that would have placed the National American on the record against segregation aboard railroad trains.

Despite Stanton's continuing outspokenness, despite Anthony's expediency, there had still been little progress. By 1900, after nearly fifty years of struggle, just four states—Wyoming, Utah, Colorado, and Idaho—had granted women the right to full suffrage. Neither woman now believed she would live to see all American women going to the polls: "We are sowing winter wheat," Stanton confided to her diary, "which the coming spring will see sprout and which other hands than ours will reap and enjoy."

Western women at the polls

Elizabeth Cady Stanton

The Solitude of Self

On January 18, 1892, Elizabeth Cady Stanton resigned as president of the National American Woman Suffrage Association. She believed this farewell speech, which she also delivered before the Judiciary Committees of the House and Senate, "the best thing I have ever written." Susan B. Anthony didn't like it much at first—it contained too little on the vote, which had become her central focus—but she later called it "the strongest and most unanswerable argument and appeal ever made by mortal pen or tongue for the full freedom and franchise of women."

The point I wish plainly to bring before you on this occasion is the individuality of each human soul; our Protestant idea, the right of individual conscience and judgement; our republican idea, individual citizenship. In discussing the rights of woman, we are to consider, first, what belongs to her as an individual, in a world of her own, the arbiter of her own destiny, an imaginary Robinson Crusoe, with her woman, Friday, on a solitary island. Her rights under such circumstances are to use all her faculties for her own safety and happiness.

Secondly, if we consider her as a citizen, as a member of a great nation, she must have the same rights as all other members, according to the fundamental principles of our Government.

Thirdly, viewed as a woman, an equal factor in civilization, her rights and duties are still the same—individual happiness and development.

Fourthly, it is only the incidental relations of life, such as mother, wife, sister, daughter, which may involve some special duties and training. . . .

The strongest reason for giving woman all the opportunities for higher education, for the full development of her faculties, her forces of mind and body; for giving her the most enlarged freedom of thought and action; a complete emancipation from all forms of bondage, of custom, dependence, superstition; from all the crippling influences of fear—is the solitude and personal responsibility of her own individual life. The strongest reason why we ask for woman a voice in the government under which she lives; in the religion she is asked to believe; equality in social life, where she is the chief factor; a place in the trades and professions, where she may earn her bread, is because of her birthright to self-sovereignty; because, as an individual, she must rely on herself. No matter how much women prefer to lean, to be protected and supported, nor how much men desire to have them do so, they must make the voyage of life alone, and for safety in an emergency, they must know something of the laws of navigation. To guide our own craft, we must be captain, pilot, engineer; with chart and compass to stand at the wheel; to watch the winds and waves, and know when to take in the sail, and to read the signs in the firmament over all. It matters not whether the solitary voyager is man or woman; nature, having endowed them equally, leaves them to their own skill and judgment in the hour of danger, and, if not equal to the occasion, alike they perish.

To appreciate the importance of fitting every human soul for independent action, think for a moment of the immeasurable solitude of self. We come into the world alone, unlike all who have gone before us, we leave it alone, under circumstances peculiar to ourselves. No mortal ever has been, no mortal ever will be like the soul just launched on the sea of life. There can never again be just such a combination of prenatal influences; never again just such

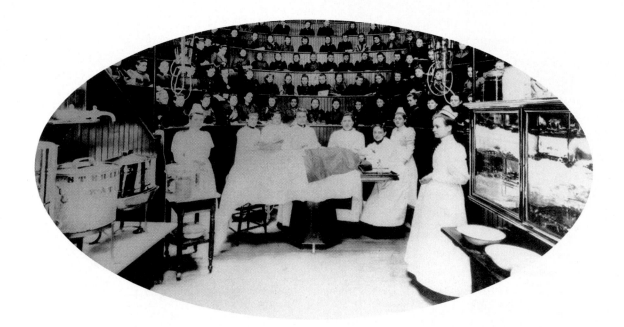

Progress: female students and staff in the operating theater at the Woman's Hospital of Philadelphia, 1895

environments as make up the infancy, youth and manhood of this one. Nature never repeats herself, and the possibilities of one human soul will never be found in another. No one has ever found two blades of ribbon grass alike, and no one will ever find two human beings alike. Seeing, then, what must be the infinite diversity in human character, we can in a measure appreciate the loss to a nation when any large class of the people is uneducated and unrepresented in the government.

We ask for the complete development of every individual, first, for his own benefit and happiness. In fitting out an army, we give each soldier his own knapsack, arms, powder, his blanket, cup, knife, fork and spoon. We provide alike for all their individual necessities; then each man bears his own burden.

Again, we ask complete individual development for the general good; for the consensus of the competent on the whole round of human interests, on all questions of national life; and here each man must bear his share of the general burden. It is sad to see how soon friendless children are left to bear their own burdens, before they can analyze their feelings; before they can even tell their joys and sorrows, they are thrown on their own resources. The great lesson

that nature seems to teach us at all ages is self-dependence, self-protection, self-support. . . .

In youth our most bitter disappointments, our brightest hopes and ambitions, are known only to ourselves. Even our friendship and love we never fully share with another; there is something of every passion, in every situation, we conceal. Even so in our triumphs and our defeats.

We ask no sympathy from others in the anxiety and agony of a broken friendship or shattered love. When death sunders our nearest ties, alone we sit in the shadow of our affliction. Alike amid the greatest triumphs and darkest tragedies of life, we walk alone. On the divine heights of human attainment, eulogized and worshipped as a hero or saint, we stand alone. In ignorance, poverty and vice, as a pauper or criminal, alone we starve or steal; alone we suffer the sneers and rebuffs of our fellows; alone we are hunted and hounded through dark courts and alleys, in byways and high-ways; alone we stand in the judgment seat; alone in the prison cell we lament our crimes and misfortunes; alone we expiate them on the gallows. In hours like these we realize the awful solitude of individual life, its pains, its penalties, its responsibilities; hours in which the youngest and most helpless are thrown on their own resources for guidance and consolation. Seeing, then, that life must ever be a march and a battle, that each soldier must be equipped for his own protection, it is the height of cruelty to rob the individual of a single natural right.

To throw obstacles in the way of a complete education is like putting out the eyes; to deny the rights of property is like cutting off the hands. To refuse political equality is to rob the ostracized of all self-respect; of credit in the market place; of recompense in the world of work, of a voice in choosing those who make and administer the law, a choice in the jury before whom they are tried, and in the judge who decides their punishment. [Think of] . . . woman's position! Robbed of her natural rights, handicapped by law and custom at every turn, yet compelled to fight her own battles, and in the emergencies of life to fall back on herself for protection. . . .

The young wife and mother, at the head of some establishment, with a kind husband to shield her from the adverse winds of life, with wealth, fortune and position, has a certain harbor of safety, secure against the ordinary ills of life. But to manage a household, have a desirable influence in society, keep her friends and the affections of her husband, train her children and servants well, she must have rare common sense, wisdom, diplomacy, and a knowledge of human nature. To do all this, she needs the cardinal virtues and the strong points of character that the most successful statesman possesses. An uneducated woman trained to dependence, with no resources in herself, must make a failure of any position in life. But society says women do not need a knowledge of the world, the liberal training that experience in public life must give, all the advantages of collegiate education; but when for the lack of all this, the woman's happiness is wrecked, alone she bears her humiliation; and the solitude of the weak and the ignorant

is indeed pitiable. In the wild chase for the prizes of life, they are ground to powder.

In age, when the pleasures of youth are passed, children grown up, married and gone, the hurry and bustle of life in a measure over, when the hands are weary of active service, when the old arm chair and the fireside are the chosen resorts, then men and women alike must fall back on their own resources. If they cannot find companionship in books, if they have no interest in the vital questions of the hour, no interest in watching the consummation of reforms with which they might have been identified, they soon pass into their dotage. The more fully the faculties of the mind are developed and kept in use, the longer the period of vigor and active interest in all around us continues. If, from a life-long participation in public affairs, a woman feels responsible for the laws regulating our system of education, the discipline of our jails and prisons, the sanitary condition of our private homes, public buildings and thoroughfares, an interest in commerce, finance, our foreign relations, in any or all these questions, her solitude will at least be respectable, and she will not be driven to gossip or scandal for entertainment.

The chief reason for opening to every soul the doors to the whole round of human duties and pleasures is the individual development thus attained, the resources thus provided under all circumstances to mitigate the solitude that at times must come to everyone. . . . Inasmuch, then, as woman shares equally the joys and sorrows of time and eternity, is it not the height of presumption in man to propose to represent her at the ballot box and the throne of grace, to do her voting in the state, her praying in the church, and to assume the position of high priest at the family altar?

Nothing strengthens the judgment and quickens the conscience like individual responsibility. Nothing adds such dignity to character as the recognition of one's self-sovereignty; the right to an equal place, everywhere conceded—a place earned by personal

Wellesley College crew, 1882

merit, not an artificial attainment by inheritance, wealth, family and position. Conceding, then, that the responsibilities of life rest equally on man and woman, that their destiny is the same, they need the same preparation for time and eternity. The talk of sheltering woman from the fierce storms of life is the sheerest mockery, for they beat on her from every point of the compass, just as they do on man, and with more fatal results, for he has been trained to protect himself, to resist, and to conquer. Such are the facts in human experience, the responsibilities of individual sovereignty. Rich and poor, intelligent and ignorant, wise and foolish, virtuous and vicious, man and woman; it is ever the same, each soul must depend wholly on itself.

Whatever the theories may be of woman's dependence on man, in the supreme moments of her life, he cannot bear her burdens. Alone she goes to the gates of death, to give life to every man that is born into the world; no one can share her fears, no one can mitigate her pangs; and if her sorrow is greater than she can bear, alone she passes beyond the gates into the vast unknown.

From the mountain-tops of Judea long ago, a heavenly voice bade his disciples, "Bear ye one another's burdens"; but humanity has not yet risen to that point of self-sacrifice; and if ever so willing, how few the burdens are that one soul can bear for another!

So it ever must be in the conflicting scenes of life, in the long, weary march, each one walks alone. We may have many friends, love, kindness, sympathy and charity, to smooth our pathway in everyday life, but in the tragedies and triumphs of human experience, each mortal stands alone.

But when all artificial trammels are removed, and women are recognized as individuals, responsible for their own environments, thoroughly educated for all positions in life they may be called to fill; with all the resources in themselves that liberal thought and broad culture can give; guided by their own conscience and judgment, trained to self-protection, by

a healthy development of the muscular system, and skill in the use of weapons and defense; and stimulated to self-support by a knowledge of the business world and the pleasure that pecuniary independence must ever give; when women are trained in this way, they will in a measure be fitted for those hours of solitude that come alike to all, whether prepared or otherwise. As in our extremity we must depend on ourselves, the dictates of wisdom point to complete individual development.

In talking of education, how shallow the argument that each class must be educated for the special work it proposes to do, and that all those faculties not needed in this special work must lie dormant and utterly wither for want of use, when, perhaps, these will be the very faculties needed in life's greatest emergencies! Some say, "Where is the use of drilling girls in the languages, the sciences, in law, medicine, theology. As wives, mothers, housekeepers, cooks, they need a different curriculum from boys who are to fill all positions." The chief cooks in our great hotels and ocean steamers are men. In our large cities, men run the bakeries; they make our bread, cake and pies. They manage the laundries; they are now considered our best milliners and dressmakers. Because some men fill these departments of usefulness, shall we regulate the curriculum in Harvard and Yale to their present necessities? If not, why this talk in our best colleges of a curriculum for girls who are crowding into the trades and professions, teachers in all our public schools, rapidly filling many lucrative and honorable positions in life?

. . . Women are already the equals of men in the whole realm of thought, in art, science, literature and government. . . . The poetry and novels of the century are theirs, and they have touched the keynote of reform, in religion, politics and social life. They fill the editor's and professor's chair, plead at the bar of justice, walk the wards of the hospital, speak from the pulpit and the platform. Such is the type of womanhood that an enlightened public sentiment wel-

Barbers in Denver, c. 1890

comes to-day, and such the triumph of the facts of life over the false theories of the past.

Is it, then, consistent to hold the developed woman of this day within the same narrow political limits as the dame with the spinning wheel and knitting needle occupied in the past? No, no! Machinery has taken the labors of woman as well as man on its tireless shoulders; the loom and the spinning wheel are but dreams of the past; the pen, the brush, the easel, the chisel, have taken their places, while the hopes and ambitions of women are essentially changed.

We see reason sufficient in the outer conditions of human beings for individual liberty and development, but when we consider the self-dependence of every human soul, we see the need of courage, judgment and the exercise of every faculty of mind and body, strengthened and developed by use, in woman as well as man.

Whatever may be said of man's protecting power in ordinary conditions, amid all the terrible disasters by land and sea, in the supreme moments of danger, alone woman must ever meet the horrors of the situation. The Angel of Death even makes no royal pathway for her. Man's love and sympathy enter only into the sunshine of our lives. In that solemn solitude of self, that links us with the immeasurable and the eternal, each soul lives alone forever. A recent writer says: "I remember once, in crossing the Atlantic, to have gone upon the deck of the ship at midnight, when a dense black cloud enveloped the sky, and the great deep was roaring madly under the lashes of demoniac winds. My feeling was not of danger or fear (which is a base surrender of the immortal soul) but of utter desolation and loneliness; a little speck of life shut in by a tremendous darkness. . . ."

And yet, there is a solitude which each and every one of us has always carried with him, more inaccessible than the ice-cold mountains, more profound than the midnight sea; the solitude of self. Our inner being which we call ourself, no eye nor touch of man or angel has ever pierced, it is more hidden than the caves of the gnome; the sacred adytum of the oracle; the hidden chamber of Eleusinian mystery, for to it only omniscience is permitted to enter.

Such is individual life. Who, I ask you, can take, dare take on himself the rights, the duties, the responsibilities of another human soul?

Members of the first class to admit women at the University of Rochester pose for their graduation picture in 1904; it was largely due to Susan B. Anthony's determination that the university became coeducational.

AN AWFUL HUSH

6

Elizabeth Cady Stanton's eightieth-birthday celebration at the Metropolitan Opera House in 1895 had seemed to signal the end of her career. She was immobilized by age and weight, virtually blind, and chronically short of breath. She had refused to stand for reelection as president of the National American three years earlier—Anthony had succeeded her—and she was now utterly uninterested in its day-to-day activities. In her New York apartment the day after the ceremonies, her son Robert remembered, she sat down at the piano and began to play and sing the "old, old songs of her youth."

> She seemed to be far away from us and the throngs that greeted her with so much enthusiasm . . . and was living over again the days of her youth, seeing life as it was to her sixty or seventy years ago. She finally stopped singing, not from exhaustion but as if she were overcome with emotion and the memories of her youth, and turning on her seat, with an expression of sadness on her face, and moistened eyes, said "Bob, life is a great mystery." That was all.

But just two weeks later, she published a new book, put herself back into the headlines—and plunged her oldest ally into still another unwanted controversy. *The Woman's Bible* was meant, Stanton said, as a direct challenge to the religious doctrine that woman was "an inferior being, subject to man," and it was for her a labor of love, the logical outcome of a lifetime of anger at the uses to which her male opponents had routinely put religious scripture. Her introduction set the caustic, tough-minded tone:

> [The Bible] teaches that woman brought sin and death into the world, that she precipitated the fall of the race, that she was arraigned before the judgment seat of Heaven, tried, condemned and sentenced. Marriage for her was to be a condition of bondage, maternity a period of suffering and anguish, and in silence and subjection, she was to play the role of a dependent on man's bounty for all her material wants, and for all the information she might desire on the vital questions of the hour, she was commanded to ask her husband at home. Here is the Bible position of woman all summed up.

She began the first volume—a second would follow two years later—by analyzing the first chapter of Genesis itself: "So God created man in His own image, in the image of God created He him; male and female created He them." "If language has any meaning," she wrote, "we have in these texts a plain declaration of the existence of the feminine element in the Godhead, equal in power and glory with the masculine: the Heavenly Mother and Father . . ." (The apparently contradictory story that woman had been created out of Adam's rib, Stanton continued, must have been added later by some "wily writer" determined to provide a pretext for male domination.)

In Judges, she noted, Samson's mother is identified only as the wife of a man named Manoah: "I suppose that it is from these Biblical examples that the wives of this Republic are known as Mrs. John Doe or Mrs. Richard Roe, to whatever Roe or Doe she may belong. If she chances to marry two or three times, the woman's identity is wholly lost."

In Kings, the Queen of Sheba is said to have told King Solomon "all that was on her mind." "This," Stanton wrote, "is the first account which we have in the Bible of a prolonged rational conversation with a woman on questions of public policy."

The Woman's Bible enraged the opposition. Clergymen denounced it as blasphemous, immoral, obscene. For those Americans for whom the Bible was the direct word of God, Stanton now seemed the handmaiden of Satan himself. She could not have been more pleased. "We have had hearings before Congress for 18 years . . . but no action," she wrote. "Our politicians are calm and complacent under our fire but the clergy jump round . . . like parched peas on a hot shovel."

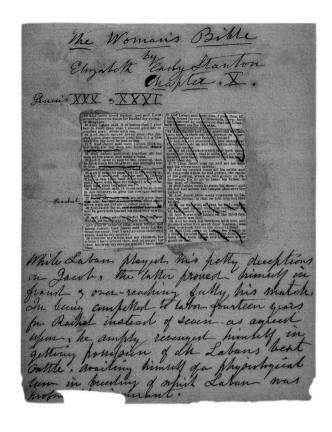

Page from Stanton's original manuscript of The Woman's Bible

Anthony and Stanton in 1900. "Well," Stanton once wrote, "as all women are supposed to be under the thumb of some man, I prefer a tyrant of my own sex, so I shall not deny the patent fact of my subjection; for I do believe that I have developed into much more of a woman under Susan's jurisdiction."

Elizabeth Cady Stanton's granddaughter Nora Stanton Blatch in an ironworking class—a course of study unthinkable for young women in her grandmother's day—at New York's Horace Mann High School in 1901

We shall some day be heeded, and . . . everybody will think it was always so, just exactly as many young people think that all the privileges, all the freedom, all the enjoyments which woman now possesses always were hers. They have no idea of how every single inch of ground that she stands upon today has been gained by the hard work of some little handful of women of the past.

SUSAN B. ANTHONY

And when a delegation of Jewish women came to call, insisting that their faith exalted women as wives and mothers, Stanton was not impressed. If that were true, she asked, why did Orthodox services begin each week with the words "I thank thee, O Lord, that I was not born a woman." That was a relatively modern interpolation, her visitors insisted; in any case, the prayer was not meant to insult or humiliate anyone.

"But it does, nevertheless," Stanton insisted. "Suppose the service read, 'I thank thee, O Lord, that I was not born a jackass.' Could that be twisted in any way into a compliment to the jackass? Oh no, ladies, the Jews afford us women no more honor than do the Gentiles."

Anthony, raised as a Quaker for whom the Bible had never been considered literally true and worried that an attack on religious orthodoxy would needlessly divide the coalition of women she had struggled to build, had refused to help Stanton with the project:

> *Stop hitting poor old St. Paul—and give your heaviest raps on the head of every Nabob—man or woman—who does injustice to a human being—for the crime of color or sex!! . . . I do wish you could center your big brain on the crimes we ourselves as a people are responsible for—to charge our offenses to false books or false interpretations—is but a way of seeking a refuge of lies.*
>
> *You say "women must be emancipated from their superstitions before enfranchisement will be of any benefit," and I say just the reverse, that women must be enfranchised before they can be emancipated from their superstitions. . . .*

Now Anthony's worst fears about the impact of her friend's provocative book on the movement they had once led together were confirmed. At the annual convention of the National American in Washington, Stanton's critics offered a resolution officially dissociating the group from her and her controversial ideas. "This association is non-sectarian," it read, "being composed of persons of all shadows of religious opinions, and has no official connection with the so-called *Woman's Bible*, or any theological publication."

Among those who favored the resolution were many of the younger delegates whom Anthony called her nieces. Anthony may have wished *The Woman's Bible* had never been published, but just before the vote she stepped down from the chair to defend her old friend one last time.

> *This resolution . . . will be a vote of censure upon a woman who is without a peer in intellectual and statesmanlike ability; one who has stood for half a century the acknowledged leader of progressive thought . . . in regard to all matters pertaining to the absolute freedom of woman. . . . When our platform becomes too narrow for people of all creeds and of no creeds, I myself shall not stand upon it. . . . I shall be pained beyond expression if the delegates . . . are so narrow and illib-*

*eral as to adopt this resolution. You [had] better not begin resolving against indi-
vidual action or you will find no limit. This year it is Mrs. Stanton; next year it
may be me or one of yourselves who will be the victim.*

In the end, not even Anthony could sway the delegates. They voted 53 to 41 officially to separate themselves from the woman who had launched their movement.

Stanton was hurt and angry. "Much as I desire the suffrage," she wrote, "I would
rather never vote than to see the policy of our government at the mercy of the
religious bigotry of such women." She wanted Anthony to resign the presidency
in protest, just as, forty-two years earlier, Anthony had resigned from the New
York State Women's Temperance Society when its members had voted to oust
Stanton from the presidency of that body. Anthony agonized for three weeks,
torn between loyalty to her oldest friend and to the organization to which they'd
both devoted their lives, but she finally decided to remain in office. "No, my
dear," she wrote Stanton; "instead of my resigning and leaving those half-fledged
chickens without any mother, I think it my duty, and the duty of yourself and
all the liberals to be at the next convention and try to reverse this miserable
narrow action."

Stanton was not easily mollified. She was now sometimes privately envious of
the laurels Anthony's young disciples were piling at her feet. "If my suffrage coadjutors had ever treated me with the boundless generosity they have my friend
Susan," she wrote, "I could have scattered my writings abundantly, from Maine

*"The apotheosis of Liberty,"
pen-and-ink drawing pub-
lished just after the 1896
National American Woman
Suffrage Association
Convention in the nation's
capital. George Washington
is at the center, flanked by
Anthony and Stanton, who
holds* The Woman's Bible
*from which the delegates had
just disassociated themselves.*

*Successors: Anna Howard
Shaw (opposite, above)
and Carrie Chapman Catt
(right)*

to Louisiana." Above all, she was tired of subsuming everything to the single cause of suffrage. "Miss Anthony has one idea and she has no patience with anyone who has two," she told a friend. "I cannot . . . sing suffrage anymore; I am deeply interested in all the questions of the day."

When Anthony wrote Stanton requesting "an argument, strong resolutions and tributes to those of our band who have died during the present year" for the next National American convention, Stanton's irritation was obvious. "One would think I were a machine that all I had to do was turn a crank and thoughts on any theme would bubble up like water," she complained to a friend. "I replied: 'Dear Susan, is it not time that some of your younger coadjutors do the bubbling?' The fact is that I am tired of bubbling on one subject. . . . In fact I have become a sort of spiritual undertaker for the pioneers of the woman suffrage movement. How much longer must I embalm the dead and weave wreaths of immortelles for the living, dwelling on their graces, virtues, and historic deeds?"

In 1900, Susan B. Anthony resigned as president of the National American. She was eighty years old and did not wish to die in office, she told the delegates, preferring instead to "see you all at work while I am alive, so I can scold you if you do not do it well." She had arranged the succession with characteristic tough-mindedness. The Reverend Anna Howard Shaw, a fine orator and personally the closest to Anthony of all her honorary nieces, had hoped to be chosen as her successor. But Anthony had also worked with Carrie Chapman Catt, whose skills at organizing and fund-raising had helped win the vote in Colorado, and she knew that it was those skills, not oratory, that the National American needed most. "In Mrs. Catt," she told the convention, "you have my ideal leader. I present you my successor."

"Miss Anthony," Catt responded, "will never have a successor."

By then Elizabeth Cady Stanton's eyesight was gone—a young woman came regularly to read aloud to her—but her mind remained as lively as it had ever been. "I am a leader of thought rather than numbers," she wrote. "I would rather be a free-lance, to say my say as opportunity offers as an individual than to speak as president of an Association."

Opportunity offered often. Stanton's views were sought on every sort of topic, and she rarely disappointed. She deplored the trend of wearing long trains that dragged through the mud, she told one reporter: "If a woman has a nicely shaped foot and a well-fitting boot, it is a much prettier sight than yards of silk filled with microbes." When war with Spain came in 1898, she professed to be delighted: "Though I hate war *per se*, I am glad that it has come in this instance. I would like to see Spain and Turkey swept from the face of the earth. They are a disgrace to the civilization of the nineteenth century." Once victory was won and the country began debating whether or not America should create an empire, she

Stanton in her New York City apartment. "As my eyes grow dimmer from day to day, my intellectual vision grows clearer," she confided to her diary in 1897. "But I have written Susan not to lay out any more work for me, but to call on our younger coadjutors to write the letters to senators and congressmen. Say to them, I write, that 'it requires no courage now to talk of suffrage; they should demand equality everywhere.'"

Carry Nation, here under arrest after smashing up a Kansas saloon, won Stanton's applause.

came out four-square for expansion: "What would this continent have been if we had left it to the Indians? I have no sympathy with all the pessimistic twaddle about the Philippines." And when Carry Nation began breaking up Kansas saloons, Stanton was jubilant: "I wish we had ten thousand 'Madame Nations,' smashing the gilded mirrors and ornaments in the haunts of vice in every state of the Union." In a single week in 1901, Stanton had seven articles in seven different newspapers, as well as two longer pieces in monthly magazines. "In a word," she proudly noted in her journal, "I am always busy, which is perhaps the chief reason why I am always well."

"We have grown a little apart since not so closely associated as of old," Anthony admitted privately of her friendship with Stanton. "She thinks the church is now the enemy to fight—and feels worried that I stay back with the children—as she says—instead of going ahead with her." But she and Stanton never broke with each other, and when she found herself in New York in June of 1902, she made it a point to call at her friend's apartment. It seemed like old times, and when Anthony was ready to leave, she embraced Stanton and began to weep.

"Shall I see you again?" she asked.

"Oh yes," Stanton answered, "if not here, then in the hereafter, if there is one—and if there isn't we shall never know it."

They agreed that Anthony would return for Stanton's eighty-seventh birthday in November. She went home to Rochester and wrote her friend a letter.

My dear Mrs. Stanton,

I shall indeed be happy to spend with you November 12, the day on which you round out your four-score and seven, over four years ahead of me, but in age as in all else I follow you closely. It is fifty-one years since we first met and we have been busy through every one of them, stirring up the world to recognize the rights of women. The older we grow, the more keenly we feel the humiliation of disfranchisement. . . .

We little dreamed when we began this contest, optimistic with the hope and buoyancy of youth, that half a century later we would be compelled to leave the finish of the battle to another generation of women. But our hearts are filled with joy to know that they enter upon this task equipped with a college education, with business experience, with the fully admitted right to speak in public—all of which were denied to women fifty years ago. They have practically but one point to gain—the suffrage; we had all. These strong, courageous, capable young women will take our place and complete our work. There is an army of them where we were but a handful. Ancient prejudice has become so softened, public sentiment so liberalized and women have so thoroughly demonstrated their ability as to leave not a shadow of doubt that they will carry our cause to victory.

And we, dear friend, shall move on to the next sphere of existence—higher and larger, we cannot fail to believe, and one where women will not be placed in an inferior position but will be welcomed on a plane of perfect intellectual and spiritual equality.

Ever lovingly yours,
Susan B. Anthony

On Sunday morning, October 26, 1902, Elizabeth Cady Stanton asked her daughter Harriot to help her dress and arrange her hair as if she were about to make a public appearance. "I placed a table for her to rest her hands on," her daughter recalled. "She drew herself up very erect . . . and there she stood seven or eight minutes, steadily looking out proudly before her. I think she was mentally making an address. When we urged her to sit down she fell asleep."

The next day, a Western Union messenger knocked at the door of Susan B. Anthony's Rochester home. Her secretary carried the telegram up to her employer's room. Anthony read it silently: "Mother passed away at three o'clock. Harriot." Her hands dropped to her lap.

As the news spread, reporters descended on her for a statement. "I cannot express myself at all as I feel," she told one of them. "If I had died first she would have found beautiful phrases to describe our friendship, but I cannot put it into words." Still, she did her best to accommodate her visitors. "To see poor Miss Anthony," a friend recalled, "questioned over and over about her early times with her dead friend and climbing up to the attic to find a picture for the reporter with her hand shaking so that she could hardly lift the cards, was a piteous thing."

She was on the train to New York City the next day for the funeral. "It is an awful hush," she wrote a friend from the Stanton apartment; "it seems impossible—that the voice is hushed that I longed to hear for fifty years—longed to hear her opinion of things—before I knew exactly where I stood—It is all at sea—but the laws of nature are still going on. . . . What a world it is—it goes right on and on—no matter who lives or who dies!!"

Elizabeth Cady Stanton had planned her funeral in advance. "I should like to be in my ordinary dress," she'd said, "no crepe or black, no fripperies or fandangos . . . and some common-sense women to conduct the services." As Stanton had requested, it was a private event over which women presided. But the mahogany table on which Stanton had written the Declaration of Sentiments that launched the suffrage movement stood at the head of her casket, and on the casket itself, surrounded by flowers, stood a framed photograph of the woman who had been her constant goad, her close friend, and most effective ally.

Susan B. Anthony's portrait atop Elizabeth Cady Stanton's flower-covered casket; and (top left) a newspaper clipping from one of the scrapbooks Anthony reverently kept

FAILURE IS IMPOSSIBLE

Susan B. Anthony soldiered on as she always had, alone. She had outlived all of her siblings except her younger sister Mary. Younger women were at least nominally in charge of the suffrage movement now, though when Carrie Chapman Catt was forced to resign from the National American's presidency in 1904 in order to care for her ailing husband, Anthony was still influential enough to see to it that the job went to the woman who had been her second choice four years earlier, the Reverend Anna Howard Shaw.

After she had suffered a second stroke in 1900, Anthony's doctors advised her to curtail her constant journeying. She paid no attention: "I feel that it would be just as well if I reached the end on the cars or anywhere else as at home." She continued to travel—to Oregon, to London, and to Berlin to attend a conference that called for woman suffrage all around the world and was, she said, "the climax of my career." She took pleasure in the near universal affection with which she was now received wherever she went. "Once I was the most hated and reviled of women," she marveled; "now it seems as if everybody loves me."

In 1902, she appeared for the last time before the Senate Select Committee on Woman Suffrage and indulged in a rare moment of bitterness. Only she survived of all the women who had petitioned the Senate in 1869, she told her listeners, "and I shall not be able to come much longer . . .

We have waited; we stood aside for the Negro; we waited for the millions of immigrants; now we must wait till the Hawaiians, the Filipinos and the Puerto Ricans [are] enfranchised; then no doubt the Cubans will have their turn. For all these ignorant, alien peoples educated American-born women have been compelled to stand aside and wait! How long will this injustice, this outrage continue?

Anthony, seated before the American flag at the table on the right, attends a banquet at the International Council of Women at Berlin in 1904. To have witnessed the women's movement spread across the globe, she said, "is the climax of my career."

Young suffragists in Oregon shade Anthony, eighty-five, and Anna Howard Shaw from the sun at the 1905 unveiling of a statue of Sacagawea, the Shoshone woman who had accompanied the Lewis and Clark expedition to the Pacific a century before. Anthony was especially pleased to take part, she said, since "This is the first statue erected in this country to a woman because of deeds of daring."

In January of 1906, despite dizzy spells and shortness of breath, she determined to attend the annual National American convention at Baltimore. She had missed just one meeting since the Civil War, and this time a host of college graduates had been invited to speak as a demonstration of the steady advancement of American women—and to endorse woman suffrage.

She couldn't bear not to be there. A howling blizzard gripped Rochester as she left for the train station, and she developed a cold. She arrived exhausted, racked by neuralgia, too weak to attend most of the sessions but still determined to accomplish things. As always, she remained anxious about the movement's finances and managed from her sickbed to persuade the presidents of Bryn Mawr and Johns Hopkins to take responsibility for raising a standing fund.

On February 15, her eighty-sixth birthday, she boarded a train for Washington, where still more friends and admirers wanted to hold a celebration in her honor. Tributes poured in from everywhere, including a carefully worded message from President Theodore Roosevelt conveying his "hearty good wishes for the continuation of her useful and honorable life." It did not impress Susan B. Anthony. "I wish the men would do something besides extend congratulations . . . ," she said. "I would rather have him say a word to Congress in favor of amending the Constitution to give women suffrage than to praise me endlessly."

At the end of an evening of unstinting praise, Anthony was finally allowed to make her frail way to the podium to thank the delegates for all the kind things that had been said about her. Before she could begin, the members of the audience stood and applauded for more than ten minutes. Anna Howard Shaw helped her remain on her feet.

Anthony seemed to know it was likely to be her last speech.

This is a magnificent sight before me, and these have been wonderful addresses and speeches I have listened to during the past week. Yet I have looked on so many such audiences, all testifying to the righteousness, the justice, and the worthiness of the cause of woman suffrage. I never saw that great woman, Mary Wollstonecraft, but I have read her eloquent and unanswerable arguments on behalf of the liberty of womankind. I have met and known most of the progressive women who came after her—Lucretia Mott, the Grimké sisters, Elizabeth Cady Stanton, Lucy Stone—a long galaxy of great women. . . . There have been others also just as true and devoted to the cause—I wish I could name every one—but with such women consecrating their lives . . . Failure is impossible!

Two days later, she returned home to Rochester, accompanied by her sister Mary and a nurse. It was a full day before she felt strong enough to climb the stairs to her room. She would never leave it. Double pneumonia now gripped her lungs. Anna Howard Shaw hurried to her side. "Just think," Anthony told Shaw, "I have been striving for over sixty years for a little bit of justice no bigger than that, and yet I must die without obtaining it. . . . It seems so cruel." She drifted in and out of consciousness, sometimes mumbling the names of suffragists she'd known. "They are still passing before me," Shaw remembered her whispering toward the end, "face after face, hundreds and hundreds of them. . . . I know how hard they have worked. I know the sacrifices they have made."

At 12:40 a.m. on Tuesday, March 13, 1906, Susan B. Anthony died. Ten thousand mourners came to Rochester for her funeral, then followed her cortege from the Central Presbyterian Church to the cemetery, where she was laid to rest alongside the parents who had first encouraged her to believe that she could become an independent woman.

Several years earlier, at a family reunion in Adams, Massachusetts, so many carriages had tied up in front of Susan B. Anthony's old home that someone said it reminded them of a funeral. She had turned to her family then and made a request: "When it *is* a funeral," she said, "remember that I want there should be no tears. Pass on, and go on with the work."

The last known photograph of Susan B. Anthony, taken upon her arrival at Baltimore in 1906. "You often seem to me like a superb warhorse," Harriot Stanton had once written to her. "You are completely swallowed up in an idea, and it's a glorious thing to be. Carlyle says, 'The end of man is an Action, not a Thought,' and what a realization of that truth has your life been. You have never stopped for idle culture or happy recreations. You are possessed by a moral force and you act. You are a Deed, not a Thinking."

Ellen Carol DuBois

A Friendship Through History

For Elizabeth Cady Stanton's gala seventieth birthday, her daughter Harriot, who was living in England, sent her mother these birthday greetings: "Kiss dear Susan for me and let her kiss you too for me. On the 12th of November I shall think of you both, for you two are not easily separated in my mind. . . . You ought to be overflowing with gratitude for each other's existence, for neither without the other would have achieved the work you have accomplished. Let your hearts praise the good fortune that brought you together every day of your lives. Friendship is the grandest relation in the world."

A decade later, in two long chapters of her autobiography dedicated to Susan B. Anthony, Elizabeth Cady Stanton lovingly described their friendship: "In thought and sympathy we were one, and in the division of labor we exactly complemented each other . . . together, we have made arguments that have stood unshaken through the storms of long years. . . . Our speeches may be considered the united product of our two brains." The affection was thoroughly mutual. In 1902, when Stanton died, Anthony wrote of her profound loss: "It seems impossible that the voice is hushed that I have longed to hear for fifty years, longed to hear her opinions of things before I knew exactly where I stood."

Why is it, then, that this friendship, so strong in the lives of Susan B. Anthony and Elizabeth Cady Stanton, has been largely lost to history? Why is it that Anthony, shorn of her political partner, has come down to subsequent generations as a lone figure, solitary in her commitment to woman suffrage, the singular historical embodiment of the movement that these two friends always thought of as the joint product of their half-century collaboration? The

answer lies in what happened to their bond in the years after their deaths, and in the dramatically different paths that their historical reputations took in the hands of twentieth-century feminists and historians entrusted with their memories. Undoubtedly, they would not have wanted their histories to be so separated. By posthumously severing their tie, subsequent generations are deprived of the fullness of their common legacy.

During their lifetimes, Stanton and Anthony disagreed often—over whether to suspend their women's-rights agitation during the Civil War, over whether to trust the flamboyant upstart Victoria Woodhull to help the cause of woman suffrage, over whether to cultivate suffrage sentiment among the conventional Christian women of the women's temperance movement. But their personal and political bond had always been strong enough to allow for their differences. Their supporters and followers were not as tolerant.

In 1895, Stanton published *The Woman's Bible*, which many of Anthony's devotees considered disrespectful of mainstream Protestantism. Anthony tried but failed to prevent her old friend from being censured and exiled to the fringes of the organized suffrage movement for her apostasy. By this time, Anthony was in quite a different situation. She was receiving public admiration and respect—often from the same moderate suffragists who criticized Stanton—which had been denied her all those long years when she had been reviled as the embodiment of strong-minded suffragism. The same year that Stanton was censured, Anthony was compared by a Chicago minister to Washington and Lincoln. He predicted that the name Susan B. Anthony would eventually "take its place among the martyrs and saints of liberty." Modest as she was, Susan could not help but enjoy these encomiums; and as much as she loved her friend, Elizabeth resented her own comparative isolation. Young suffragists "have given Susan thousands of dollars, jewels, laces, silks and satins," she complained bitterly to a friend, "and me criticisms for my radical ideas."

Underlying these different responses were divergent political paths that the two old friends were following. By the end of her career, after so many failed alliances, Anthony had come to believe that suffragists must single-mindedly pursue women's political rights; no other issue must be allowed to intrude on the primacy of woman suffrage. Stanton, for her part, believed more strongly than ever that woman suffrage must be linked to a broad vision, both of women's emancipation and of social justice. By the 1890s, she was beginning to talk about socialism, as well as to criticize Christianity. Her vision of women's emancipation looked far beyond woman suffrage to the distant horizon of women's full "self-sovereignty," to a lifting of "women's social and religious bondage" as well as their disfranchisement.

After their deaths, these perspectives, by which Stanton and Anthony had enriched each other over the long years of their collaboration, became separated, even counterpoised, in the minds of their followers. Especially during the last phases of the drive for woman suffrage, when overcoming the final political obstacles to votes for women required extraordinary devotion and concentrated commitment, Stanton's "many idea'd feminism" dropped out of suffragism's collective memory. Instead, Anthony's single-mindedness became the lone standard of devotion to women's political empowerment. One could not be fully devoted to suffrage, it seemed, and to other political visions and goals as well.

The Anthony cult was begun by Anna Howard Shaw, minister and temperance advocate, who served as third president of the National American Woman Suffrage Association. Of all the second-generation suffragists, Shaw had been personally the closest to Anthony. Even so, when it came time for Anthony to retire and pick her successor, Anthony skipped over Shaw in favor of Carrie Chapman Catt, whose organizing skills offered more to suffragism than Shaw's oratorical abilities. When Shaw succeeded to the presidency in 1904, she dramatized her privileged relationship with Anthony to hold on to power. Shaw claimed that as Anthony lay dying, with virtually her last breath, she had begged her young follower to "keep the presidency of the association as long as you are well enough to do 'the work.'" Anna Howard Shaw kept the presidency until 1915.

Shaw's claim to exert sole control over Anthony's memory did not go unchallenged. During her presidency of the organization, the votes-for-women movement split into two rival camps. Shaw led the larger, moderate group, while Alice Paul headed a younger and more militant faction. Twenty years Shaw's junior, Paul had never met Susan B. Anthony, but this did not stop her from claiming that she, not Anna Howard Shaw, was the true inheritor of the great woman's mantle of leadership. She was quick to point out that, like Anthony, she was a Quaker. Like Anthony, she believed in suffrage "single-mindedly." And as if to prove some divine quality to their bond, she noted that their birthdays were only one day apart. In 1914, Paul and her militant followers began

Elizabeth Cady Stanton

to refer to the pending woman-suffrage addition to the U.S. Constitution as "the Susan B. Anthony Amendment." The label, which ignored Stanton's role in first introducing this version of the amendment in 1878, stuck.

In laying historical claim to Anthony's memory, subsequent generations of feminists did not always do justice to her legacy. Nowhere was this more the case than with respect to the politics of racial justice. In the 1850s, Anthony had been a dedicated abolitionist and had traveled around New York and New England speaking on behalf both of women's rights and antislavery. In the years following the Civil War, when the Constitution was being revised to ensure the permanent abolition of slavery and equal rights to the former slaves, she and Stanton had pushed mightily to have the Constitution prohibit disfranchisement on the basis of "sex" as well as "race, color, or previous condition of servitude." They failed, and in response, broke with their former allies in the abolitionist movement, in an acrimonious and painful bid to make the woman-suffrage cause an independent movement.

In the heat of the moment, Anthony and especially Stanton, who disparaged black men's new political rights, were not without blame through this historic conflict, but Anthony's political descendants ignored the complexities of this episode in favor of a single lesson from the past. Speaking as if in Anthony's name, they declared that women demanding their own enfranchisement had suffered the greatest of all humiliations when African-American men had won suffrage before them; and that the rule to be derived was that all "men's politics" should be

Susan B. Anthony

avoided lest they lead women in pursuit of their own rights astray.

It is hard to imagine that Anthony would have gone along with these conclusions. Over the years, she looked to various "men's" political parties—in the 1890s it was the radical Populists—for help in winning woman suffrage. And despite the grievous disappointments of the 1860s, she remained a committed antiracist till the end of her life. She would have probably objected to the use of her name to continue to drive a wedge between the struggles for racial and gender justice. African-American women had good reason when they appealed to her memory for historical inspiration. In 1921, when a group of African-American suffragists wanted to call attention to the mounting obstacles they faced in enjoying de facto the right to vote that they just been granted de jure, they named themselves the Women's Anthony League in her honor.

One factor contributing to the historical elevation of Anthony's memory over Stanton's was Anthony's childlessness. For subsequent generations of feminists, looking for an authoritative ancestor for their convictions, Susan B. Anthony came to serve as "The Mother of Us All" (the title of Gertrude Stein's 1940s opera about Anthony). Stanton, of course, had descendants aplenty, and they had a proprietary interest in their mother's memory. Among her seven children, the two who became feminist activists, Harriot Stanton Blatch and Theodore Stanton, were particularly determined to control her historical reputation.

Soon after their mother's death, Theodore and Harriot began editing a collection of Stanton's letters to serve as a record of her life. But by the time they finally published their "epistolary autobiography," Stanton's memory was already being eclipsed by that of Anthony. Harriot had her own suspicions about why Anthony had been elevated to the suffrage pantheon without her lifelong partner. Unlike Anthony, she observed, her mother had subscribed to various "heresies," such as free love and free thought. Harriot was convinced that later guardians of the suffrage legacy, intent on keeping its prestige "pure," had seen to it that Stanton's provocative ideas were deleted from their movement's history.

Harriot, a suffrage leader in her own right, shared her mother's expansive approach to feminist militancy. Once women were armed with the vote, she believed, they needed to work for peace, for children's rights, for birth control, and for their own economic empowerment. In 1920, just as the Nineteenth Amendment, finally granting women the right to vote, was being ratified, Harriot joined the Socialist Party, claiming that she was following Elizabeth Cady Stanton's precedent. "My mother," she explained, "could not conceive of suffrage as standing by itself, as an issue unrelated to other issues. For her it was inseparable from the antislavery agitation, from women's demand for entry into the field of labor, into the universities and professions. Later when she saw how narrow the American suffrage movement had become, she was much disturbed."

Harriot's ideas about how women should use their new political power conflicted with Alice Paul's conviction that feminism could be carried forward only by a "single issue" strategy. With the Nineteenth Amendment secured, Paul proposed another highly focused constitutional campaign, this time for an Equal Rights Amendment, which she believed would obliterate all remaining legal discriminations against women. To inaugurate the campaign, in 1923 Paul planned a seventy-fifth-anniversary commemoration of the first women's-rights convention, which Elizabeth Cady Stanton had organized in Seneca Falls, New York, in 1848. Yet Harriot did not share Paul's enthusiasm for the ERA. And unlike Susan B.

Anthony, whose historical authority was everyone's to claim, Harriot got to say how the memory of Elizabeth Cady Stanton could be used.

Thus, when Harriot looked into the plans for the Seneca Falls celebration, she was horrified to discover that they were proceeding as if her mother had had nothing to do with the original event. In all the precelebration publicity, Elizabeth Cady Stanton's name went virtually unmentioned. Instead, everyone was under the false impression that Anthony—who had not even met Stanton or learned about women's rights until 1851—had called the 1848 convention. Harriot was furious and demanded that her mother be given her due. "You may admire above all women Mary Queen of Scots and I Queen Elizabeth," she complained. "But . . . when you take off the belongings of my queen and dress your queen up in them it is a high offense." Her protests did little good. In 1936, Susan B. Anthony was still mistakenly being given the credit for writing the 1848 Seneca Falls Declaration of Sentiments.

In a final bid to revive her mother's reputation, Harriot arranged for "a very aggressive biography . . . a stirring, fighting volume." Although Anthony already had three biographies, this was to be the first full account of the life of Elizabeth Cady Stanton. Harriot was deeply resentful, if not at Anthony, at the way her memory was being used to obliterate that of Elizabeth Stanton. Her response was to belittle the historical figure of Susan B. Anthony whenever she could. Intent as she was on correcting the stubborn misapprehension that Anthony was "the only leader in those early days," she showered her mother's biographer, Alma Lutz, with notes about Stanton's "infinite superiority" and "unusual brain power." Hers was yet another posthumous attack on the memory of the Stanton-Anthony friendship. Everyone involved, it seemed, wanted to preserve the historical legacy of each woman at the expense of the other.

By the middle of the twentieth century, few remembered and even fewer honored the dramatic, seventy-five-year battle for women's votes. There are many reasons for the precipitous decline in the historical reputation of the woman-suffrage movement. After 1920, women took to voting comfortably if not energetically. Over the next few decades, the extravagant claims that suffragists had made for the uplifting and democratizing impact of female enfranchisement on the American political process seemed so much empty rhetoric. Postsuffrage generations of women had their own expanded vistas, but they were private and individualistic rather than political and collective; and the solidarity of sex so important to the suffragists did not inspire them. Economic depression, two world wars, and the anxious return to domestic "normalcy" in the 1950s proved barren ground for the growth of feminist sympathies. In the midst of World War II, Carrie Chapman Catt sadly predicted that "the women's movement will be forgotten and almost buried in the great tragedies that have succeeded it."

Through the decades during which public knowledge of the woman-suffrage movement faded to the vanishing point, a handful of feminists tried in vain to nurture the memory of Susan B. Anthony. Throughout the 1930s and 1940s, they tracked down and preserved all sorts of Anthony memorabilia—letters, books, reminiscences, even locks of hair—and came up with ways to memorialize their heroine. In California, they had a giant sequoia tree named after her, and the U.S. Postal Service issued a stamp with her likeness. But like the Susan B. Anthony dollar minted fifty years later, instead of stemming the tide of forgetfulness, these gestures only worked to underline Anthony's historical irrelevance and to confirm her diminished historical status. Rather than functioning as a stirring memory, the figure of Susan B. Anthony had come to be regarded as a historical joke. The single-mindedness with which her memory was identified seemed, without the breadth of vision on which Stanton had insisted, fanatical rather than forward-looking, obsessive rather than inspir-

ing. It is just possible that if Stanton and Anthony had been remembered together, their historical legacy might have had a bit more staying power.

In the late 1960s, feminism was rediscovered, and along with it the history of the woman-suffrage movement. Women looking toward new dimensions of female emancipation needed the legitimacy of predecessors, foremothers, a tradition. In this context, Stanton and Anthony were revived in their mutual legacy. Writing in 1963 to housebound women who were discontent with the "Feminine Mystique," Betty Friedan declared that Anthony was not the "bitter spinster" of popular history but an accomplished activist who shared a lifelong commitment to women's emancipation with her "spirited" companion Elizabeth Cady Stanton. A few years later, the youthful radical Shulamith Firestone, spokeswoman for the women of "the sixties generation," offered the same lesson from the past. Women needed to know what had too long been forgotten: that the early women's-rights movement had been unflinching in its attacks on women's subordination "in the Family, in the Church, and in the State," and that Elizabeth Cady Stanton and Susan B. Anthony had been that movement's "most militant feminists."

Will we forget these two women again? There is that danger. When feminist victories are won, we get used to them very quickly. It is as if women had always been educated, always voted, always had the right to expect equality in the labor force, always had the right to expect equality in their family lives. But the truth is that each of these rights was fought for long and hard and by many generations of women that came before us. Each of these victories—and each of the future dimensions to women's emancipation that we cannot yet really imagine—require breadth of vision combined with depth of dedication. This is what the memory of Stanton and Anthony best stand for, and why their joint history can always be such a rich resource for a better future.

Epilogue

Winter Wheat

It would take American women fourteen more years to realize the dream of Elizabeth Cady Stanton and Susan B. Anthony—fourteen years during which the women of Australia, Finland, Norway, the newly created Soviet Union, Canada, Germany, Great Britain, Austria, Poland, and Czechoslovakia all won the vote.

"To get the word male out of the Constitution cost the women of the country . . . years of pauseless campaigning," Carrie Chapman Catt wrote when victory was finally theirs. "Hundreds of women gave the accumulated possibilities of an entire lifetime, thousands gave interest and such aid as they could. It was a continuous, seemingly endless chain of activity. Young suffragists who helped forge the last links of that chain were not born when it began. Old suffragists who forged the first links were dead when it ended."

Generations: Elizabeth Cady Stanton's daughter Harriot Stanton Blatch, in the back seat, and granddaughter Nora Blatch de Forest, behind the wheel, take their struggle to the streets of New York City in 1908.

Cincinnati suffragists spread the word, 1912.

"What can be done to strike these dull minds and awaken them to the deep significance of our agitation?" Stanton asked shortly before her death. "Something sensational." By the spring of 1912, ten years after her death, twenty thousand suffragists, dressed in white to demonstrate their unity and discipline, were marching up Fifth Avenue in New York City and more (top right) lobbied delegates to the National Democratic Convention in Baltimore.

Of one thing suffrage opponents could be certain, Elizabeth Cady Stanton had warned, the next generation would not display "the infinite patience we have for half a century." Many members of that new generation found the National American too slow, too sedate. They formed their own organizations and began marching in the streets.

When conventional suffragists worried that by so doing they would expose the movement to ridicule, Harriot Stanton Blatch was unmoved. "Ridicule, ridicule, ridicule," she said, "blessed be ridicule." And when America entered World War I, suffragists refused to put aside their cause as their forebears had done during the Civil War. Ninety-six members of the militant National Woman's Party, led by its president, Alice Paul, picketed the White House. Jailed for "obstructing traffic," some were manhandled and force-fed when they refused to eat.

Meanwhile, Carrie Chapman Catt, Anthony's hand-picked successor as president of the National American, continued to pursue what she called her "winning plan"—a long-term strategy by which she hoped first to secure suffrage in at least thirty-six states (the number needed to ratify a Federal Amendment) and then to organize women voters into an irresistible force behind it.

Washington police wrest banners from suffragists marching near the White House during World War I.

In the spring of 1919, the House and Senate finally passed the Nineteenth Amendment. Suffragists still had to persuade thirty-six states to ratify.

By midsummer of 1920, everything came down to Tennessee. Victory in the state senate came easily, but no one was sure what would happen in the house.

Roses filled the chamber for the vote on August 18: yellow for suffrage, red for those opposed to it. The Antis moved to table the amendment and lost. As the fateful roll call began, suffragists needed one more vote to win—and had no idea where it might come from.

Harry Burn from McKinn County, at twenty-four, was the youngest man in the legislature. He entered the chamber with a red rose in his buttonhole, which seemed to signal one more vote for the Antis. But he also carried folded in his pocket a letter from his mother:

> Dear son . . .
> Vote for suffrage and don't keep them in doubt. I notice some of the speeches against. They were very bitter. I have been watching to see how you stood, but have not seen anything yet. Don't forget to be a good boy . . .
>
> With lots of love,
> Mama

When the roll call reached him, he voted to ratify. Suffragists in the balcony exploded in cheers. Seventy-two years of struggle were finally over.

Asked to explain himself later he simply said, "I know that a mother's advice is always safest for a boy to follow."

That fall, for the first time in history, American women would go to the polls in every precinct in America. Only the oldest among them could remember the two extraordinary women who had done more than anyone else to make it possible.

Mother knows best: Febb E. Burn (above), whose letter persuaded her son to cast his momentous vote. Harry Burn himself (right), on the lowest step, and other legislators receiving thanks from suffragists.

To mark the victory, suffragist leader Alice Paul, president of the National Woman's Party, unfurls a suffrage flag from the balcony of its headquarters in Washington, D.C. Each star represents a state that voted for ratification.

Acknowledgments

Like Elizabeth Cady Stanton and Susan B. Anthony, who marshalled the help and support of a vast army of coworkers across the country to aid them in their cause, we came to depend upon the hard work of many other people in the making of this book and documentary film.

Buddy Squires and Allen Moore—assisted by Roger Haydock—filmed the Stanton and Anthony homes as well as the environs of the Genesee Country Village and Museum (our stand-in for nineteenth-century Seneca Falls and Rochester, New York) with exquisite care and a keen eye for detail. Susanna Steisel faced the daunting task of compiling photographs to evoke a story for which few documented "action" photos exist, and came up with stunning solutions at every juncture. Sarah Hill, for whom this film was her first major project, did a masterful job of editing—ably assisted by Peter Smith and Christine Rose Lyon.

Extra-special thanks must go to our nineteen-year-old, fresh-out-of-high-school assistant to the producer, David Waingarten, who lugged equipment, helped set up film shoots, ran errands, organized and scheduled voice recordings, researched historical documents for script revisions, wrote letters to help secure stock footage and music rights, etc., etc., etc. Dave's spirit and enthusiasm kept us all going. Without Dave there would be no film.

Thanks to our own field soldiers in the cause at Florentine Films—Pam Tubridy Baucom, Brenda Heath, Patty Lawlor, Susan Yeaton Butler, Aaron Vega, and Craig Mellish, all of whom helped out in indispensible ways. And to our interns without whose help we would not have survived—Heather Autry, Christian Imperato, Jessica LaClair, Matthew L. McGrail, Mary Lynn Ring, and Tim Clark, who went on to lend his talents as postproduction assistant.

We are deeply grateful for the knowledge, advice, and insights of all of our consultants and interviewees who have worked so hard to rescue this story from the dustbin of history—Elisabeth Griffith, Kathleen Barry, Ellen Carol DuBois, Lynn Sherr, Judith Wellman, Sally Roesch Wagner, and especially Ann Gordon, whose good sense and good humor always kept us on the right track. When completed, her superb ongoing twenty-year compilation of the papers of Stanton and Anthony (undertaken in collaboration with Pat Holland) will provide historians and biographers with the material they need for a fuller understanding of these two remarkable women. Anyone interested in supporting this project can send a check—payable to Rutgers University Foundation— to Ann D. Gordon, History Department, 16 Seminary Place, Rutgers University, New Brunswick, NJ 08901-1108.

When the film was first conceived, back in 1988, we were faced with the task of casting the voices of our heroines. Our first choices were Ronnie Gilbert for Stanton and Julie Harris for Anthony. Luckily for us, they both agreed and then proceeded to deliver two of the most beautiful voice performances to grace any of the films we've made. Their consummate artistry was augmented by Sally Kellerman's splendid reading of the narration, and the superb work of Adam Arkin, Tim Clark, Wendy Conquest, Kevin Conway, Keith David, Ann Dowd, Ann Duquesnay, Charles Durning, Carolyn McCormick, Amy Madigan, and George Plimpton.

Special thanks to Stanton's great-granddaughter Rhoda Barney Jenkins, who opened to us the family's private collection of photographs and papers, and to Rhoda's daughter and son, Coline Jenkins-Sahlin and Morgan Jenkins, for their support.

Much of the story of Stanton and Anthony unfolded against the backdrop of upstate New York, and we are grateful for the help of its kind and generous people. In Seneca Falls, we would like to thank the staff of the Seneca Falls Historical Society, especially the indefatigable Frances Barbieri, who was always there with whatever we needed, and the Society's temporary director, Carolyn Zogg. Members of the staff of the Women's Rights National Historical Park offered invaluable help, especially rangers Mary Ellen Snyder, Felicia Moss, and Leroy Renniger, who guided us through the Stanton home and were a font of information in helping to furnish and film the individual rooms. Special thanks to the National Park Service and to park director Joanne M. Hanley for giving us access to the site and allowing us to bring furniture into the Stanton house. Park historian Vivien Rose gave us invaluable help, as well. Thanks also to Francis and Gail Caraccilo of the Urban Cultural Park and Sarah Suggs and Mary Gratton of the Women's Hall of Fame for their advice and for opening their archives to us.

In Rochester, we are very grateful to the staff of the Susan B. Anthony House, especially executive director Lorie Barnum and archivist Judy Emerson for their permission, guidance, and help in filming the individual rooms and the photo collection; to historian Colleen Hurst for her insights into Anthony's character and career; and to Libby Moore and Cindy Rosenbloom for helping in numerous ways to make our work there easier. The Rochester Museum and Science Center was an important source of Anthony photos and artifacts and we were well taken care of there by Leatrice Kemp, Victoria Schmitt, and Lizabeth Dailey. Special thanks are also due to the staff of the Rochester Public Library, who allowed us the freedom to spend several days going through their photograph files. Mary Huth expertly guided us through the Anthony archives at the University of Rochester Library. The Rochester Finger Lakes Film and Video Office and its director, Jerry Stoeffhaas, provided much practical advice on local film technicians, equipment services, and locations, and found us David Waingarten. Finally, our everlasting gratitude to Rochester photographer Michael Hager, who so graciously and quickly responded to our every need.

In Mumford, the fine staff of the Genesee Country Village and Museum were especially hospitable to our production. Special thanks to president and CEO Douglass McDonald for granting permission to film there (and coming to our rescue one evening when we were particularly hungry); to curator Peter Wisby for his knowledge and willingness to share it; to Keith Bonnlander for his technical help; and to public relations director Grace Lazzara and her assistant Rebecca Schichler for taking such good care of us.

And finally thanks to Kathleen D. Sweeney and Judge Frederick T. Henry Jr. at the Ontario County Courthouse in Canandaigua for all their help in filming the historic courtroom where Susan B. Anthony was put on trial.

Well over one hundred archives, museums, historical societies, and private collectors supplied photographs, newspapers, and other graphic material. A collective thanks to them all for their time, patience, and generosity. In particular, we would like to thank first Virginia Putnam from our local Walpole Historical Society. Special thanks for their generous assistance also go to Lansing Lord from the Johnstown Historical Society, Marie-Hélène Gold from the Schlesinger Library, Courteney Holden from the Sewall Belmont House, Susan Barker from the Sophia Smith Collection, Marguerite Lavin from the Museum of the City of New York, Allen Reuben from Culver Pictures, Jan Grenci, Rosemary Plakas, and Jeff Flannery from the Library of Congress, Bea Contant from the Terwilliger Museum, collectors Peter Palmquist, George Whiteley, and Greg French, and both Martha Wheelock from Ishtar Films and Robert Cooney for their invaluable research assistance. We are also, as always, extremely grateful to archival photographer Stephen Petegorsky who has served us so kindly and skillfully for so many years.

Our film could not have been made without the generous financial support of General Motors; the Corporation for Public Broadcasting and the Public Broadcasting Service; the PEW Charitable Trusts; the Arthur Vining Davis Foundations; Helen and Peter Bing; the New York State Department of Economic Development; the Wayne–Finger Lakes BOCES District, and the People of the State of New York. Our good friends at WETA-TV, especially Sharon Rockefeller, David Thompson, Phylis Geller, and Karen Kenton, were once again crucial in making this project possible.

The book produced its own ledger of debts: to our essayists Martha Saxton, Ann D. Gordon, and Ellen Carol DuBois; to Gerry McCauley, to Ash Green and Leyla Aker at Alfred A. Knopf; and to Wendy Byrne, who has once again fashioned a beautiful, coherent volume from a host of disparate historical materials.

Finally, we wish to thank our families—Sarah and Lilly Burns, and Vernon James and Melissa Laliberte—for their constant support of our work; for putting up with our prolonged absences and obsessive attention to this project; and for providing a safe haven for us to come home to.

Ken Burns
Paul Barnes
Walpole, New Hampshire

Selected Bibliography

Anthony, Katherine. *Susan B. Anthony: Her Personal History and Her Era.* New York: Doubleday, 1954.

Banner, Lois. *Elizabeth Cady Stanton: A Radical for Woman's Rights.* Boston: Little, Brown, 1980.

Barry, Kathleen. *Susan B. Anthony: A Biography of a Singular Feminist.* New York: New York University Press, 1988.

Bordin, Ruth. *Frances Willard: A Biography.* Chapel Hill: University of North Carolina Press, 1983.

Cazden, Elizabeth. *Antoinette Brown Blackwell: A Biography.* Old Westbury, N.Y.: The Feminist Press, 1983.

Cott, Nancy. *Bonds of Womanhood.* New Haven: Yale University Press, 1977.

Cullen-DuPont, Kathryn. *Elizabeth Cady Stanton and Woman's Liberty.* New York: Facts on File, 1992.

Davis, Angela. *Women, Race and Class.* New York: Random House, 1982.

Dorr, Rheta Childe. *Susan B. Anthony: The Woman Who Changed the Mind of a Nation.* New York: Stokes, 1928.

DuBois, Ellen Carol. *Feminism and Suffrage: The Emergence of an Independent Woman's Movement 1848–1869.* Ithaca, N.Y.: Cornell University Press, 1978.

————. *Harriot Stanton Blatch and the Winning of Woman Suffrage.* New Haven: Yale University Press, 1997.

————. *Woman Suffrage & Women's Rights.* New York: New York University Press, 1998.

————, ed. *The Elizabeth Cady Stanton–Susan B. Anthony Reader.* Boston: Northeastern University Press, 1992.

Edwards, G. Thomas. *Sowing Good Seeds: The Northwest Suffrage Campaigns of Susan B. Anthony.* Portland: Oregon Historical Society, 1990.

Flexner, Eleanor. *Century of Struggle.* New York: Atheneum, 1968.

Frost, Elizabeth, and Kathryn Cullen-DuPont. *Women's Suffrage in America: An Eyewitness History.* New York: Facts on File, 1992.

Giddings, Paula. *When and Where I Enter: The Impact of Black Women on Race and Sex in America.* New York: William Morrow, 1984.

Goldsmith, Barbara. *Other Powers: The Age of Suffrage, Spiritualism, and the Scandalous Victoria Woodhull.* New York: Alfred A. Knopf, 1998.

Gordon, Ann D. (editor). *The Selected Papers of Elizabeth Cady Stanton and Susan B. Anthony.* Vol. 1, *In the School of Anti-Slavery 1840–1856.* New Brunswick, N.J.: Rutgers University Press, 1997.

Griffith, Elisabeth. *In Her Own Right: The Life of Elizabeth Cady Stanton.* New York: Oxford University Press, 1984.

Gurko, Miriam. *The Ladies of Seneca Falls: The Birth of the Woman's Rights Movement.* New York: Macmillan, 1974.

Harper, Ida Husted. *Life and Work of Susan B. Anthony,* 3 vols. Salem, N.H.: Ayer Co., 1983.

Harper, Judith E. *Susan B. Anthony: A Biographical Companion.* Santa Barbara, Calif.: Clio, 1998.

Kerr, Andrea Moore. *Lucy Stone: Speaking Out for Equality.* New Brunswick, N.J.: Rutgers University Press, 1992.

Lutz, Alma. *Created Equal: A Biography of Elizabeth Cady Stanton.* New York: Day, 1940.

————. *Susan B. Anthony: Rebel, Crusader, Humanitarian.* New York: Beacon Press, 1959.

Marilley, Suzanne M. *Woman Suffrage and the Origins of Liberal Feminism in the United States 1820–1920.* Cambridge: Harvard University Press, 1996.

Marshall, Susan E. *Splintered Sisterhood: Gender and Class Against Woman Suffrage.* Madison: University of Wisconsin Press, 1997.

O'Neill, William. *Feminism in American History.* New Brunswick, N.J.: Transaction Publishers, 1994.

Rossi, Alice S. (editor). *The Feminist Papers: From Adams to Beauvoir.* New York: Columbia University Press, 1973.

Scott, Ann Firor, and Andrew MacKay Scott. *One Half the People: The Fight for Women's Rights.* Urbana: University of Illinois Press, 1975.

Shaw, Anna Howard. *Anna Howard Shaw: The Story of a Pioneer.* Cleveland: Pilgrim Press, 1994.

Sherr, Lynn. *Failure Is Impossible: Susan B. Anthony in Her Own Words.* New York: Times Books, 1995.

Stanton, Elizabeth Cady (Introduction by Ellen Carol DuBois; Afterword by Ann D. Gordon). *Eighty Years and More: Reminiscences 1815–1897.* Boston: Northeastern University Press, 1993.

Stanton, Elizabeth Cady, and the Revising Committee. *The Woman's Bible.* Seattle: Ayer Press, 1974.

Stanton, Elizabeth Cady, Susan B. Anthony, and Matilda

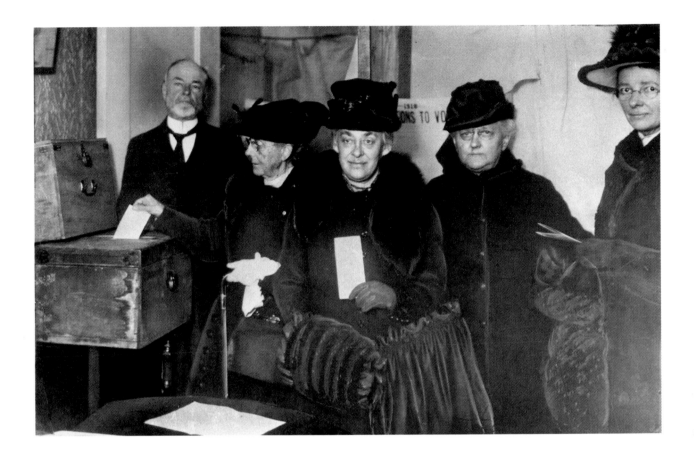

Joslyn Gage (editors). *History of Woman Suffrage*, vols. 1–3. New York: Fowler & Wells, 1884.

Stanton, Henry B. *Random Recollections*. New York: Harper & Brothers, 1887.

Stanton, Theodore, and Harriot Stanton Blatch. *Elizabeth Cady Stanton*, 2 vols. New York: Arno Press, 1969.

Terborg-Penn, Rosalyn. *African Women in the Struggle for the Vote, 1850–1920*. Bloomington: Indiana University Press, 1998.

Wheeler, Leslie (editor). *Loving Warriors: Selected Letters of Lucy Stone and Henry B. Blackwell 1853–1893*. New York: Dial Press, 1981.

Wheeler, Marjorie Spruill (editor). *One Woman, One Vote: Rediscovering the Woman Suffrage Movement*. Troutdale, Oreg.: Newsage Press, 1995.

We benefited greatly from *The Road to Seneca Falls: Elizabeth Cady Stanton and the First Woman's Rights Convention*, an unpublished manuscript kindly lent to us by Judith Wellman.

(Top) Carrie Chapman Catt, center, and three other suffragists exercise their right to vote in a Presidential election for the first time in New York City on November 2, 1920. For black women like those above seeking to sign up voters in Louisville, Kentucky, that same year, the struggle for equality at the polls would continue for another four decades.

Index

Illustration Credits

**ARCHIVE
ABBREVIATIONS**

CP: Culver Pictures
HL: The Henry E. Hunting-
    ton Library
LOC: Library of Congress
LOC/RB/SBA: Library of
    Congress, Rare Books,
    Susan B. Anthony
    Scrapbooks
MCNY: Musuem of the
    City of New York
NA: National Archives
NPG: National Portrait
    Gallery, Smithsonian
    Institution
PP: Peter Palmquist
RJ/CJS: Rhoda Jenkins/
    Coline Jenkins-Sahlin
RPL: Rochester Public
    Library
SBAH: Susan B. Anthony
    House
SFHS: Seneca Falls Histori-
    cal Society
SC: Smith College, Sophia
    Smith Collection
SL: Schlesinger Library,
    Radcliffe College
UR: University of
    Rochester Library

ENDPAPERS

National Museum of Ameri-
can History, Smithsonian
Institution, #78-17195

FRONTISPIECE

SBAH

**PREFACE
OUR BIG TIME**

9: LOC, #LCUSZ62-10845

HALF-TITLE PAGE

left RJ/CJS; **right** SBAH

**CHAPTER I
SO ENTIRELY ONE ARE WE**

2–3: Church of Latter-Day
Saints #P 100 15; **5: top**
Rutgers University, Douglass

Library; **5: bottom**
LOC/RB/SBA vol. 23,
p. 342; **6:** SC; **7:** RJ/CJS;
8: George Whiteley; **10:**
both RJ/CJS; **11:** Johnstown
Historical Society; **13:** PP;
15: both Emma Willard
School; **16:** Oberlin College
Archives; **17:** NPG, #NPG.
80.118; **18:** Donna Burdick;
19: RJ/CJS; **21: both**
SBAH; **22 and 23:** Adams
Historical Society; **25:** PP;
29: National Portrait
Gallery, London/Super
Stock, #454/120/I/P30F;
31: both LOC, #USZ61-
1608-903994, #USZ61-
1609-903994; **32:** SC; **33:**
top Gilman Paper Company,
bottom Chester County
Historical Society, #Dg327
Bx29; **34–35:** George
Eastman House, #29344;
36: Canajoharie Libaray and
Art Gallery; **37:** SBAH;
38: Microfilm, NY Tribune:
July 28, 1848; **39: top both**
Terwilliger Museum, Waterloo, NY; bottom SC;
40: RJ/CJS; **43:** RJ/CJS;
44: George Whiteley;
48: SBAH; **49: top** UR, **bottom** American Antiquarian
Society; **50:** J. Paul Getty
Musuem, #84.XT.1582.5,
51: SC; **52:** Adams
National Historic Park;
55: Tate Gallery, London/
Art Resouce, NY,
#S0077071 N1167;
56: NPG, #NPG.77.217.

**CHAPTER 2
BIGGER FISH TO FRY**

62–63: Metropolitan
Musuem of Art, #MM85595
B 37.14.56; **64:** SBAH;
65: LOC, #LCUSZC4-1629;
66: Buffalo and Erie County
Historical Society; **68:**
LOC, #LCZ6-2055-715612;

69: LOC/RB/SBA vol. 1, p.15; 70: Seneca Falls Historical Society, #1426.1; 71: LOC, #LCZ62-50991; 73: Albany Institute of History and Art, #P-6/23; 74: RJ/CJS; 75: RJ/CJS; 76: PP; 78: Ontario County Historical Society; 79: SBAH; 81: Ontario County Historical Society; 82: SL #A-77-114-4; 83: HL; 86-87: PP; 89: Stanton/Anthony Papers microfilm, Rutgers University; 90: LOC #BH82-5166-712723; 91: MCNY P.A. Astor Place #7; 93: CP, #WED006 CP001 047; 94: both LOC #BH8201-5004-A, #LCZ62-16680.

CHAPTER 3
LET NONE STAND ALONE

96–97: Musuem of The Confederacy; 98: top RJ/CJS; bottom SC, *The Liberator* Jan. 25, 1861; 99: MCNY; 101: top NA, #RG46 SEN 38A-H20, bottom American Numismatic Society; 102: Valentine Musuem, Cook, #1388 ; 103: NA #RG 233, 39th Cong., 1st Sess., House 39A-H14.9; 104: LOC/RB/SBA vol.2 p.15; 105: Western Reserve Historical Society; 106: NPG, #NPG.85.106; 107: top CP, #PE0146 CP015 004, bottom LOC, #LCUSZ62-31328; 108: top UR, bottom LOC/RB/SBA vol.2 p.70; 109: Nebraska Historical Society, #RG2608, 2182, 110: SC; 111: New York State Historical Association; 112: Source unknown; 113: MCNY; 114–115: Kansas State Historical Society, #FK2.01 Q.73

N.Kan*1; 117: SBAH; 118: LOC/RB/SBA vol.2 p.151; 121: CP, # Pe0006 Cp001 007; 122: left State Historical Society of Wisconsin, #Whi (X3) 51329, right SL, #11; 125: SBAH; 126–127: SBAH; 129: RPL, #RPF 2 Architecture, Domestic.

CHAPTER 4
UNDER SUCH FIRE

130–131: Wyoming State Musuem, #2298; 132: SL, #Wrc-633 3; 133: HL; 134: Nebraska Historical Society, #RG2669-5; 135: CP, #PE0140 CP008 018; 136–137: Montana Historical Society; 138: LOC/RB/SBA vol.8 p.147; 140: CP, #PE0160 CP011 037; 141: left SC; right NPG/Art Resouce, NY #NPG.78.93; 142: HL; 143: left Supreme Court of the United States, right RPL, #RPF 2-Portraits; 144: Ontario County Historical Society; 146: LOC/RB/SBA vol.6(4b) p.126; 147: LOC/RB/SBA vol. 6(4b) p.23 148: NA,# RG233, 42nd Cong. 3rd sess.House, R2A-H8.11; 150: Free Library of Philadelphia #OPEP 189; 151: CP, #FA1005 CP001 061; 152: top RPL, #Manuscripts/Box 2 bottom LOC/RB/SBA vol. 8 p.105; 153: Bergen Evening Record Corp., Hackensack, NJ; 154: SBAH; 155: LOC, 43rd Congress, Senate 1874; 156: Massillon Musuem, OH; 157: Oakland Musuem, #131A; 158–159: Nevada Historical Society, #WA-1671; 161: RJ/CJS; 165: Colorado Historical Society, #F10512; 166–167: Anoka County Historical Society,

#Clubs & Organizations 1.2; 168: Denver Public Library, #McC733.

CHAPTER 5
THE ONE & SOLE POINT

170–171: Gilcrease Musuem, #4326.3501; 172: MCNY, #93.1.1.17320; 173: LOC/Manuscripts; 174–175: Frances E. Willard Memorial Library; 176: LOC Z61-79080-3806; 177: top State Historical Society of North Dakota, #239; 134, bottom LOC, #LC-USZ62-683; 178: Frederick Douglass National Historic Site #3888; 179: left UR, right SC; 180–181: LOC, #LCUSZ62-7142; 182: State Historical Society of Wisconsin, #Whi (X3) 30205 PH3390; 184: Friends Historical Library, Swarthmore College; 185: University of Chicago Library, #IBW 2; 186: LOC/RB/SBA vol. 25; 187: top SL, #12454: bottom HL, #323.2.1; 188: Denver Public Library, #F12978; 190: Allegheny University of the Health Sciences, #P.724; 192–193: LOC, # 814073-J694-14; 194–195: Wellesley College Archives; 197: Denver Public Library, #F32629.

CHAPTER 6
AN AWFUL HUSH

198–199: UR; 200: LOC, Manuscripts; 201: LOC, #LCUSZ62-37938; 202: RJ/CJS; 204: LOC, #712725-Z62-10862 205: top SL, #1323, bottom State Historical Society of Wisconsin, #Whi (X3) 42028; 206: Brown Brothers; 207: Kansas State Historical Society, #B*21; 208: SBAH, courtesy UR;

209: Rutgers University, Douglass Library; 210: UR; 211: Oregon Historical Society, #OrHi 37240; 212: SL, #12198; 214: LOC, #Z62-29801; 215: SFHS, #1394.

EPILOGUE
WINTER WHEAT

218: RJ/CJS 219: LOC, #LC-USZ62-30534; 220: RJ/CJS; 221: SBAH; 222–223: LOC, National Woman's Party; 224: Knox County Public Library, McClung Collection; 225: Sewall Belmont House, #Page 58; 226–227: LOC, #USZ62-14447-903328; 231: top Brown Brothers, bottom University of Louisville, Ekstrom Library, #CS33312-C.

Film Credits

For our mothers
LYLA and GRACE
and
for our daughters
SARAH, LILLY and
MELISSA

A film by
KEN BURNS
and
PAUL BARNES

Written by
GEOFFREY C. WARD

Produced by
PAUL BARNES
KEN BURNS

Edited by
SARAH E. HILL

Cinematography
BUDDY SQUIRES
ALLEN MOORE
KEN BURNS

Associate Producer
SUSANNA STEISEL

Narrated by
SALLY KELLERMAN

Voices

RONNIE GILBERT
Elizabeth Cady Stanton

JULIE HARRIS
Susan B. Anthony
with
AMY MADIGAN
ADAM ARKIN
TIM CLARK
WENDY CONQUEST
KEVIN CONWAY
KEITH DAVID
ANN DOWD
ANN DUQUESNAY
CHARLES DURNING
CAROLYN McCORMICK
GEORGE PLIMPTON

Assistant Editors
CHRISTINE ROSE LYON
PETER R. SMITH

Assistant to the Producer
DAVID WAINGARTEN

Senior Creative Consultant
GEOFFREY C. WARD

Program Consultants
KATHLEEN BARRY
ELLEN CAROL DUBOIS
ANN GORDON
ELISABETH GRIFFITH
LYNN SHERR
JULIE DUNFEY

Coordinating Producer
PAM TUBRIDY BAUCOM

Additional Cinematography
ROGER HAYDOCK
TOM MARINI

Assistant Camera
ROGER HAYDOCK
ELIZABETH DORY
TIM CLARK

Sound Recording
ERIK EWERS
GREGG GOODHEW
BRENDA RAY

Chief Financial Officer
BRENDA HEATH

Administrative Assistants
SUSAN YEATON
BUTLER
PATTY LAWLOR

Supervising Sound Editor
IRA SPIEGEL

Dialogue Editor
MARLENA
GRZASLEWICZ

Music Editor
JENNIFER
DUNNINGTON

Assistant Sound Editor
MARIUSZ GLABINSKI

Re-Recording Mixer
LEE DICHTER
DOMINICK TAVELLA

Production Assistants
DAVID WAINGARTEN
JAKE ZOLLER
JODI CAMPBELL
MALCOLM FRANKLIN
CURT MARKHAM

Post-Production Assistant
TIM CLARK

Animation
Stand Photography
THE FRAME SHOP
EDWARD JOYCE and
EDWARD SEARLES

Archival Still Photography
MICHAEL HAGER
STEPHEN PETEGORSKY

Voice-Over Recording
A&J RECORDING
STUDIOS
LOU VERRICO
WAVES SOUND
RECORDERS, INC.
JOHN WALKER
MIKE KLINGER

Sound Department
ERIK EWERS
CRAIG MELLISH
MATTHEW L. McGRAIL

Post-Production Interns
HEATHER AUTRY
CHRISTIAN IMPERATO
JESSICA LACLAIR
MATTHEW L. McGRAIL
MARY LYNN RING

Negative Matching
NOELLE PENRAAT

Title Design
JAMES MADDEN

Color
DUART FILM LABS

Spirit Data
Cine Film Transfer
THE TAPE HOUSE
JOHN J. DOWDELL III

On-Line Editing
THE TAPE HOUSE
JAY TILIN

Digital Imaging
TIM THRASHER
STEPHEN PETEGORSKY

Legal Services
ROBERT N. GOLD

Associate Music Producers
TRICIA REIDY
ERIK EWERS
TEESE GOHL

Instrumentalist and
Studio Arrangements
BOBBY HORTON

Traditional Music
JACQUELINE SCHWAB,
piano
JAY UNGAR,
violin, mandolin
MOLLY MASON, guitar
MATT GLASER, violin
L. E. McCULLOUGH,
flute, whistle, bones
REINMAR SEIDLER, cello
BILL TOMCZAK, clarinet
GLEN D'EON, drums
JUDITH SERKIN, cello
TEESE GOHL, piano

Music Recorded at
SOUND DESIGN
BRATTLEBORO, VT.

Music Engineers
ALAN STOCKWELL
BILLY SHAW

Locations

SUSAN B. ANTHONY
HOUSE

GENESEE COUNTRY
VILLAGE AND MUSEUM

ONTARIO COUNTY
COURTHOUSE

PARKMINSTER
PRESBYTERIAN
CHURCH,
ROCHESTER, N.Y.

HOME OF ANN &
THOMAS DIETERICH,
TENAFLY, N.J.

GARDEN OF GORDON
& MARY HAYWARD,
PUTNEY, VT.

JOHN B. FOWLER
PRINTING COMPANY
and
WOMEN'S RIGHTS
NATIONAL
HISTORICAL PARK

DEPARTMENT OF THE
INTERIOR, NATIONAL
PARK SERVICE

Extra Special Thanks
Rhoda Barney Jenkins
Frances Barbieri
Lorie Barnum
Judy Emerson
Philip Guarascio

Susan Barker
Lisa Baskin
Luana Floccuzio
Donna Fontana
Marie-Hélène Gold
Judy Hu
Colleen Hurst
Mary Huth
Vernon James
Coline Jenkins-Sahlin
Morgan Jenkins
Leatrice Kemp
Lansing Lord
Felicia Moss
Rosemary Plakas
Leroy Renninger
Skip Roberts
Vivien Rose
Nan Scofield
Stanton Foundation
Mary Ellen Snyder
Carolyn Zogg

National Publicity
DAN KLORES
ASSOCIATES, INC

Produced in
Association with
WETA-TV,
WASHINGTON

Executive in Charge of
Production for WETA
PHYLIS GELLER

Project Director for WETA
DAVID S. THOMPSON

Associate Producer
for WETA
KAREN KENTON

Publicity for WETA
DEWEY BLANTON

SHARON P.
ROCKEFELLER,
President & CEO

A Production of
Florentine Films
Executive Producer
KEN BURNS

Funding provided by

General Motors
Corporation

The PEW Charitable Trusts

Public Broadcasting Service

Corporation for Public
Broadcasting

Helen and Peter Bing

The Wayne-Finger Lakes
BOCES District

New York State Department
of Economic Development

The Arthur Vining Davis
Foundations

A NOTE ABOUT THE AUTHORS

GEOFFREY C. WARD, historian, screenwriter, and former editor of *American Heritage*, was the coauthor of *The Civil War* and *Baseball* and principal writer of the television series on which they were based, and was author of *The West* and cowriter of the script for that series. He has also written seven other books, including *A First-Class Temperament: The Emergence of Franklin Roosevelt*, which won the 1989 National Book Critics Circle Award for biography and the 1990 Francis Parkman Prize from the Society of American Historians. He is currently at work on the script for *Jazz*, a series for Public Television, as well as two books: *Jazz: An Illustrated History* and *A Disposition to Be Rich*.

KEN BURNS, director and producer of *Not for Ourselves Alone: The Story of Elizabeth Cady Stanton and Susan B. Anthony*, has been making award-winning documentary films for more than twenty years. He was director of the landmark PBS series *The Civil War* and *Baseball* and executive producer of *The West*. His other films include the Academy Award–nominated *Brooklyn Bridge*; *The Shakers*; *The Statue of Liberty* (also nominated for an Oscar); *Huey Long*; *Thomas Hart Benton*; *The Congress*; *Empire of the Air*; *Jefferson*; *Lewis & Clark*, and, most recently, the acclaimed *Frank Lloyd Wright*. He is currently producing a series on the history of jazz.

A NOTE ABOUT THE CONTRIBUTORS

PAUL BARNES has been a documentary film editor for over twenty-five years. Among his credits are *The Thin Blue Line*, *Say Amen Somebody*, *Wasn't That a Time!*, and *No Maps on My Taps*. He has been filmmaker Ken Burns's supervising film editor for ten years, working with him on *The Civil War*, *Baseball*, *The Statue of Liberty*, and, currently, *Jazz*. *Not for Ourselves Alone* is Barnes's first film as codirector and coproducer with Burns. He lives in Walpole, New Hampshire.

MARTHA SAXTON teaches in the American History and Women and Gender Studies Departments at Amherst College. She has written a biography of Louisa May Alcott and is working on a book about women's moral standards in early America. She lives in New York City with her husband and two children.

ANN D. GORDON coedited *Papers of Elizabeth Cady Stanton and Susan B. Anthony, Microfilm Edition* with Patricia G. Holland. As project director and editor of the ongoing project to publish *Papers of Elizabeth Cady Stanton and Susan B. Anthony*, she has published volume 1 in that series, *In the School of Anti-Slavery, 1840–1866*, and is working on further volumes. She also wrote the afterword to the 1993 reissue of Stanton's memoir, *Eighty Years and More*. She is Associate Research Professor of History at Rutgers, the State University of New Jersey.

ELLEN CAROL DUBOIS is the author of *Harriot Stanton Blatch and the Winning of Woman Suffrage* and *Feminism and Suffrage: The Emergence of an Independent Women's Movement in America*. She wrote the introduction to the 1993 reissue of Stanton's memoir, *Eighty Years and More*, and is the editor of *The Elizabeth Cady Stanton/Susan B. Anthony Reader*. She is Professor of History at the University of California, Los Angeles.

A NOTE ON THE TYPE

The text of this book has been set in Goudy Old Style, one of the more than one hundred typefaces designed by Frederic William Goudy (1865–1947).

Although Goudy began his career as a bookkeeper, he was so inspired by the appearance of several newly published books from the Kelmscott Press that he devoted the remainder of his life to typography in an attempt to bring a better understanding of the movement led by William Morris to the printers of the United States.

Produced in 1914, Goudy Old Style reflects the absorption of a generation of designers with things "ancient." Its smooth, even color combined with its generous curves and ample cut marks it as one of Goudy's finest achievements.

Composed by North Market Street Graphics,
Lancaster, Pennsylvania

Printed and bound by World Color,
Taunton, Massachusetts

Picture research by Susanna Steisel

Designed by Wendy Byrne